Asian American Sexualities

Asian American Sexualities

Dimensions of the
Gay and Lesbian Experience

Edited by Russell Leong

Routledge
New York and London

Published in 1996 by

Routledge
29 West 35th Street
New York, NY 10001

Published in Great Britain by
Routledge
11 New Fetter Lane
London EC4P 4EE

Design: David Thorne
Printed in the United States of America on acid-free paper.

Library of Congress Cataloging-in-Publication Data
Asian American sexualities: dimensions of the gay and lesbian experience
edited by Russell Leong.
   p.   cm.
Includes bibliographical references.
ISBN 0-415-91436-1 (cl) — ISBN 0-415-91437-X (pb)

     1. Asian American gays.   2. Leong, Russell.

HQ76.2.U5A75   1995   95-538
305.9'0664—dc20   CIP

Contents

Acknowledgments

Without the insights and contribution of each writer *Asian American Sexualities* would not have come into being. I would like to thank each individual in this volume for permission to publish their article. Gratitude is due to the Regents of the University of California for permission to republish a number of essays from "Dimensions of Desire," *Amerasia Journal* 20:1 (1994), to Daniel C. Tsang to reprint Michiyo Cornell's speech, "Living in Asian America" from *Gay Insurgent*, and to West End Press, Albuquerque New Mexico to reprint "Aloes" from *The Country of Dreams and Dust* by Russell Leong.

The Bay Press, Seattle kindly gave permission to reprint Richard Fung's article, "Looking for My Penis: The Eroticized Asian in Gay Video Porn," in *How Do I Look? Queer Film and Video*, edited by Bad Object-Choices, 1991.

The editorial committee of "Dimensions of Desire" (*Amerasia Journal*)— Elsa E'der, Alice Hom, Lawrence Padua, Hanh Thi Pham, Dana Takagi, Daniel C. Tsang—provided support and insightful writing.

For the Routledge edition, Allan deSouza, David L. Eng, Abraham Ferrer, Richard Fung, Terry S. Gock, Marjorie Lee, James Chan Leong, James Kyung Jin Lee, Janice Mirikitani, Ric Parish, Celine Parrenas, Eric Estuar Reyes, Steven Masami Ropp, Joël B. Tan, Jennifer Ting, Daniel Tsang, Teresa Williams, Gust A. Yep, and members of the Asian Pacific AIDS Intervention Team generously shared their insights and materials with me. Candace Fujikane shared her literary materials; Alice Hom supplied biographical information on Michiyo Cornell; Daniel C. Tsang provided invaluable references, and Chandan Reddy led me to new authors.

Eugene Ahn, King-Kok Cheung, Daniel C. Tsang, and Allan deSouza read and critiqued earlier drafts of the introductory essay; Mari Saso aided in proofreading. Artists and photographers, we are indebted to your vision: Gaye Chan, Allan deSouza, Ming Yuen S. Ma, Yong Soon Min, Steve Nowling, Hanh Thi Pham, and Stanley Blair Roy.

Don. T. Nakanishi, director of the UCLA Asian American Studies Center, and Glenn Omatsu, Mary Kao, and Jean Pang Yip of Resource Development and Publications supported this project in many ways, and allowed me time to work on the book.

At Routledge, Jayne M. Fargnoli, the sociology and education editor, supported this project from its inception, and Anne Sanow, senior editorial assistant, guided this book through to production with optimism and dedication. Kimberly Herald, production editor, brought the book to publication.

Home Bodies and the Body Politic

Russell Leong

Home bodies, homelands, homosexuals.... This litany begins at home. Through words and ideas we seek ourselves, as we seek others. Asian American, Pacific Islander, American. But not homogeneous. Homegirls and homeboys.

Where is home? Home is just around the corner or may originate in communities halfway around the world. We were born colored. Somewhere between brown, yellow, black, and red relative to the light and sea, the continent, and your angle of vision. We might be Malaysian, Chinese, Japanese, Trinidadian, Goan, Vietnamese, Guamanian, Pakistani, Filipino, Indonesian, Thai, Korean—and more.

In the United States, Asian Americans were seven million in 1990 and will be twenty million in 2020. Pacific Island peoples who live in their island nations or in the continental U.S., because of their smaller numbers, still struggle for visibility. Asian American or Pacific Islander. Afroasian or Amerasian. *Hapa*— half-white. *Bu Doi*—children of the dust.[1]

Whose body? Lesbian, gay, or straight. Bisexual or transgendered. HIV positive or negative. Asian American activists or academics who articulate the body politic. Queer or just *qurious.* The subject of Asian American sexualities is more complex than any of the names we give it.

Through these writings we pursue our politics and claim our pleasures, taking both racial identities and sexual differences into account. This is the first book to do so from an interdisciplinary Asian American perspective. Here we cross boundaries, bridging the work of academics and artists who are mainly lesbian and gay, but also bisexual and heterosexual—activists and scholars, writers and journalists, poets and artists. We utilize various strategies from scholarly rumination to ethnographic research, from poetry to novel, from a speech given at the 1979 March on Washington to personal confession and polemic around the effects of AIDS today. Visually, artists capture our lives, be they queries into culture or photographic exposures of the Asian body.

To explore linkages between race and same-sex sexuality, *Asian American Sexualities* brings together works that address a number of overlapping questions and concerns, including but not limited to the following:[2]

—How do the political and personal identities of Asian American gays, lesbians, and bisexuals emerge out of the intersections of history, race, and sexuality?
—How do theories and practices of alternative sexualities underscore "decisive moments" of crisis, conflict, or change in our thinking about Asian American communities and cultures?
—How do sexual difference, interracial sexuality, the AIDS crisis, and the politicization of homosexuality among Asian Americans shape our production of literature, media, and the arts?
—What is the relationship between the gay and lesbian liberation movement, the Asian American Movement, and Asian American Studies ?

For Asian Americans and Pacific Islanders, looking at same-sex sexuality, means looking at the development of racial formation in the United States. Because race can no longer be conceived within fixed biological boundaries or sociological categories, ideas around the formation of racial identity must take into account white racism. E. San Juan, Jr., states that:

By "racism" is meant ideas, systems of thought, institutional practices, and all behavior that deterministically ascribe fixed roles and negatively evaluated group characteristics (moral, intellectual, cultural) to peoples on the basis of selected physical attributes whereby their oppression and exploitation are legitimized and perpetuated. I call "racial formation" the sociohistorical field of forces that racism inhabits.[3]

Homosexuality is not only an issue that involves gender, class, and psyche, but has as much to do with how racial and sexual categories have been developed for Asians, Pacific Islanders, African Americans, Native Americans, or

Latinos. Within the "Asian" or "Pacific" category itself are subcategories of gendered sexual and racialized traits ascribed to different groups by white Americans, e.g. Hawaiians, Chinese, Filipino, Thai, and Japanese.[4]

Popular ideas around Asian American homosexuality have been confounded with broader notions of exotic Asian or "oriental" sexuality, especially in popular culture, film, and media.[5] The pornography industry for instance, in producing homosexual or heterosexual printed and film material on Asians and Asian Americans, configures our most visible racial features—skin, hair, complexion, and size—in sexual terms for the primary consumption of the white male voyeur.[6] Not surprisingly, some Asian Americans themselves view same-sex sexuality as a sign of western decadence. Others acknowledge the fact that homosexuality has always existed in Asia and the Pacific—though not necessarily in the form of the western gay lifestyle.

In the United States, the myth of Asian Americans as a homogeneous, heterosexual "model minority" population since the 1960s has worked against exploration into the varied nature of our sexual drives and gendered diversity. Asian Americans "are presumed to practice the typical values of individualism, self-reliance, the work ethic, discipline, and so on."[7] Our mythical successful assimilation is used to pit us against other minority groups such as African Americans and Latinos. In terms of sexuality, the model minority view simply denies diversity as an issue. Yet struggles around same-sex sexuality in the home, workplace, and community can often be connected to other Asian American concerns such as immigrant rights, labor, and workplace issues, women's rights, interracial relations, and anti-Asian violence. In relation to HIV and AIDS, health education and care for women, men, and youth remain critical arenas of political struggle.

North American studies on theory, sexuality, and gender have largely excluded racial minorities and same-sex sexuality in their discussions.[8] As part of the Racial/Ethnic Other within the sexual "Other," Asian Americans and Pacific Islanders who are "gender non-conformists" have been met with silence or token inclusion at best. In looking at societal assumptions, practices, and discourses that oppress women and sexual minorities, Sandra Lipsitz Bem, in her otherwise excellent analysis on cultural oppression, does not differentiate between the racial and sexual constructions of marginalized groups:

> Although the concepts of heterosexuality, homosexuality, and bisexuality may be historically and culturally created *fictions*, like the concepts of masculinity and femininity and the concepts of black, Hispanic, Asian, Native American, and white, they are fictions that come to have psychological reality if they are institutionalized by the dominant culture. Accordingly, they can have extraordinary political power both for cultural oppression and for the resistance to cultural oppression.[9]

"But not all differences are created equally," as Dana Takagi reminds us in her essay, "Maiden Voyage," included here. Thus to differentiate ourselves from other "minorities," and to clarify our own political positions, lesbian, gay, and bisexual Asian Americans and Pacific Islanders have had to rely on our own media and literary networks, political organizations, and community groups. Moreover, our sexual differences have received scant attention from scholars in Asian American Studies since it was established twenty-five years ago. One early exception was *Asian Women*, published by the Asian Women's Journal collective in 1971. Today, North American scholars, writers, and cultural workers are foregrounding the subject; many have written for this book.[10] Independent film and video filmmakers are producing alternative work.[11] Literary collections include works by lesbians, gays, and bisexuals, but usually in separate volumes.[12]

During the last decade, not only Asian American lesbian and gay publications, but the ethnic press including the *KoreAm Journal, Asian Week,* and the *International Examiner,* have helped to disseminate perspectives on gays, lesbians, and bisexuals.[13] *Amerasia Journal* in its annual 3,000 item bibliography compiled by Glenn Omatsu includes citations on same-sex and women's issues, as well as on literary culture and media arts. This cultural work, viewed as a whole, can add a comparative dimension to emerging studies on Asians, sexuality, and "Black" British studies. In Britain, some writers, artists, and cultural activists, mainly of South Asian or Caribbean descent, identify themselves and their work as "black."[14]

Video still from *Aura* (1991), by Ming-Yuen S. Ma.

I. Home Bodies

"Just at the moment that we attempt to rectify our ignorance by adding say, the lesbian, to Asian American history, we arrive at a stumbling block, an ignorance of how to add her," states Dana Takagi in her introductory essay, "Maiden

Voyage: Excursion into Sexuality and Identity Politics in Asian America." Takagi rails against merely *adding* the Asian American lesbian—or gay man—as another ad-hoc subject. Instead, she argues for a plurality of sexual identifications and relations located in the Asian American experience. She describes the experience of the worlds of Asian America and gay America as separate places—"emotionally, physically, intellectually," sustained by, in her view, the "family-centeredness and supra-homophobic beliefs of ethnic communities." The domain of the Asian American "home" is usually kept separate from the desire of the sexual and emotional "body."

In delving into "stories from the homefront," Alice Y. Hom in her essay supports Takagi's observations on Asian American communities. Hom interviews Chinese, Japanese, Filipina, Vietnamese, and Korean mothers and fathers with lesbian daughters and gay sons. At the same time, her research reveals that Asian parents do not necessarily see homosexuality as a western import. First generation immigrants, for instance, recall knowing same-sex couples in their homelands. For the parents also, "coming out" is a process that not only involves their children, but is a disclosure of their most intimate feelings—as parents—with one another.

In a personal account, Eric C. Wat addresses the paradox of his parents hating "queers," but still loving him as an Asian son. As Hong Kong immigrants, his parents separate his gay identity from his familial and cultural one. From the personal, Wat then proceeds to the public arena, looking at the case of Truong Loc Minh, a Vietnamese immigrant who was savagely beaten by a group of young white men in Laguna Beach, California in 1993. While mainstream media reported the incident as a gay-bashing, the Asian media assured its readers that the victim was not gay and was beaten because of his race. Again, we see the division in the perception that occurs between race and sexuality within and outside the Asian community.

For Asian Americans, how to reconfigure personal, sexual, and racial identities takes both individual and collective forms. For Vietnamese artist Hanh Thi Pham, profiled in an essay by Erica L. H. Lee, the process was a gradual one. Pham was married for a twelve years and attempted to be a female role model in a traditional Vietnamese family. It was only after her divorce that she came into her own as a lesbian artist and writer.

In "Searching for Community," Martin F. Manalansan IV analyzes how social class, family roots, the AIDS pandemic, and the American experience work to shape the lives of gay Filipino immigrants in New York City. His study, based on interviews with fifty men, also explores how a traditional Catholic celebration, the Santacruzan, has been reconfigured by gay Filipino men to include their own religious iconography in the creation of community.

II. The Body Politic

> The civil rights movement and the anti-war movement gave inspiration to the student movements of the sixties, and then there were the modern women's movement and the post-Stonewall lesbian/gay movement. I am one of the beneficiaries of these movements: I have gotten an education to affirm not only who I am, an Asian American lesbian woman, but I also got support in terms of physical survival—I got work because of these movements.[15]
>
> —Merle Woo

Asian American lesbians, like Merle Woo, were part of the Black Power, Women's Liberation, Ethnic Studies, and anti-Vietnam War Movements of the 1960s and 70s. The Asian American Movement began as a political struggle twenty-five years ago at San Francisco State College in 1968 and spread to other campuses across the country.[16] The State Strike involved students from local Black, La Raza, Asian, and Native American communities who demanded open admissions, community control of education, ethnic studies, and an education relevant to their needs. Students, community, and cultural workers joined forces in the struggle for social justice and change. Within the movement, some progressive Asian American women recognized that "gay women must also have the right to self-definition." They stated in 1971 that:

> The gay movement has provided one of the most challenging criticisms of the radical movement for it has questioned the basic issues of chauvinism within the movement as well as the alienation of gay women from women's groups. "Lesbianism" can be seen as revolutionary in that it is a challenge to the basic assumptions of the present system, representing an alternative life style.
>
> As revolutionary women seeking the liberation of all women, we support a united front with our sisters against all arbitrary and rhetorical social standards.[17]

During that time, however, Asian American activists who were lesbian or gay often did not reveal their sexual preferences. Unlike those who could make opposition to the heterosexual world as the center of their political identity, activist Gil Mangaoang had a more complex understanding of his situation in the 1960s and 70s. As a community worker involved in activities around social justice for Filipinos in the United States. and in the anti-Marcos movement in the Philippines, he chose to keep his homosexuality hidden in order not to jeopardize his organizing efforts.

As a gay man of color, his situation was problematic. In the 1970s there were few gay organizations that were not dominated by white males. "Minorities who were members of these gay organizations were generally seen as subordinates reflecting the dominant racist attitudes in society," he states in his essay. For Asian and Pacific lesbians and gays, politicization involved confronting white racism, whether in heterosexual mainstream or gay and lesbian institutions. It involved a world view that included the Asian community and the history of Asians in the United States and the Americas. Factors such as colonization and the relationship of Asian Americans to Third World struggles in Central America, Southern Africa, Southeast Asia, China, and Cuba had to considered.

During October 12–15, 1979, activist Daniel Tsang attended the first national Third World Lesbian Gay conference at Howard University, which coincided with the First National Lesbian and Gay March on Washington. "The early morning march through the Black neighborhood and through Chinatown was the first time Black and Asian lesbians and gay men had paraded through their own neighborhoods," he said.[18] The Asian contingent was made up of lesbians and gay men of Chinese, Japanese, Indonesian, Indian, Malaysian, and Filipino backgrounds from North America, Asia, and the Caribbean. In front of the Washington Monument, Michiyo Cornell represented the Lesbian and Gay Asian Collective. Speaking as an Asian American woman, a mother and a lesbian, she emphasized that Third World men and women shared the historical oppression of white racism (see her speech, reprinted in this volume).[19]

Thus, for individuals such as Cornell, Mangaoang, Tsang, and Woo, liberation went far beyond issues of sexual emancipation or the affirmation of individual identity. Their community-based political activism, and those of others, helped to pave the ground for many of the Asian Pacific lesbian and gay organizations and support networks that emerged regionally and nationally in the late 1980s.[20] Fifteen years after the 1979 March on Washington, Eric Estuar Reyes joined the 1993 March and proposed an extended activist agenda also rooted in community needs.

Asian, Pacific, and biracial lesbians see *multiple* community needs that may include language and generational issues within specific groups, e.g. Vietnamese, Chinese, or South Asian, and women's struggles in relation to immigration, family relations, and the white lesbian movement. "It's never the same for a woman of color, a person of color, in the world," says Cristy Chung, coauthor of "In Our Own Way," with Aly Kim, Zoon Nguyen, Trinity Ordona, and Arlene Stein.

The creation of same-sex communities and movements is not necessarily tied to a single space, place, or even nation, but traversed and determined by politics, migrations, lovers, and families across seas and continents. Siong-huat Chua, who founded one of the first gay and lesbian Asian groups in North America in 1979, observed that:

A distinctive feature of the North American gay Asian Movement is its international perspective. Many individual activists and organizations maintain ties with gay groups and activists in East and South Asia—the political and cultural exchanges that have developed have enriched the movement on both sides of the Pacific.[21]

Lisa Kahaleole Chang Hall and J. Kehaulani Kauanui in their essay, "Same-Sex Sexuality in Pacific Literature," argue that indigenous Pacific peoples are often subsumed under rubrics of "Asian American" and "Asian Pacific." Yet these terms fail to address the particular colonial histories of the Pacific peoples of Hawaii, Eastern Samoa, Guam, the Republic of the Marshall Islands, the Federated States of Micronesia, the Commonwealth of the Northern Mariana Islands, and Belau. Colonization had imposed western constructions of sexuality upon native worldviews. According to Hall and Kauanui, "The discrete analytical categories of 'homosexuality,' and more fundamentally 'sexuality' itself are a colonial imposition which only address the realities of a small part of the spectrum of Pacific people who have sexual and love relationships with members of their own sex."

Their essay raises fundamental questions about terms and concepts currently employed to describe the Asian, Asian American, and Pacific Islander experiences including "Pacific Rim," "diaspora," and "transnational." Too often, the Pacific discourse on transnationalism is a thin intellectual disguise for the U.S., European, and Japanese incursion of Pacific economies and peoples, and appropriation of their sexualities and cultures.[22] Along these lines, Gayatri Gopinath, in "Notes on a Queer South Asian Planet," delves into the possibilities, limitations, and dangers of "conceptualizing a diasporic or transnational South Asian queer sexuality."

III. Figuring Desire

How do Asian Americans figure as the subjects, rather than the objects, of homosexual history and desire? Essays in this section explore the representation of Asian Americans as the subject of theater and film, of popular culture and cyberspace, and of commercial gay pornography. David L. Eng's essay, "In the Shadows of a Diva: Committing Homosexuality in David Henry Hwang's M. Butterfly," desconstructs sexual boundaries from homosexual to heterosexual—and the various psychological closets in which the West has placed itself in. The essay brings a queer reading onto a play written by an Asian American. At the same time, Eng challenges lesbian and gay studies to bring race fully into the dialogue.

In refiguring desire, Took Took Thongthiraj in her essay "Love between Women in Thailand," has interviewed women in Thailand and the United States. Unlike studies of Thai sexuality and homosexuality that have focused on the gay male subculture, usually from a western perspective, Thongthiraj looks at working and upper-class women, in rural and urban lifestyles, in popular and elite Thai culture in light of lesbian relationships. Presenting the terms and concepts that women themselves use to describe their identities, Thongthiraj allows Thai women to emerge as the subjects, rather than the objects of discourse.

Daniel C. Tsang enters the world of cyberspace and electronic bulletin boards with its gay Asian members in "Notes on Queer 'N' Asian Virtual Sex." The online environment allows users to continually reinvent their personal, sexual, and political histories and identities. The very nature of desire, according to Tsang, is being redefined by those who may engage in telephone sex, for example, as new configurations of visual and textual desire emerge from the internet.

How Asian American gay desire is translated into film and video is the subject of Kimberly Yutani's essay on Los Angeles filmmaker Gregg Araki, a leading figure in "Queer New Wave." Despite Araki's success alongside that of independent white artists, Yutani points to the relative absence of Asian lesbian filmmakers. But for those Asians who are more isolated from urban gay support groups or lifestyles, it is mainstream pornography rather than New Wave filmmaking that is more accessible. Richard Fung's "Looking for My Penis: The Eroticized Asian in Gay Video Porn," included here, was first published in 1991. The article focuses on the commercial gay representation of Asian men in video, within the context of the white fetishization of bodies (and bodily parts) of color. Fung believes that pornography is an important, but overlooked site of political struggle. He argues that porn "affirms gay identity articulated almost exclusively as white" with blacks depicted as hypersexual, Asians as passive and less sexual, and whites occupying the middle ground.

IV. Bloodlines

When Olympic diver Greg Louganis announced he had AIDS in February 1995, it was uncertain how Asian and Pacific Islander communities would respond to his medical condition and to his homosexuality.[23] Of mixed Samoan/white background, Louganis is a sports hero, as was tennis star Arthur Ashe and basketball player Magic Johnson. Of the three male athletes of color infected with the HIV virus, however, only Louganis had stated he was gay.

At the time Louganis had tested positive for HIV—six months before the Seoul Olympic Games in 1988—the Center for Disease Control and Prevention in Atlanta had only just recognized Asian Americans as a discrete category in their epidemiological reports. Prior to 1987, Asians were not listed as a separate group although Blacks, Latinas, and Latinos were already categorized. Metropolitan areas such as San Francisco, Los Angeles, Hawaii, and New York revealed increasing cases of HIV and AIDS among Asians and Pacific Islanders.[24]

Although the numbers change monthly, the fact is that all groups—well over 2,000 male and female—Cambodian, Chinese, Filipino, Koreans, Taiwanese, Thai, Vietnamese, and others are affected by the disease. The majority of reported cases are males who have been exposed to the retrovirus HIV through high risk sexual behavior.

"Communion" is a collaborative work on Asian Pacific males, their lovers and AIDS. Ric Parish, James Sakakura, Brian Green, and Robert Vázquez-

Pacheco are four men of color—Afro-Asian, Japanese American, African American, and Puerto Rican—who live each day with HIV and AIDS. Joël B. Tan is a founder of the Asian Pacific AIDS Intervention Team in Los Angeles and the lover of an HIV-positive man. In this collaboration, these individuals speak about how AIDS has affected their lives, how they live with it, continue to nurture bonds based on the mortality that affects them and how they make love and have sex with men who are seropositive.

Although "Communion" only deals with gay men of color—the population with the highest incidence rate—it is women of color who constitute the majority of women with AIDS in the United States. Asian and Pacific Islander women have the lowest percentage of reported cases in comparison to whites, Blacks, Latinas, and Native Americans. Nonetheless, women as a group are "undercounted, overlooked, misdiagnosed, and undiagnosed," for various political, medical, and cultural reasons. Women of Asian and Pacific Islander descent—lesbian, bisexual, and heterosexual—are no exception.[25]

V. A Tongue in Your Ear

The erotic has its own etymologies. Like me, it defines itself.

From a poem that opens the final section on literature, this line is from Thelma Seto's "My Grandmother's Third Eye." The writing included here is but a sampling of the vast amount of literature now being published by gay, lesbian, and bisexual Asian American writers.

Asian American gays and lesbians were writing about their "sexuality long before their narratives were published."[26] Lesbian-themed works have been written since the 1940s, such as Margaret Chinen's play *All, All Alone* (1947), although the first book of poetry and novel were published in 1971 and 1985 by Willyce Kim. Two of the earliest-gay themed short stories, by Lonny Kaneko and myself, can be found in Asian American anthologies of literature, *Aiiieeeee!* (1974) and *The Big Aiiieeeee!* (1991). I wrote "Rough Notes for Mantos" under the pseudonymn Wallace Lin about the conflict among the protagonist, a father, and a Vietnam war veteran. Around that time I remember reading Lonny Kaneko's "The Shoyu Kid" (first published in 1976 in *Amerasia Journal*) a tale that recounted the molestation of a young Japanese American boy by a white soldier in a World War II internment camp. By linking homosexuality and sexual abuse with race and war—World War II and the Viet Nam conflict—the two stories provide alternate readings of the Asian American experience within a U.S. colonial and neocolonial context.

Novelist R. Zamora Linmark offers a piece entitled "Tita Aida," or Auntie AIDS, a passionate plea that turns the English language on its head. In "Queer Pilpino Rebolusiyon," Joël B. Tan satirizes mass media and offers instead an authentic "one word poem."

In elegiac tones, Lisa Asagi describes an affair with a married woman in her short story, "Fascination, Gravity and a Deeply Done Kiss," just as Elsa E'der in her poem celebrates "all those pretty women/drowning at the gates/love looking for home." Both writers build upon the Asian American lesbian literary tradition established by Willyce Kim, Barbara Noda, Merle Woo, Canyon Sam, and Kitty Tsui in the 1970s.

An excerpt from Kitty Tsui's forthcoming historical novel, *Bak Sze, White Snake* graces these pages. Based upon fifteen years of research on China, Hong Kong, and the United States, the novel's protagonist is a lesbian Chinese opera singer. I have also included a short story, "Grandma's Tales," by Vietnamese journalist Andrew Lam, not only for its bisexual narrator, but for its parody of Asian and Asian American social and sexual mores. Lam's story and Tsui's novel excerpt are examples of literature in which race and ethnicity are not short-changed but neither is sexuality sacrificed. Race and sexuality coexist as part of a literature of desire. "Aloes," the final poem, links desire with suffering and a return both to origins and to the future.

"Upon the Origins of Other Things"

In the domain of Asian and Pacific homosexualities, there are hidden doors and unknown rooms. Decades before Stonewall and the gay/lesbian liberation movement of the 1960s, there were stirrings within family compounds. Beyond familiar figures of mothers and fathers, daughters and sons, there have always been other folk: the odd bachelor uncle or lone aunt, the niece or nephew whose silences or syllables never chimed with tradition. What were the contents of their rooms—windows opaqued with warm breath and walls pinned with images of their own desire? I decided to query my uncle, a painter and a keen observer of life around him.

Pioneer Square: Seattle, Washington, 1994. The rain falls without ceasing on the tall studio windows that face the waters of Elliot Bay. My Uncle Jimmy's loft is filled with paintings he had done during the past thirty-five years.[27] The wooden room echoes with the sounds of his wife and son talking in an adjoining room.

Born in the United States, he is in his sixties, with a smooth face and a shock of black hair turning grey. I ask him about growing up in San Francisco Chinatown in the 1930s and 40s before World War II. I ask him about gays and lesbians before I was born. He laughs. He says that there were many white homosexuals in North Beach "who had a thing for Asian and Black boys," at the time. But that there were also many spinsters and unmarried sisters in the families he knew about.

After World War II, he says, San Francisco became known as a good place for people who didn't quite fit in. The Beat Generation. They read, drank, smoked, and slept around. "But what about Asian Americans?" I ask.

He tells me that his first wife was white, and because of that, he was considered an oddball and ostrasized during those times. "Once your community ostrasizes you, then there are no longer any barriers."

He ended up painting and hanging around with other artists, some of whom were gay or bisexual. "So whom you loved or slept with", he says, "was just another difference." Among the people whom he knew were gay or lesbian were a well-known Chinese American lawyer, a dress designer, and a few dancers and singers. There were Asian American homosexuals of both sexes. Because of the restrictive atmosphere in Chinatown, however, many who were lesbian or gay fled to other parts, such as the Midwest, New York, or even Europe—to find themselves or live their lives elsewhere.

In fact, he says, he remembered that back in the 1930s a friend of his, a young photographer, had died mysteriously of what people said was pneumonia, but with all the wasting syndromes that people today associate with AIDS. In uncovering stories and memories, he says, "We may stumble upon the origins of other things."

I pondered what he told me. A year later, as I write this essay, his words hit home. If we have a memory, we have a future. As we imagine our lives, we invent ourselves. We are positive; we are negative. Personal and political. Children of history, desire, and rebirth. [28]

We become what we call ourselves.

Notes

Author's note: I dedicate this essay to Alejandro Fu-Chang (1966–1993), labor organizer, political activist, and friend.

1. Leadership Education for Asian Pacifics, Inc. and the UCLA Asian American Studies Center, *The State of Asian Pacific America: A Public Policy Report* (Los Angeles: LEAP and UCLA, 1993), see articles on immigration, population, women, media, language, and labor rights, cultural preservation, and legal and civil rights. Also, Herbert Barringer, Robert W. Gardner, and Michael J. Levin, *Asian and Pacific Islanders in the United States* (New York: Russell Sage Foundation, 1993). *Bu Doi*—a Vietnamese term meaning "dust of life" or "homeless," and *hapa*—a Hawaiian term meaning "half."

2. Russell Leong, ed., "Dimensions of Desire," *Amerasia Journal*, vol. 20, no. 1. 1994 special issue on gay, lesbian, and bisexual Asian and Pacific Americans, from which a number of articles were selected and reprinted in this volume.

3. See E. San Juan, Jr., *Racial Formations/Critical Transformations: Articulations of Power in Ethnic and Racial Studies in the United States,* (New Jersey: Humanities Press, 1992), 3, and Introduction, 1–21; Michael Omi and Howard Winant, "By the Rivers of Babylon: Race in the United States." *Socialist Review* 71 (Sept.–Oct. 1983): 31–65 and *Racial Formation in the United States from the 1960s to the 1980s* (New York: Routledge,

1986). On Asian Americans, theory formation and political and cultural change in relation to Asian American Studies, see "Thinking Theory" a special issue of *Amerasia Journal* (1995) 21:1 ed. by Dana Takagi and Michael Omi, especially articles by Gordon Chang, Dorinne Kondo, Lisa Lowe, and Sauling Wong. Lisa Lowe's essay, "On Contemporary Asian American Projects," suggests lines of inquiry around culture, Marxism and capitalism that can be linked with race, racialization, and sexuality.

4. Richard Fung, "Looking for My Penis: The Eroticized Asian in Gay Video Porn," in *How Do I Look? Queer Film and Video*, ed. Bad Object-Choices (Seattle: Bay Press, 1991), 145–68, and reprinted in this book. See also, Russell Leong, ed. *Moving the Image: Independent Asian Pacific American Media Arts* (Los Angeles: UCLA Asian American Studies Center and Visual Communications, 1991), especially the articles by gay filmmakers Gregg Araki, "The (Sorry) State of (Independent Things)," 68–70 and Richard Fung, "Center the Margins," 62–67. See also, L. T. Goto, "The Asian Penis: The Long and Short of It," in *Yolk Magazine* 1: 1, 1994.

5. Eugene Franklin Wong, *On Visual Media Racism: Asians in the American Motion Pictures* (New York: Arno Press, 1978); John Kuo Wei Tchen, "Believing Is Seeing: Transforming Orientalism and the Occidental Gaze," in *Asian America: Identities in Contemporary Asian American Art* (New York: The Asia Society Galleries and The New Press, 1994), 13–23; Gina Marchetti, *Romance and the "Yellow Peril": Race, Sex and Discursive Strategies in Hollywood Fiction* (Berkeley and Los Angeles: University of California Press, 1994); James S. Moy, *Marginal Sights: Staging the Chinese in America* (Iowa City: University of Iowa Press, 1993). Also, Renee Tajima, "Lotus Blossoms Don't Bleed: Images of Asian Women," *The Anthology of Asian American Film and Video* (New York: Third World Newsreel, n.d.); and Russell Leong, "Unfurling Pleasure, Embracing Race," in *On a Bed of Rice: An Asian American Erotic Feast*, ed. Geraldine Kudaka (New York: Anchor Books, 1995).

6. Two examples of orientalized sexual fetishism—one heterosexual and one gay, follow: Alan Rifkin, in "Asian Women / L.A. Men," with a subcaption of "Why Do So Many Hollywood Types Go Looking For Love In Bangkok, Hong Kong, and Tokyo?" (*Buzz Magazine*, September 1993) reports that the new passion and fetish of white Hollywood movie industry males are Asian women as lovers or wives. One cinematographer ended up bringing a Thai wife to Hollywood:

> He saw women. Lithe, coy women with eyes that either hid or smiled at themselves in his own eyes; women who endured men's flaws and giggled in the hollow of men's shoulders; women of waist-high embraces; women with flawless skin wearing gloves and shoulderless dresses; women who loved-hated the erotic dance and eternally kept men guessing; laugh-bringing, praying good-bye, trusting the heavens with every human mystery.

In *O.G. Oriental Guys*, a soft-porn gay magazine with photos, articles and personal ads of Asian men mainly from Thailand, the Philippines and the United States, a typical letter to the editor from a white reader reads as follows (issue no. 13, 1994):

> The images of Sakoi, the handsome Thai adonis featured in this issue took my breath away. To me he epitomizes that tantalizing fusion of androgynous beauty and potent masculinity, that set Asian males apart.... The buns shot is a real prick teaser, firm rounded buns and hairless scrotum, leading ones eye to the centre of ones desire....

Another letter that objectifies the racial, sexual, and class aspects of Asian men in terms of white western male desire:

> I really enjoy George Stanley's photography of young rural Filipino boys from those enchanting islands. The boys come across as charming and innocent. Unlike the city boys from Manila who are so commercial and streetwise in their behavior....

7. See, E. San Juan, Jr., *Racial Formations*, 133–34. For a counterpoint and critique to assimilation and the model minority syndrome, see the introduction on "racist love" by Frank Chin, Jeffery Chan, Shawn Wong, and Lawson Inada, editors of *Aiiieeeee! An Anthology of Asian American Writers* (Washington, D.C. : Howard University Press, 1974).

8. For instance, see Lynne Segal, *Straight Sex: Rethinking the Politics of Pleasure* (Berkeley: University of California Press, 1994), a useful survey of post-World War II American and British sexuality and culture, including feminist, lesbian, and gay challenges to "straight sex." Like other studies, however, the only other racial or ethnic group it discusses in any detail besides whites are African Americans.

9. Sandra Lipsitz Bem, *The Lenses of Gender, Transforming the Debate on Sexual Inequality* (New Haven and London: Yale University Press, 1993), 175.

10. Asian Women's Journal, *Asian Women* (University of California, Berkeley, 1971 and UCLA Asian American Studies Center) had articles on Asian American and Third World women including Vietnamese, Arab, and Persian; on Taoism and sex; and on birth control, male chauvinism, the gay issue, and birth control. See also Daniel C. Tsang, "Gay Awareness," in *Bridge Magazine*, vol. 3–4 (February 1975), an early "coming out" account. Emma Gee taught the first course on Asian women at U.C. Berkeley; Teresa Williams taught the first course at UCLA on Gay, Lesbian and Bisexual Asian and Pacific Islanders twenty-five years later. At Brown University, Jennifer Ting, in teaching about Asian American sexuality, states that "reading through the conceptual lenses of Queer Studies, we can recognize that when we teach about families, marriages, prostitutes, representations of effeminacy and hyperfemininity; when we teach the political histories of miscegenation and standards of beauty; we are teaching, self-consciously or unself-consciously, about Asian American sexuality." From "Asian American Studies, Get Bent! or Teaching against Heteronormativity," forthcoming in the Association of Asian American Studies, *Asian American Studies: Pedagogies and Prospects*. Also, see Asian Women United of California, *Making Waves: An Anthology of Writings by and about Asian American Women* (Boston: Beacon Press, 1989). Recent works on Asian Americans such as Ronald Takaki, *Strangers from a Different Shore: A History of Asian Americans* (Boston: Little, Brown, 1989) and Sucheng Chan, *Asian Americans: An Interpretive History* (Boston: Twayne Publishers, 1991), which survey migration and settlement, exclusion and discrimination, labor and family, community, culture and arts, do not cover sexuality.

11. North American gay, lesbian, and bisexual-identified film and video makers include: Desireena Almoradie, Gregg Araki, Pablo Bautisa, Yau Ching, Arthur Dong, Quentin Lee, Paul Lee, Richard Fung, Ming-Yuen S. Ma, Shani Mootoo, Meena Nanji, Midi Onodera, Ian Rashid, and Paul Wong. For catalogues and information on Asian American filmmakers and festivals, write: NAATA, 346 Ninth St. 2nd. Floor, San Francisco, CA. 94103; Third World Newsreel, 335 West 38th St., New York, NY 10018;

Visual Communications, 263 South Los Angeles Street, Los Angeles, CA 90012; and Asian CineVision, 32 E. Broadway, New York, NY 10012.

12. See Alice Y. Hom and Ming-Yuen S. Ma, "Premature Gestures: A Speculative Dialogue on Asian Pacific Islander Lesbian and Gay Writing," in *Journal of Homosexuality*, vol. 26, no. 2/3 (1993), 21–51. Also, Sharon Lim-Hing, editor, *The Very Inside: An Anthology of Writing by Asian and Pacific Islander Lesbian and Bisexual Women* (Toronto: Sister Vision Press, 1994); and Loraine Hutchins and Lani Kaahumanu, ed., *Bi Any Other Name* (Boston: Alyson Publications, 1991) with articles and essays by Asian and Pacific bisexuals including: Chandini Goswami, Lani Kaahumanu, Shu Wei Chen, Kei Uwano, Selena Julie Whang, and Amanda Yoshizaki.

Other collections include: Curtis Chin, Gayatri Gopinath, Joo-Hyun Kang, and Alvin Realuyo, editors, "Witness Aloud: Lesbian, Gay and Bisexual Asian American/Pacific Writings," *The Asian/Pacific American Journal* 2: 1 (1993). C. Chung, A. Kim, and A. K. Lemeshewsky, ed., *Between the Lines: An Anthology by Pacific/Asian Lesbians of Santa Cruz, California,* (Santa Cruz: Dancing Bird Press, 1987). See Jessica Hagedorn, ed., *Charlie Chan is Dead: An Anthology of Contemporary Asian American Fiction,* (New York: Penguin, 1993), which contain a few gay and lesbian stories and accounts.

For a listing of thousands of Asian American works through 1988, see King-Kok Cheung and Stan Yogi, *Asian American Literature: An Annotated Bibliography* (New York: Modern Language Association of America, 1988).

13. See, *KoreAm Journal*, vol. 4, no. 11 (November 1993), special issue on HIV and AIDs, with articles by John H. Lee, Dredge Byung-Chu Kang, Risa Denenberg, Kyung-min Kim, Tae Soo Chung, Lucy J. Kim, Joo Hyun Lee, Johnnie Lee Norway, and Jeff Kim; and "The Queer Issue," vol. 4 no. 8 (August 1993), with articles by Tae Soo Chung, C. H. Young, Charles Choe, John H. Lee, Tom Choi, and Kang Byung-Chu Dredge. Also, Bob Shimabukuro, ed., "Speaking Out: Rethinking AIDS in the Asian Pacific Communities," in *International Examiner* (16 December 1993), a special supplement. *AsianWeek* provides continuous coverage of Asian gays and lesbians: see, for example, Elisa Lee, "API Gays and Lesbians Celebrate Stonewall 25," vol. 15, no. 48 (24 June 1994); Milyoung Cho, "Asian Pacifics Hold Their Own at Gay March in D.C.," vol. 14, no. 37 (7 May 1993); Kenneth R. Ong and Joanna Omi, "We are Not Immune: APIs and AIDS," vol. 15, no. 43 (20 May 1994); Daniel C. Tsang, "Loc Truong's Attack: Race, Sexual Orientation, Violence Intersect," vol. 14, no. 26 (19 February 1993).

Asian lesbian and gay newsletters include: Asian Lesbians of the East Coast (ALOEC) Newsletter, P.O. Box 850, New York, NY 10002; Asian Pacifica Sisters (API), *Phoenix Rising*, P.O. Box 170596, San Francisco, CA 94117; Gay Asian Pacific Alliance (GAPA), *Lavender Godzilla Newsletter*, P.O. Box 421884, San Francisco, CA 94142–1884. See back issues of *Amerasia Journal*, (est. 1971, interdisciplinary, three times yearly), UCLA Asian American Studies Center, 3230 Campbell Hall, Los Angeles, CA 90024, and *The Asian Pacific American Journal*, (est. 1992, literary— semi-annual) 296 Elizabeth St., New York, NY 10012.

14. Nayan Shah, "Sexuality, Identity and the Uses of History," in Rakesh Ratti, ed., *A Lotus of Another Color: An Unfolding of the South Asian Gay and Lesbian Experience* (Boston: Alyson Publications 1993), 113–32. In the same volume, see also Khush, "Fighting

back: an interview with Pratibha Parmar," 34–40; and Sharmeen Islam, "Toward a global network of Asian lesbians," 41–46. See also, *Rungh: A South Asian Quarterly of Culture, Comment and Criticism* (Tsar Publications, Box 6996, Station A, Ontario, MSW 1x7); Ian Iqbal Rashid, *Black Markets White Boyfriends and other Acts of Elision* (Toronto: Tsar Publications, 1991); and Allan deSouza, "Re-placing Angels: Extracts and Extractions," in *Tracing Cultures: Art History, Criticism, Critical Fiction* (New York: Whitney Museum of American Art, 1994), 29–51.

15. Merle Woo, "What Have We Accomplished? From the Third World Strike Through the Conservative Eighties," in *Amerasia Journal* 15: 1 (1989), 81–89, "Salute to the 60s and 70s: Legacy of the San Francisco State Strike," with issue editor Glenn Omatsu. Chris Bull, "Arbitrator tells Berkeley to reinstate lesbian prof: Merle Woo wins latest round in discrimination case against University of California," *gay community news* (12–18 March 1989), vol. 16, no. 34: 3.

16. On the Asian American movement, see Glenn Omatsu, "The 'Four Prisons' and the Movements of Liberation," in *Amerasia Journal*, 15: 1 (1989), Salute to the 60s and 70s Legacy of the San Francisco State Strike Issue, xv–xxx.

17. See "Politics of the Interior," editorial essay in *Asian Women* (University of California, Berkeley, 1971; UCLA Asian American Studies Center 1975): 128, 129.

18. Daniel Tsang, "Third World Lesbians and Gays Meet," in *Gay Insurgent* 6 (Summer 1980), 11; and Siong-huat Chua, "Asian-Americans, Gay and Lesbian," entry in Wayne R. Dynes, ed., *Encyclopedia of Homosexuality* (New York and London: Garland Publishing, 1990), 84–85.

19. Michiyo Cornell, "Living in Asian America: An Asian American Lesbian's Address before the Washington Monument," *Gay Insurgent* 6,16 (Summer 1980).

20. Trinity A. Ordona, in "The Challenges Facing Asian and Pacific Islander Lesbian and Bisexual Women in the U.S.: Coming Out, Coming Together, Moving Forward" in Sharon Lim-Hing, ed., *The Very Inside*, lists Asian Pacific lesbian organizations in the U.S. and Canada, including: (1970s) Asian Women United (San Francisco Bay Area) and their sucessor, Asian Pacifica Sisters. In the 1980s: Asian Lesbians of the East Coast (New York); South Asian lesbian and bisexual women's newsletters *Anamika* and *Shamakami* (Toronto, New York, and San Francisco), and others. Conferences have included the first Asian/Pacific Lesbian West Coast Regional Retreat (1987); the first National Retreat that brought women from the U.S., Canada, and England (1989). International gatherings include the 1988 North American Conference of Lesbians and Gay Men in Toronto and the Asian Lesbian Network Conferences in Thailand (1990), Japan (1992), and Taiwan (1995).

    Eric E. Reyes provided additional listings of organizations founded in the 1980s: Barangay; Asian Pacific AIDS Council (Seattle); Alliance of MA Asian Lesbians and Gay Men (Boston); Asian and Pacific Islander Coalition on HIV/AIDS (New York); Asian AIDS Project (San Francisco); Dragon Flies (Texas); Filipino Task Force on AIDS (San Francisco); Gay Asian Pacific Islander Men of NY; Gay Asian Pacific Support Network (Los Angeles); Gay Asian Pacific Alliance (San Francisco); MAHU (UCLA, Los Angeles); Trikon (Los Angeles and San Francisco); Asian Pacific AIDS Intervention Team (Los Angeles); and Trikone (San Francisco).

21. From Chua, "Asian-Americans, Gay and Lesbian," 85. Also, Daniel C. Tsang, "Founder

of First Gay and Lesbian Asian Group Sucumbs to AIDS" in *AsianWeek*, vol. 16, (2 September 1994). Chua founded Boston Asian Gay Men and Lesbians (BAGMAL), the first co-gender lesbian and gay organization in North America. Later, he was profiled in Richard Fung's *Fighting Chance* (1990), the first video to record the lives of Asians with AIDS. Fung founded Gay Asians Toronto after the 1979 march, inspired by the creation of BAGMAL, according to Tsang.

22. Arif Dirlik, ed., *What Is in a Rim: Critical Perspectives on the Pacific Region Idea*, (Boulder, Colorado: Westview Press, 1993).

23. John Weyler, "Olympic Diver Louganis Reveals That He Has AIDS," *Los Angeles Times*, 23 February 1995, 1.

24. Terry S. Gock, "Acquired Immunodeficiency Syndrome," in *Confronting Health Issues of Asian and Pacific Islander Americans*, ed. Nolan W. S. Zane, David T. Takeuchi, and Kathleen N.J. Young, (Thousand Oaks: Sage Publications, 1994), 247–65; Kenneth R. Ong and Joanna Omi, "We are Not Immune: APIs and AIDS, *AsianWeek*, vol. 15, no. (20 May 1994). Current Asian Pacific AIDS statistics available from (Asian Pacific AIDS Education Project, Asian Pacific Health Care Venture, 1313 W. Eighth St. #201, Los Angeles, CA 90017), and Centers for Disease Control, HIV/AIDS surveillance: annual year-end edition. (Division of HIV/AIDS, Center for Infectious Diseases, Centers for Disease Control, Atlanta, GA 30333).

25. "Unique Aspects of HIV Infection in Women," compiled by Risa Denenberg, *KoreAm Journal*, vol. 4: 11 (November 1993). Also, Jo Ann Tsark, Governor's Pacific Health Promotion and Development Center, Report of September 16, 1993 (Asian AIDS Project, San Francisco) and F. Alavao, "AIDS in the Pacific," *Samoa News*, 22 August 1991 (Pago Pago, American Samoa).

26. David L. Eng and Candace Fujikane, "Asian American Gay and Lesbian Literatures," *The Gay and Lesbian Literary Heritage*, ed. Claude Summers (New York: Holt, 1995). What follows is a partial list of works by individual authors: Margaret Chinen, *All, All Alone. College Plays*, (Honolulu: University of Hawaii Department of English, 1947–48); Willyce Kim, *Curtains of Light*, (self-published, 1971) and *Dancer Dawkins and the California Kid* (Boston: Alyson, 1985); Barbara Noda, *Strawberries* (Berkeley: Shameless Hussy Press, 1979); Kitty Tsui *Words of a Woman Who Breathes Fire* (San Francisco: Spinsters Ink, 1983); Wallace Lin, "Rough Notes for Mantos," in *Aiiieeeee! An Anthology of Asian American Writers;* and Russell Leong, *The Country of Dreams and Dust* (West End Press: Albuquerque, 1993); Lonny Kaneko, "The Shoyu Kid," in *The Big Aiiieeeee! An Anthology of Chinese American and Japanese American Literature*, ed. Jeffery Paul Chan, Frank Chin, Lawson Inada, and Shawn Wong (New York: Meridian, 1991); Dwight Okita, *Crossing with the Light* (Chicago: Tia Chucha Press, 1992); Paul Stephen Lim *Homerica: A Triology on Sexual Liberation* (Louisville: Aran Press, 1985); Timothy Liu, *Vox Angelica* (Cambridge: alicejamesbooks, 1992); Norman Wong, *Cultural Revolution* (New York: Persea Books, 1994); Chea Villanueva *Chinagirls*, (n.p.: Lezzies on the Move Productions, 1991) and *Girlfriends* (New York: Outlaw Press, 1987). On heterosexual and gay Asian American masculinity, see King-Kok Cheung, "Of Man and Man: Reconstructing Chinese American Masculinity," in Sandra Kumamoto Stanley, ed., *Women of Color and Literary Theory* (Urbana: University of Illinois Press,1995).

27. On Chinese American painter, James Chan Leong, see Ian Findlay, "In From Exile," in *Asian Art News* (November/December 1994): 88–92.

28. For more on the world of Desire, *Samsara*—suffering, and rebirth, see Narada Maha Thera, *The Buddha and His Teachings* (Singapore: Singapore Buddhist Meditation Centre, n.d.) and Richard A. Gard, ed., *Buddhism,* (New York: George Braziller, 1962). See also *Tricycle: The Buddhist Review* (Fall 1994) section on "Dharma, Diversity and Race" with articles by bell hooks, Victor Sogen Hori, and Russell Leong. On Buddhist mind/body theory, see Yuasa Yasuo, *The Body, Toward an Eastern Mind-Body Theory* (Albany: State University of New York Press, 1987).

Dana Takagi has pointed out there are at least two ways of speaking of desire: in queer studies desire is theorized as part of subject identity but in Buddhist thought desire is related to suffering. I venture a third viewpoint: that "subject identity" is inclusive of suffering, sexuality—and of joy—and that we ought to overcome the split, fractured ways in which we analyze our nature.

part I

"Within me, there is this wanting to be larger than the Asian
concept of largeness."

—Hanh Thi Pham

Home Bodies

overleaf: from "Angel on a Folding Chair" series
(1986–88), by Gaye Chan.
Quotation from "Breaking through the Chrysalis: Hanh
Thi Pham," *Amerasia Journal* 20: 1 (1994).

I

Maiden Voyage
Excursion into Sexuality and Identity Politics in Asian America

Dana Y. Takagi

> Like black men and women who refused to be the exceptional "pet" Negro for whites, and who instead said they were "niggers" too (the original "crime" of "niggers" and lesbians is that they prefer themselves), perhaps black women writers and non-writers should say, simply, whenever black lesbians are being put down, held up, messed over, and generally told their lives should not be encouraged, We are all lesbians. For surely it is better to be thought a lesbian, and to say and write your life exactly as you experience it, than to be a token "pet" black woman for those whose contempt for our autonomous existence makes them a menace to human life.[1]
>
> —Alice Walker

The topic of sexualities—in particular, lesbian, gay, and bisexual identities—is an important and timely issue in that place we imagine as Asian America. All of us in Asian American Studies ought to be thinking about sexuality and Asian American history for at least two compelling reasons.

One, while there has been a good deal of talk about the "diversity" of Asian American communities, we are relatively uninformed about Asian American subcultures organized specifically around sexuality. There are Asian American gay and lesbian social organizations, gay bars that are known for Asian clientele, conferences that have focused on Asian American lesbian and gay experiences, and as Tsang notes in this issue, electronic bulletin boards catering primarily to gay Asians, their friends, and their lovers. I use the term "subcultures" here rather loosely and not in the classic sociological sense, mindful that the term is somewhat inaccurate since gay Asian organizations are not likely to view themselves as a gay subculture within Asian America any more than they are likely to think of themselves as an Asian American subculture within gay America. If anything, I expect that many of us view ourselves as on the margins of both communities. That state of marginalization in both communities is what prompts this essay and makes the issues raised in it all the more urgent for all of us—gay, straight, or somewhere-in-between. For as Haraway has suggested, the view is often clearest from the margins where, "The split and contradictory self is the one who can interrogate positionings and be accountable, the one who can construct and join rational conversations and fantastic imaginings that change history."[2]

To be honest, it is not clear to me exactly how we ought to be thinking about these organizations, places, and activities. On the one hand, I would argue that an organization like the Association of Lesbians and Gay Asians (ALGA) ought to be catalogued in the annals of Asian American history. But on the other hand, having noted that ALGA is as Asian American as Sansei Live! or the National Coalition for Redress and Reparation, the very act of including lesbian and gay experiences in Asian American history, which seems important in a symbolic sense, produces in me a moment of hesitation. Not because I do not think that lesbian and gay sexualities are not deserving of a place in Asian American history, but rather, because the inscription of non-straight sexualities in Asian American history immediately casts theoretical doubt about how to do it. As I will suggest, the recognition of different sexual practices and identities that also claim the label Asian American presents a useful opportunity for rethinking and reevaluating notions of identity that have been used, for the most part, unproblemmatically and uncritically in Asian American Studies.

The second reason, then, that we ought to be thinking about gay and lesbian sexuality and Asian American Studies is for the theoretical trouble we encounter in our attempts to situate and think about sexual identity and racial identity. Our attempts to locate gay Asian experiences in Asian American history render us "uninformed" in an ironic double sense. On the one hand, the field of Asian American Studies is mostly ignorant about the multiple ways that gay identities are often hidden or invisible within Asian American communities. But the irony is that the more we know, the less we know about the ways of knowing. On the other hand, just at the moment that we attempt to rectify our ignorance by adding say, the lesbian, to Asian American history, we arrive at a stumbling block, an ignorance of how to add her. Surely the quickest and simplest way to add her is to think of lesbianism as a kind of ad hoc subject-position, a minority within a minority. But efforts to think of sexuality in the same terms that we think of race, yet simultaneously different from race in certain ways, and therefore, the inevitable "revelation" that gays/lesbians/bisexuals are like minorities but also different too, is often inconclusive, frequently ending in "counting" practice. While many minority women speak of "triple jeopardy" oppression—as if class, race, and gender could be disentangled into discrete additive parts—some Asian American lesbians could rightfully claim quadruple jeopardy oppression—class, race, gender, and sexuality. Enough counting. Marginalization is not as much about the quantities of experiences as it is about qualities of experience. And, as many writers, most notably feminists, have argued, identities whether sourced from sexual desire, racial origins, languages of gender, or class roots, are simply not additive.[3]

Not Counting

A discussion of sexualities is fraught with all sorts of definition conundrums. What exactly does it mean, sexualities? The plurality of the term may be unsettling to some who recognize three (or two, or one) forms of sexual identity: gay, straight, bisexual. But there are those who identify as straight, but regularly indulge in homoeroticism, and, of course, there are those who claim the identity gay/lesbian, but engage in heterosexual sex. In addition, some people identify themselves sexually but do not actually have sex, and, there are those who claim celibacy as a sexual practice. For those who profess a form of sexual identity that is, at some point, at odds with their sexual practice or sexual desire, the idea of a single, permanent, or even stable sexual identity is confining and inaccurate. Therefore, in an effort to capture the widest possible range of human sexual practices, I use the term sexualities to refer to the variety of practices and identities that range from homoerotic to heterosexual desire. In this essay, I am concerned mainly with homosexual desire and the question of what happens when we try to locate homosexual identities in Asian American history.

Writing, speaking, acting queer. Against a backdrop of lotus leaves, sliding shoji panels, and the mountains of Guilin. Amid the bustling enclaves of Little Saigon, Koreatown, Chinatown, and Little Tokyo. Sexual identity, like racial identity, is one of many types of recognized "difference." If marginalization is a qualitative state of being and not simply a quantitative one, then what is it about being "gay" that is different from "Asian American?"

The terms "lesbian" and "gay," like "Third World," "woman," and "Asian American," are political categories that serve as rallying calls and personal affirmations. In concatenating these identities we create and locate ourselves in phrases that seem a familiar fit: black gay man, third world woman, working class Chicana lesbian, Asian American bisexual, etc. But is it possible to write these identities—like Asian American gay—without writing oneself into the corners that are either gay and only gay, or, Asian American and only Asian American? Or, as Trinh T. Minh-ha put it, "How do you inscribe difference without bursting into a series of euphoric narcissistic accounts of yourself and your own kind?"[4]

It is vogue these days to celebrate difference. But underlying much contemporary talk about difference is the assumption that differences are comparable things. For example, many new social movements activists, including those in the gay and lesbian movement, think of themselves as patterned on the "ethnic model."[5] And for many ethnic minorities, the belief that "gays are oppressed too" is a reminder of a sameness, a common political project in moving margin to center, that unites race-based movements with gays, feminists, and greens. The notion that our differences are "separate but equal" can be used to call attention to the specificity of experiences or to rally the troops under a collective banner. Thus, the concept of difference espoused in identity politics may be articulated in moments of what Spivak refers to as "strategic essentialism" or in what Hall coins "positionalities." But in the heat of local political struggles and coalition building, it turns out that not all differences are created equally. For example, Ellsworth recounts how differences of race, nationality, and gender, unfolded in the context of a relatively safe environment, the university classroom:

> Women found it difficult to prioritize expressions of racial privilege and oppression when such prioritizing threatened to perpetuate their gender oppression. Among international students, both those who were of color and those who were White found it difficult to join their voices with those of U.S. students of color when it meant a subordination of their oppressions as people living under U.S. imperialist policies and as students for whom English was a second language. Asian American women found it difficult to join their voices with other students of color when it meant subordinating their specific oppressions as Asian Americans. I found it difficult to speak as a White woman about gender oppression when I occupied positions of institutional power relative to all students in the class, men and women, but positions of gender oppression relative to students who were White men, and in different terms, relative to students who were men of color.[6]

The above example demonstrates the tensions between sameness and difference that haunt identity politics. Referring to race and sexuality, Cohen suggests that the "sameness" that underlies difference may be more fiction than fact:

> The implied isomorphism between the "arbitrariness of racial categorizations" and the "sexual order" elides the complex processes of social differentiation that assign, legitimate, and enforce qualitative distinctions between different types of individuals. Here the explicit parallel drawn between "race" and "sexuality," familiar to so many polemical affirmations of (non-racial) identity politics, is meant to evoke an underlying and apparently indisputable common sense that naturalizes this particular choice of political strategy almost as if the "naturalness" of racial "identity" could confer a corollary stability on the less "visible" dynamics of sexuality.[7]

There are numerous ways that being "gay" is not like being "Asian." Two broad distinctions are worth noting. The first, mentioned by Cohen above, is the relative invisibility of sexual identity compared with racial identity. While both can be said to be socially constructed, the former are performed, acted out, and produced, often in individual routines, whereas the latter tends to be more obviously "written" on the body and negotiated by political groups.[8] Put another way, there is a quality of voluntarism in being gay/lesbian that is usually not possible as an Asian American. One has the option to present oneself as "gay" or "lesbian," or alternatively, to attempt to "pass," or, to stay in "the closet," that is, to hide one's sexual preference.[9] However, these same options are not available to most racial minorities in face-to-face interactions with others.

As Asian Americans, we do not think in advance about whether or not to present ourselves as "Asian American," rather, that is an identification that is worn by us, whether we like it or not, and which is easily read off of us by others.

A second major reason that the category "gay" ought to be distinguished from the category "Asian American" is for the very different histories of each group. Studying the politics of being "gay" entails on the one hand, an analysis of discursive fields, ideologies, and rhetoric about sexual identity, and on the other hand, knowledge of the history of gays/lesbians as subordinated minorities relative to heterosexuals. Similarly, studying "Asian America" requires analysis of semantic and rhetorical discourse in its variegated forms, racist, apologist, and paternalist, and requires in addition, an understanding of the specific histories of the peoples who recognize themselves as Asian or Asian American. But the specific discourses and histories in each case are quite different. Even though we make the same intellectual moves to approach each form of identity, that is, a two-tracked study of ideology on the one hand, and history on the other, the particular ideologies and histories of each are very different.[10]

In other words, many of us experience the worlds of Asian America and gay America as separate places—emotionally, physically, intellectually. We sustain the separation of these worlds with our folk knowledge about the family-centeredness and supra-homophobic beliefs of ethnic communities. Moreover, it is not just that these communities know so little of one another, but, we frequently take great care to keep those worlds distant from each other. What could be more different than the scene at gay bars like "The End Up" in San Francisco, or "Faces" in Hollywood, and, on the other hand, the annual Buddhist church bazaars in the Japanese American community or Filipino revivalist meetings?[11] These disparate worlds occasionally collide through individuals who manage to move, for the most part, stealthily, between these spaces. But it is the act of deliberately bringing these worlds closer together that seems unthinkable. Imagining your parents, clutching bento box lunches, thrust into the smoky haze of a South of Market leather bar in San Francisco is no less strange a vision than the idea of Lowie taking Ishi, the last of his tribe, for a cruise on Lucas' Star Tours at Disneyland. "Cultural strain," the anthropologists would say. Or, as Wynn Young, laughing at the prospect of mixing his family with his boyfriend, said, "Somehow I just can't picture this conversation at the dinner table, over my mother's homemade barbecued pork: 'Hey, Ma. I'm sleeping with a sixty-year-old white guy who's got three kids, and would you please pass the soy sauce?'"[12]

Thus, "not counting" is a warning about the ways to think about the relationship of lesbian/gay identities to Asian American history. While it may seem politically efficacious to toss the lesbian onto the diversity pile, adding one more form of subordination to the heap of inequalities, such a strategy glosses over the particular or distinctive ways sexuality is troped in Asian America. Before examining the possibilities for theorizing "gay" and "Asian American" as non-mutually exclusive identities, I turn first to a fuller description of the chasm of silence that separates them.

Silences

The concept of silence is a doggedly familiar one in Asian American history. For example, Hosokawa characterized the Nisei as "Quiet Americans" and popular media discussions of the "model minority" typically describe Asian American students as "quiet" along with "hard working" and "successful." In the popular dressing of Asian American identity, silence has functioned as a metaphor for the assimilative and positive imagery of the "good" minorities. More recently, analysis of popular imagery of the "model minority" suggests that silence ought to be understood as an adaptive mechanism to a racially discriminatory society rather than as an intrinsic part of Asian American culture.[13]

If silence has been a powerful metaphor in Asian American history, it is also a crucial element of discussions of gay/lesbian identity, albeit in a somewhat different way. In both cases, silence may be viewed as the oppressive cost of a racially biased or heterosexist society. For gays and lesbians, the act of coming out takes on symbolic importance, not just as a personal affirmation of "this is who I am," but additionally as a critique of expected norms in society, "we are everywhere." While "breaking the silence" about Asian Americans refers to crashing popular stereotypes about them, and shares with the gay act of "coming out" the desire to define oneself rather than be defined by others, there remains an important difference between the two.

The relative invisibility of homosexuality compared with Asian American identity means that silence and its corollary space, the closet, are more ephemeral, appear less fixed as boundaries of social identities, less likely to be taken-for-granted than markers of race, and consequently, more likely to be problematized and theorized in discussions that have as yet barely begun on racial identity. Put another way, homosexuality is more clearly seen as constructed than racial identity.[14] Theoretically speaking, homosexual identity does not enjoy the same privileged stability as racial identity. The borders that separate gay from straight, and, "in" from "out," are so fluid that in the final moment we can only be sure that sexual identities are as Dianna Fuss notes, "in Foucaldian terms, less a matter of final discovery than a matter of perpetual invention."[15]

Thus, while silence is a central piece of theoretical discussions of homosexuality, it is viewed primarily as a negative stereotype in the case of Asian Americans. What seems at first a simple question in gay identity of being "in" or "out" is actually laced in epistemological knots.

For example, a common question asked of gays and lesbians by one another, or by straights, is, "Are you out?" The answer to that question (yes and no) is typically followed by a list of who knows and who does not (e.g., my coworkers know, but my family doesn't...). But the question of who knows or how many people know about one's gayness raises yet another question, "how many, or which, people need to know one is gay before one qualifies as "out?" Or as Fuss says, "To be out, in common gay parlance, is precisely to be no longer out; to be out is to be finally outside of exteriority and all the exclusions and deprivations such outsider-hood imposes. Or, put another way, to be out is really to be in— inside the realm of the visible, the speakable, the culturally intelligible."[16]

Returning to the issue of silence and homosexuality in Asian America, it seems that topics of sex, sexuality, and gender, are already diffused through discussions of Asian America.[17] For example, numerous writers have disclosed, and challenged, the panoply of contradictory sexually-charged images of Asian American women as docile and subservient on the one hand, and as ruthless mata-hari, dragon-lady aggressors on the other. And of course, Frank Chin's tirades against the feminization of Asian American men has been one reaction to the particular way in which Asian Americans have been historically (de)sexualized as racial subjects. Moving from popular imagery of Asian Americans, the people, to Asia, the nation, Chow uses Bertolucci's blockbuster film, The Last Emperor, to illustrate what she calls, "the metaphysics of feminizing the other (culture)" wherein China is predictably cast as a "feminized, eroticized, space."[18]

That the topic of homosexuality in Asian American studies is often treated in whispers, if mentioned at all, should be some indication of trouble. It is noteworthy, I think, that in the last major anthology on Asian American women, Making Waves, the author of the essay on Asian American lesbians was the only contributor who did not wish her last name to be published.[19] Of course, as we all know, a chorus of sympathetic bystanders is chanting about homophobia, saying, "she was worried about her job, her family, her community..." Therefore, perhaps a good starting point to consider lesbian and gay identities in Asian American studies is by problematizing the silences surrounding homosexuality in Asian America.

It would be easy enough for me to say that I often feel a part of me is "silenced" in Asian American Studies. But I can hardly place all of the blame on my colleagues. Sometimes I silence myself as much as I feel silenced by them. And my silencing act is a blaring welter of false starts, uncertainties, and anxieties. For example, on the one hand, an omnipresent little voice tells me that visibility is better than invisibility, and therefore, coming out is an affirming social act. On the other hand, I fear the awkward silences and struggle for conversation that sometimes follow the business of coming out. One has to think about when and where to time the act since virtually no one has ever asked me, "Are you a lesbian?" Another voice reminds me that the act of coming out, once accomplished, almost always leaves me wondering whether I did it for myself or them. Not only that, but at the moment that I have come out, relief that is born of honesty and integrity quickly turns to new uncertainty. This time, my worry is that someone will think that in my coming out, they will now have a ready-made label for me, lesbian. The prospect that someone may think that they knowme because they comprehend the category lesbian fills me with stubborn resistance. The category lesbian calls up so many different images of women who love other women that I do not think that any one—gay or straight—could possibly know or find me through that category alone. No wonder that I mostly find it easier to completely avoid the whole issue of sexual identity in discussions with colleagues.

There are so many different and subtle ways to come out. I am not much of a queer nation type, an "in your face" queer—I catalogue my own brand of lesbian identity as a kind of Asian American "take" on gay identity. I do not wear pink triangles, have photos of girls kissing in my living room, or, make a point of bringing up my girlfriend in conversation. In effect, my sexual identity is often backgrounded or stored somewhere in between domains of public and private. I used to think that my style of being gay was dignified and polite— sophisticated, civilized, and genteel. Work was work and home was home. The separation of work and home has been an easy gulf to maintain, less simple to bridge. Recently, however, I have come to think otherwise.

But all this talk about me is getting away from my point, which is that while it would be easy enough for me to say many of us feel "silenced," which alone might argue for inclusion of gay sexualities in discourse about the Asian American experience, that is not enough. Technically speaking then, the terms "addition" and "inclusion" are misleading. I'm afraid that in using such terms, the reader will assume that by adding gay/lesbian experiences to the last week's topics in a course on Asian American contemporary issues, or, by including lesbians in a discussion of Asian women, the deed is done. Instead, I want to suggest that the task is better thought of as just begun, that the topic of sexualities ought to be envisioned as a means, not an end, to theorizing about the Asian American experience.

For example, one way that homosexuality may be seen as a vehicle for theorizing identity in Asian America is for the missteps, questions, and silences that are often clearest in collisions at the margins (identities as opposed to people). In the following discussion, I describe two such confrontations—the coming out of a white student in an Asian American Studies class and the problem of authenticity in gay/lesbian Asian American writing. Each tells in its own way the awkward limits of ethnic-based models of identity.

The Coming Out Incident

Once, when I was a teaching assistant in Asian American Studies at Berkeley during the early 1980s, a lesbian, one of only two white students in my section, decided to come out during the first section meeting. I had asked each student to explain their interest, personal and intellectual, in Asian American Studies. Many students mentioned wanting to know "more about their heritage," and "knowing the past in order to understand the present." The lesbian was nearly last to speak. After explaining that she wanted to understand the heritage of a friend who was Asian American, her final words came out tentatively, as if she had been deliberating about whether or not to say them, "And, I guess I also want you all to know that I am a lesbian." In the silence that followed I quickly surveyed the room. A dozen or so Asian American students whom I had forced into a semicircular seating arrangement stared glumly at their shoes. The two white students, both of whom were lesbians, as I recall, sat together, at one end of the semicircle. They glanced expectantly around the circle, and then, they too, looked at the ground. I felt as though my own world had split apart, and the two pieces were in front of me, drifting, surrounding, and at that moment, both silent.

I knew both parts well. On the one side, I imagined that the Asian American students in the class, recoiled in private horror at the lesbian, not so much because she was a lesbian or white, but because she insisted on publicly baring her soul in front of them. I empathized with the Asian American students because they reminded me of myself as an undergraduate. I rarely spoke in class or section, unless of course, I was asked a direct question. While my fellow white students, most often the males, chatted effortlessly in section about readings or lectures, I was almost always mute. I marveled at the ease with which questions, thoughts, answers, and even half-baked ideas rolled off their tongues and floated discussion. For them, it all seemed so easy. As for me, I struggled with the act of talking in class. Occasionally, I managed to add a question to the discussion, but more often, I found that after silently practicing my entry into a fastmoving exchange, the discussion had moved on. In my silence, I chastised myself for moving too slowly, for hesitating where others did not, and alternately, chastised the other students for their bull-dozing, loose lips. I valorized and resented the verbal abilities of my fellow classmates. And I imagined how the Asian American students who sat in my class the day the lesbian decided to come out, like me, named the ability to bare one's soul through words, "white." On the other side, I empathized as well with the lesbian. I identified with what I imagined as her compelling need to claim her identity, to be like the others in the class, indeed to be an "other" at all in a class where a majority of the students were in search of their "roots." I figured that being a lesbian, while not quite like being Asian American, must have seemed to the intrepid student as close to the ethnic model as she could get. Finally, I thought she represented a side of me that always wanted, but never could quite manage, to drop the coming out bomb in groups that did not expect it. Part of the pleasure in being an "outsider" can be in the affirmation of the identity abhorred by "insiders." I imagined that she and her friend had signed up for my section because they knew I too was a lesbian, and I worried that they assumed that I might be able to protect them from the silence of the closet.

In the silence that followed the act of coming out, and indeed, in the ten weeks of class in which no one spoke of it again, I felt an awkwardness settle over our discussions in section. I was never sure exactly how the Asian American students perceived the lesbian—as a wannabe "minority," as a comrade in marginality, as any White Other, or perhaps, they did not think of it at all. Nor did I ever know if the lesbian found what she was looking for, a better understanding of the Asian American experience, in the silence that greeted her coming out.

The silences I have described here dramatize how dialogue between identities is hampered by the assumption of what Wittig calls the "discourses of heterosexuality." She says:

> These discourses of heterosexuality oppress us in the sense that they prevent us from speaking unless we speak in their terms. Everything which puts them into question is at once disregarded as elementary. Our refusal of the totalizing interpretation of psychoanalysis makes the theoreticians say that we neglect the symbolic dimension. These discourses deny us every possibility of creating our own categories. But their most ferocious action is the unrelenting tyranny that they exert upon our physical and mental selves.[20]

More important, the coming out incident suggests that marginalization is no guarantee for dialogue. If there is to be an interconnectedness between different vantage points, we will need to establish an art of political conversation that allows for affirmation of difference without choking secularization. The construction of such a politics is based implicitly on our vision of what happens, or, what ought to happen, when difference meets itself—queer meets Asian, black meets Korean, feminist meets Greens, etc., at times, all in one person.[21] What exactly must we know about these other identities in order to engage in dialogue?

The Question of Authenticity

What we do know about Asian American gays and lesbians must be gleaned from personal narratives, literature, poetry, short stories, and essays. But first, what falls under the mantle, Asian American gay and lesbian writings? Clearly, lesbians and gays whose writings are self-conscious reflections on Asian American identity and sexual identity ought to be categorized as Asian American gay/lesbian writers. For example, Kitty Tsui, Barbara Noda, and Merle Woo are individuals who have identified themselves, and are identified by others, as Asian American lesbian voices. Similarly, in a recent collection of essays from a special issue of *Amerasia Journal*, "Burning Cane," Alice Hom ruminates on how an assortment of Others—white dykes, Asian dykes, family, and communities—react to her as butchy/androgynous, as Asian American, as a lesbian. These writers are lesbians, and they write about themselves as lesbians which grants them authorial voice as a lesbian. But they also identify as Asian American, and are concerned with the ways in which these different sources of community—lesbian and Asian American—function in their everyday lives.

But what then about those who do not write explicitly or self-consciously about their sexuality or racial identity? For example, an essay on AIDS and mourning by Jeff Nunokawa, while written by a Japanese-American English professor, does not focus on issues of racial and sexual identity, and as such, is neither self-consciously gay nor Asian American.[22] What are we to make of such work? On the one hand, we might wish to categorize the author as a gay Asian American writer, whether he wishes to take this sign or not, presuming of course, that he is gay since his essay appears in an anthology subtitled, "gay theories," and, in addition presuming that he is Asian American, or at least identifies as such given his last name. On the other hand, we might instead argue that it is the author's work, his subject matter, and not the status of the author, that marks the work as gay, Asian American, or both. In this case, we might infer that since the topic of the essay is AIDS and men, the work is best categorized as "gay," but not Asian American.

This may seem a mundane example, but it illustrates well how authorial voice and subject matter enter into our deliberations of what counts and what does not as Asian American gay/lesbian writings. The university is filled with those of us, who while we live under signs like gay, Asian, feminist, ecologist, middle-class, etc., do not make such signs the central subject of our research. And what about those individuals who write about gays/lesbians, but who identify themselves as heterosexual? In the same way that colonizers write about the colonized, and more recently, the colonized write back, blacks write about whites and vice versa, "we" write about "them" and so on.

I want to be clear, here. I am not suggesting that we try to locate Asian American gay/lesbian sensibilities as if they exist in some pure form and are waiting to be discovered. Rather, I think we ought to take seriously Trinh T. Minh-ha's warning that,"Trying to find the other by defining otherness or by explaining the other through laws and generalities is, as Zen says, like beating the moon with a pole or scratching an itching foot from the outside of a shoe."[23] My concern here is to turn the question from one about a particular identity to the more general question of the way in which the concept of identity is deployed in Asian American history.

Thus, not only is marginalization no guarantee for dialogue, but the state of being marginalized itself may not be capturable as a fixed, coherent, and holistic identity. Our attempts to define categories like "Asian American" or "gay" are necessarily incomplete. For example, as Judith Butler has noted:

> To write or speak as a lesbian appears a paradoxical appearance of this "I," one which feels neither true nor false. For it is a production, usually in response to a request, to come out or write in the name of an identity which, once produced, sometimes functions as a politically efficacious phantasm.
> ...This is not to say that I will not appear at political occasions under the sign of the lesbian, but that I would like to have it permanently unclear what precisely that sign signifies.[24]

A politics of identity and whatever kind of politics ensues from that project— multiculturalism, feminism, and gay movements—is first of all a politics about identity. That is, about the lack of a wholistic and "coherent narrative" derived from race, class, gender, and sexuality.... Because no sooner do we define, for example, "Japanese American" as a person of Japanese ancestry then we are forced back to the drawing board by the biracial child of Japanese American and an African American who thinks of herself as "black" or "feminist."

Rethinking Identity Politics

Lisa Lowe in her discussion of identity politics affirms the articulation of "Asian American" identity while simultaneously warning us of its overarching, consuming, and essentializing dangers. She (Lowe) closes her discussion saying:

> I want simply to remark that in the 1990s, we can afford to rethink the notion of ethnic identity in terms of cultural, class, and gender differences, rather than presuming similarities and making the erasure of particularity the basis of unity. In the 1990s, we can diversify our political practices to include a more heterogeneous group and to enable crucial alliances with other groups—ethnicity-based, class-based, and sexuality-based—in the ongoing work of transforming hegemony.[25]

I have intended this essay, in part, as an answer to Lowe's call to broaden the scope of Asian American discourse about identity. But there is a caveat. The gist of this essay has been to insist that our valuation of heterogeneity not be ad hoc and that we seize the opportunity to recognize non-ethnic based differences—like homosexuality—as an occasion to critique the tendency toward essentialist currents in ethnic-based narratives and disciplines. In short, the practice of including gayness in Asian America rebounds into a reconsideration of the theoretical status of the concept of "Asian American" identity. The interior of the category "Asian American" ought not be viewed as a hierarchy of identities led by ethnic-based narratives, but rather, the complicated interplay and collision of different identities.

At the heart of Lowe's argument for recognizing diversity within Asian American, generational, national, gender, and class, as well as my insistence in this essay on a qualitative, not quantitative view of difference, is a particular notion of subjectivity. That notion of the subject as non-unitary stands in sharp contrast to the wholistic and coherent identities that find expression in much contemporary talk and writing about Asian Americans. At times, our need to "reclaim history" has been bluntly translated into a possessiveness about the Asian American experience (politics, history, literature) or perspectives as if such experiences or perspectives were not diffuse, shifting, and often contradictory. Feminists and gay writers, animated by post-structuralism's decentering practices offer an alternative, to theorize the subject rather than assume its truth, or worse yet, assign to it a truth.

Concretely, to theorize the subject means to uncover in magnificent detail the "situatedness"[26] of perspectives or identities as knowledge which even as it pleas for an elusive common language or claims to establish truth, cannot guarantee a genuine politics of diversity, that is, political conversation and argument, between the margins.[27] Such a politics will be marked by moments of frustration and tension because the participants will be pulling and pushing one another with statements such as, "I am like you," and "I am not like you." But the rewards for an identity politics that is not primarily ethnic-based or essentialist along some other axis will be that conversations like the one which never took place in my Asian American studies section many years ago, will finally begin. Moreover, our search for authenticity of voice—whether in gay/lesbian Asian American writing or in some other identity string—will be tempered by the realization that in spite of our impulse to clearly (de)limit them, there is perpetual uncertainty and flux governing the construction and expression of identities.

Notes

My special thanks to Russell Leong for his encouragement and commentary on this essay.

1. Alice Walker, *Conditions: Five, the Black Women's Issue* (1984): 288–89.
2. See Donna Haraway, "Situated Knowledges: The Science Question in Feminism and the Privilege of Partial Perspective," *Feminist Studies* 14: 3 (1988): 575–99.
3. See Teresa de Lauretis, "Feminist Studies/Critical Studies: Issues, Terms, and Contexts," in *Feminist Studies/Critical Studies*, ed. Teresa de Lauretis (Bloomington: Indiana University Press, 1986), 1–19; bell hooks, *Yearning: Race, Gender and Cultural Politics* (Boston: South End Press, 1990); Trinh T. Minh-ha, *Woman, Native, Other* (Bloomington: Indiana University Press, 1989); Chandra Talpade Mohanty, "Under Western Eyes: Feminist Scholarship and Colonialist Discourses," in *Third World Women and the Politics of Feminism*, ed. Chandra Talpade Mohanty, Ann Russo and Lourdes Torres (Bloomington: Indiana University Press, 1991), 52–80; Linda Alcoff, "Cultural Feminism versus Post-Structuralism: The Identity Crisis in Feminist Theory," *Signs*, 13: 3 (1988): 405–37.
4. Trinh T. Minh-ha, 28.
5. Epstein (1987). Jeffrey Escoffier, editor of *Outlook* magazine made this point in a speech at the American Educational Research Association meetings in San Francisco, April 24, 1992.
6. See Elizabeth Ellsworth, "Why Doesn't This Feel Empowering? Working through the Repressive Myths of Critical Pedagogy," 59: 3 (1989): 297–324.
7. Ed Cohen, "Who Are We? Gay 'Identity' as Political (E)motion," *inside/out*, ed. Diana Fuss (New York and London: Routledge, 1991), 71–92.
8. Of course there are exceptions, for example, blacks that "pass" and perhaps this is where homosexuality and racial identity come closest to one another, amongst those minorities who "pass" and gays who can also "pass."
9. I do not mean to suggest that there is only one presentation of self as lesbian. For example, one development recently featured in the *Los Angeles Times* is the evolution of "lipstick lesbians" (Van Gelder, 1991). The fashion issue has also been discussed in gay/lesbian publications. For example, Stein (1988) writing for *Outlook* has commented on the lack of correspondence between fashion and sexual identity, "For many, you can dress as femme one day and a butch the next...."
10. Compare for example the histories: Richard Takaki's *Strangers from a Different Shore: A History of Asian Americans* (Boston: Little, Brown, and Company, 1989) with Jonathan Katz' *Gay American History* (New York: Meridian, 1992), Michel Foucault's *The History of Sexuality* (New York: Vintage, 1980), and David Greenberg, *The Construction of Homosexuality* (Chicago: University of Chicago Press, 1988).
11. See Steffi San Buenaventura, "The Master and the Federation: A Filipino-American Social Movement in California and Hawaii," *Social Process in Hawaii* 33 (1991): 169–93.
12. Wynn Young, "Poor Butterfly" *Amerasia Journal* 17:2 (1991): 118.
13. See Keith Osajima, "Asian Americans as the Model Minority: An Analysis of the Popular Press Image in the 1960s and 1980s," *Reflections on Shattered Windows:*

Promises and Prospects for Asian American Studies, ed. Gary Y. Okihiro, Shirley Hune, Arthur A. Hansen and John M. Liu (Pullman: Washington State University Press, 1988), 165–74.

14. See Judith Butler, *Gender Trouble* (New York: Routledge, 1990).

15. Diana Fuss, "Inside/Out," *inside/out*, ed. Diana Fuss (New York: Routledge, 1991), 1–10.

16. Ibid.

17. Consider for example debates in recent times over intermarriage patterns, the controversy over Asian Americans dating white men, the Asian Men's calendar, and the continuation of discussions started over a decade ago about gender, assimilation, and nativism in Asian American literature.

18. See Rey Chow, *Woman and Chinese Modernity* (Minneapolis: University of Minnesota Press, 1991).

19. See Asian Women United, *Making Waves* (Boston: Beacon Press, 1989).

20. Monique Wittig, "The Straight Mind," *The Straight Mind and Other Essays*, 25.

21. All too often we conceptualize different identities as separate, discrete, and given (as opposed to continually constructed and shifting). For an example of how "identity" might be conceptualized as contradictory and shifting moments rather than discrete and warring "homes," see Elly Bulkin, Minnie Bruce Pratt, and Barbara Smith, "Identity: Skin Blood Heart," in *Yours In Struggle* (Ithaca: Firebrand Books, 1988).

22. See Jeff Nunokawa, "'All the Sad Young Men': Aids and the Work of Mourning," *inside/out*, ed. Diana Fuss, 311–23.

23. Trinh T. Minh-ha, 76.

24. Judith Butler, "Imitation and Gender Subordination," *inside/out*, ed. Diana Fuss, 13–31.

25. Lisa Lowe, "Heterogeneity, Hybridity and Multiplicity: Marking Asian American Differences," *Diaspora* (Spring 1991): 24–44.

26. Haraway.

27. I am indebted to Wendy Brown for this point. See Wendy Brown, "Feminist Hesitations, Postmodern Exposures," *Differences* 2: 1 (1991).

2

Stories from the Homefront

Perspectives of Asian American Parents with Lesbian Daughters and Gay Sons

Alice Y. Hom

Having been a classroom teacher since 1963, I have new knowledge that ten percent of all the students who came through my classroom have grown up and are gay and lesbian.... Because I cannot undo the past, I want to teach people the truth about homosexuality so people will not abandon these children.[1]

These are stories from the homefront; the emotions, responses, and attitudes of Asian American parents regarding their lesbian daughters or gay sons.[2] The stories attempt to shed some light on parents' attitudes, and inform lesbians and gay men about the various ways that parents may react and respond to their coming out.

I focus on four themes that illustrate important concepts around understanding Asian American parents and their views on homosexuality. These themes emerged from the interviews: 1) the attitudes of parents before disclosure/discovery; 2) the attitudes and reactions of parents after disclosure/discovery; 3) disclosure to friends and their communities; and 4) advice for other parents.

Sexuality is an issue rarely or never discussed amongst Asian families, yet it remains a vital aspect of one's life. What are the implications of alternative sexualities in family situations? Coming out stories and experiences of Asian

American lesbians and gay men have had some exposure and publication,[3] however the voices of the parents are rarely presented or known.

I found the majority of interviewees through personal contacts with individuals in organizations such as Asian Pacifica Sisters in San Francisco, Mahu Sisters and Brothers Alliance at UCLA, and Gay Asian Pacific Alliance Community HIV Project in San Francisco. I met one set of parents through the Parents and Friends of Lesbians and Gays group in Los Angeles. Obviously this select group of people, who were willing to talk about their child, might represent only certain perspectives. Nonetheless, I managed to pool a diverse set of parents despite the small size in terms of disclosing time and time lapse— some parents have known for years and a few have recently found out. I did receive some "no" answers to my request. I also offered complete anonymity in the interviews; most preferred pseudonyms. Names with an asterisk sign denote pseudonyms.

I interviewed thirteen parents altogether, all mothers except for two fathers.[4] The interviewee pool consisted of four single mothers by divorce, a widower, two couples, and four married mothers. The ethnicities included four Chinese, four Japanese, three Pilipinas, one Vietnamese, and one Korean. Most live in California with one in Portland and another in Hawaii. All of the interviews occurred in English with the exception of one interview conducted in Japanese with the lesbian daughter as translator. Ten out of the thirteen interviewees are first generation immigrants. The other three are third generation Japanese American. I interviewed four mothers of gay sons including one mother with two gay sons. The rest had lesbian daughters including one mother with two lesbian daughters. Six were told and seven inadvertently discovered about their children's sexual orientation.[5]

Most books on the topic of parents of lesbian and gay children report mainly on white middle-class families.[6] *Beyond Acceptance: Parents of Lesbians and Gays Talk about Their Experiences*, by Carolyn W. Griffin, Marian J. Wirth, and Arthur G. Wirth, discusses the experiences of twenty-three white middle-class parents from a Midwestern metropolitan city involved with Parents and Friends of Lesbians and Gays (PFLAG).[7] Another book titled, *Parents Matter: Parents' Relationships with Lesbian Daughters and Gay Sons*, by Ann Muller, relates the perspectives of lesbian and gay children with a few stories by the parents. Seventeen percent of the seventy-one people interviewed were black.[8] These examples present mainly an Anglo picture and fail to account for the diversity of lesbian and gay communities as well as different experiences of parents of color.

Attitudes of Parents towards Gays and Lesbians Pre-disclosure

The knowledge of lesbians and gay men in their native countries and in their communities in the United States serves as an important factor in dismantling the oft-used phrase that a son or daughter is gay or lesbian because of assimilation and acculturation in a western context. The parents interviewed did not utter "it's a white disease," a phrase often heard and used when discussing coming out in an Asian American community and context. Connie S. Chan in her essay, "Issues of Identity Development among Asian American Lesbians and Gay Men," found in her study that nine out of ninety-five respondents were out to their parents. Chan suggested that this low number might be related to, "specific cultural values defining the traditional roles, which help to explain the reluctance of Asian-American lesbians and gay men to 'come out' to their parents and families."[9]

Nonetheless, the parents interviewed recounted incidents of being aware of lesbians and or gays while they were growing up and did not blame assimilation and Anglo American culture for their children's sexual orientation. One quote by Lucy Nguyen*, a fifty-three year old Vietnamese immigrant who has two gay sons, does however, imply that the environment and attitudes of the United States allowed for her sons to express their gay identity. She stated:

> In an environment like this—with all the gay activities—I think I'm lesbian. You know, I'll be honest. When I was young in Vietnam society was so strict. Yet, I had a really close friend, I loved her. That was just a friendship nothing else. In my mind now, I say, well this country is freer. There's no restraints, so that's why I accept it, whatever they [my sons] are.[10]

This revealing remark assumes that an open environment allows for freedom of sexual expression. Nevertheless, it does not necessarily suggest lesbians and gay men exist solely because of a nurturing environment. Rather lesbians and gay men must live and survive in different ways and/or make choices depending on the climate of the society at the time.

Midori Asakura*, a sixty-three-year-old Japanese immigrant with a lesbian daughter, related an example of lesbianism in Japan. She remembered, while studying to be a nurse, talk in the dorm rooms about "S," which denotes women who had really close friendships with one another.[11] She recalled,

> One day you'd see one woman with a certain blouse and the next day, you'd see the other woman with the same blouse. They would always sit together, they went everywhere together. There was talk that they were having sex, but I didn't think they were…. People used to say they felt each other out. I thought, 'Nah, they're not having sex, why would they?' Everyone thought it was strange but no one really got into it.[12]

*These names have been changed.

When asked what she thought of the "S" women, Midori replied, "I didn't think much of it, although I thought one was man-like, Kato-san, and the other, Fukuchi-san, who was very beautiful and sharp-minded was the woman."[13]

Another parent, George Tanaka*, a fifty-three-year-old Japanese American who grew up in Hawaii and has a lesbian daughter, remembers a particular person known as mahu.[14] Toni Barraquiel, a fifty-four-year-old Pilipina single mother with a gay son, commented on gay men in Manila because of their effeminacy and admission of being gay. Toni asserted these men would be in certain careers such as manicurists and hairdressers. When asked of the people's attitudes towards them she replied,

> that they look down on those gays and lesbians, they make fun of them…. It seems as if it is an abnormal thing. The lesbian is not as prominent as the gays. They call her a tomboy because she's very athletic and well built.[15]

Maria Santos*, a fifty-four-year-old Pilipina immigrant with two lesbian daughters, spoke of gays and lesbians in Luzon. She said, "There were negative attitudes about them. 'Bakla' and 'Tomboy'—it was gay-bashing in words not in physical terms. There was name-calling that I did not participate in."[16]

Lucy Nguyen* had lesbian classmates in her all-girls high school. She said, "They were looked down upon, because this isn't normal. They were called 'homo'."[17] A common thread throughout the observations of the parents about gays and lesbians lies in stereotypical gender role associations. For example, Margaret Tsang*, a sixty-year-old Chinese single parent who has a gay son, recalled a family member who might possibly be gay, although there was not a name for it. She observed, "He was slanted towards nail polish and make-ups and all kinds of things. And he liked Chinese opera. He behaved in a very feminine fashion."[18]

Similarly, Liz Lee, a forty-two-year old Korean single parent with a lesbian daughter, clearly remembered lesbians in Seoul. "My mother's friend was always dressed like man in suit. She always had mousse or grease on her hair and she dressed like a man. She had five or six girlfriends always come over."[19] Liz related that she did not think anything about it and said they were respected.[20] When asked of people's attitudes toward these women, Liz responded, "They say nature made a mistake. They didn't think it was anybody's choice or anybody's preference."[21]

For the most part the interviewees, aware of gays and lesbians during their growing up years, associated gender role reversals with gays and lesbians. The men were feminine and the women looked male or tomboy with the women couples in a butch-femme type relationship. The belief and experiences with lesbians and gay men who dress and act in opposite gender roles serve as the backdrop of what to compare their children with when faced with their coming out. Most of what these parents see is a part of homosexuality, the dress or behavior. They have not seen the whole range of affectional, emotional, intellectual, and sexual components of a person. Although I asked the interviewees if they had any thoughts or attitudes about lesbians or gay men, most said they did not think about them and did not participate in the name calling or bashing. This might not be necessarily true because they were able to relate quite a few incidents of homophobic opinions which might have been internalized. Moreover, once they know they have a lesbian or gay child, that distance or non-judgmental attitude radically changes. As one mother remarked, "the fire is on the other side of the river bank. The matter is taking place somewhere else, it's not your problem."[22]

Disclosure or Discovery

For the most part, parents experience a wide range of emotions, feelings, and attitudes when they find out they have a lesbian daughter or gay son. Parents find out through a variety of ways, ranging from a direct disclosure by the child themselves, discovering the fact from a journal, confronting the child because of suspicions, or by walking in on them.

For example, Liz Lee, who walked in on her daughter Sandy, said, "[it was] the end of the world. Still today I can't relate to anything that's going on with my daughter, but I'm accepting."[23] She found out in 1990 and said,

> I was hoping it was a stage she's going through and that she could change. I didn't accept for a long time. I didn't think she would come out in the open like this. I thought she would just keep it and later on get married. That's what I thought but she's really out and open.... I said to myself I accept it because she is going to live that way.[24]

Because Sandy serves as the co-chair of the Gay, Lesbian, and Bisexual Association at school, her mother sees Sandy as happy and politically fulfilled from this position, which assists her process in accepting Sandy's sexual orientation. However, like many of the parents interviewed, she initially thought she had done something wrong. "I didn't lead a normal life at the time either. But Sandy always accept me as I was and she was always happy when I was happy and I think that's love. As long as Sandy's happy."[25]

Toni Barraquiel responded differently when Joel told her at an early age of thirteen or fourteen that he was gay back in the mid 1980s. She plainly asked him if he felt happy, and he replied affirmatively. Thus her response, "Well, if you're happy I'll support you, I'll be happy for you."[26] Their relationship as a single mother and only child has always been one of closeness and open communication so problems did not arise in terms of disclosing his sexual orientation. Toni Barraquiel experienced confusion because at the time Joel had girlfriends and she did not think of him as a typical feminine gay man, since he looked macho. She also wondered if her single mother role had anything to do with Joel's gay orientation:

> Maybe because I raised him by myself, it was a matriarchal thing. I have read now that these gays, there is something in the anatomy of their bodies that affect the way they are. So it is not because I raised him alone, maybe it's in the anatomy of the body. Even if I think that because I raised him alone as a mother, even if he came out to be gay, he was raised as a good person. No matter what I would say I'm still lucky he came out to be like that.[27]

In the end she accepted Joel no matter what caused his sexual orientation.

Katherine Tanaka*, a fifty-three-year-old Japanese American from Hawaii, found out about Melissa's lesbianism through an indirect family conversation. George Tanaka* brought up the issue of sexuality and asked Melissa* if she was a lesbian. He suspected after reading her work on the computer. Katherine* remembered her own response:

> I was in a state of shock. I didn't expect it, so I didn't know how to react. It was the thing of disbelief, horror and shame and the whole thing. I guess I felt the Asian values I was taught surface in the sense that something was wrong. That she didn't turn out the way we had raised her to be.[28]

George Tanaka* recalled, "After we hugged, she went off to her bedroom. As she was walking away from us, all of a sudden I felt like she was a stranger. I thought I knew [her]. Here was a very important part of her and I didn't know anything about it."[29] The idea of not knowing one's children anymore after discovering their sexual orientation remains a common initial response from the interviewees. Because of this one aspect, parents believe their child has changed and is no longer the person they thought they knew. For example, one parent said:

> The grieving process took a long time. Especially the thing about not being a bride. Not having her be a bride was a very devastating change of plans for her life. I thought I was in her life and it made me feel when she said she was a lesbian that there was no place for me in her life. I didn't know how I could fit into her life because I didn't know how to be the mother of a lesbian.[30]

Upon finding out, the parents interviewed spoke of common responses and questions they had. What did I do wrong? Was I responsible for my child's lesbian or gay identity? What will others think? How do I relate to my child? What role do I have now that I know my child is a lesbian or gay man? The emotions a parent has ranged from the loss of a dream they had for their child to a fear of what is in store for them as a gay or lesbian person in this society.

Nancy Shigekawa*, a third-generation Japanese American born and residing in Hawaii, recalled her reaction:

I had come home one night and they were in the bedroom. Then I knew it wasn't just being in the room. My reaction was outrage, to say the least. I was so angry. I told them to come out...and I said [to her girlfriend] "I'm going to kill you if you ever come back." That's how I was feeling. I look back now and think I must have been like a crazy lady.[31]

Maria Santos* remembered her discovery.

I found out through a phone call from the parents of [her] best friend. They [Cecilia* and her friend] were trying to sneak out and they had a relationship. I thought it would go away. Let her see a psychiatrist. But she fooled me. In her second year at college she told me she was a lesbian. It broke my heart. That was the first time I heard the word lesbian, but I knew what it meant. Like the tomboy.[32]

She also had a feeling about her youngest daughter, Paulette*:

At Cecilia's graduation I saw them talking secretly and I saw the pink triangle on her backpack. I can't explain it. It's a mother's instinct. I prayed that it would not be so [starts to cry]. Paulette told me in a letter that she was a lesbian and that Cecilia had nothing to do with it. I wanted it to change. I had the dream, that kids go to college, get married and have kids.[33]

Maria Santos* did not talk to anyone about her daughters. She grew up having to face the world on her own without talking to others. However, she said, "But I read books, articles all about gays and lesbians as members of the community. They are normal people. I did not read negative things about them."[34]

In this sense parents also have a coming out process that they go through. They must deal with internalized homophobia and reevaluate their beliefs and feelings about lesbians and gay men. One method in this process includes reading about and listening to gay men and lesbians talk about their lives. Having personal contact or at least information on lesbian and gay life takes the mystery out of the stereotypes and misconceptions that parents might have of lesbian and gay people. What helped some women was the personal interaction and reading about lesbian and gay men's lives. They had more information with which to contrast, contradict, and support their previous notions of lesbians and gay men.

Yet sometimes some parents interviewed have not yet read or do not seek outside help or information. Some of the parents did not talk to others and have remained alone in their thinking. This does not necessarily have negative effects. Liz Lee said, "Still today I don't think I can discuss with her this matter because I can't relate.... I can't handle it. I wouldn't know how to talk to her about this subject. I just let her be happy."[35]

MG Espiritu*, a sixty-year-old Pilipina immigrant, believes her daughter's lesbianism stems from environmental causes such as being with other lesbians. Nonetheless, less than a couple of years after finding out about her daughter Michelle, she went with her daughter to an Asian Pacific lesbian Lunar New Year banquet. MG* did so because her daughter wanted it and she wanted to please her. When asked how she felt at the event, MG* replied, "Oh, it's normal. It's just like my little girls' parties that they go to."[36] She speaks of little by little trying to accept Michelle's lesbianism.

Parents, Friends, and their Ethnic Communities

For some parents having a lesbian or gay child brings up the issue of their status and reputation in the community and family network. Questions such as: What is society going to think of me? Will the neighbors know, and what will it reflect upon us? Did we raise a bad child?

> I told her we would have to move away from this house. I felt strongly neighbors and friends in the community would not want to associate with us if they knew we had a child who had chosen to be homosexual.[37]

The above quote reflected one parent's original reaction. Now she feels differently but is still not quite out to her family in Hawaii.

Some parents have told their siblings or friends. Others do not talk to relatives or friends at all because of fear they will not understand.

The following quote highlighted a typical anxiety of parents:

> I was ashamed. I felt I had a lot to do with it too. In my mind I'm not stupid, I'm telling myself, I know I didn't do it to her. I don't know if it's only because I'm Japanese...that's the way I saw it. I felt a sense of shame, that something was wrong with my family. I would look at Debbie* and just feel so guilty that I have these thoughts that something's wrong with her. But mostly I was selfish. I felt more for myself, what I am going to say? How am I going to react to people when they find out?[38]

Despite her apprehension in the beginning, she did disclose Debbie's lesbianism to a close friend:

I have a dear friend who I finally told because she was telling me about these different friends who had gay children. I couldn't stand it, I said, "You know, Bea, I have to tell you my daughter is gay." She was dumfounded. I'm starting to cheer her up and all that. That was a big step for me to come out.

Nancy Shigekawa's* quote emphasizes the complexity of feelings that parents have when adjusting to their children's sexual orientation.

If parents are not close to their immediate family, they might not have told them. Others have not spoken because they do not care whether or not their family knows. Some parents do not disclose the fact of their gay son or lesbian daughter to protect them from facing unnecessary problems.

When asked how their respective ethnic communities feel about lesbians and gay men, some parents responded with firm conviction. Liz Lee, who spoke about the Korean community, said, "As long as they're not in their house, not in their life, they accept it perfectly."[39] She mentioned her daughter's lesbianism to a nephew but not to others in her family. "I'm sure in the future I have to tell them, but right now nobody has asked me and I don't particularly like to volunteer."[40] Jack Chan*, a sixty-one-year-old Chinese immigrant claimed, "Shame, that's a big factor. Shame brought upon the family. You have to remember the Chinese, the name, the face of the family is everything. I don't know how to overcome that."[41]

Lucy Nguyen* gave this answer about the Vietnamese community, "They won't accept it. Because for a long, long time they say they [gays and lesbians] are not good people, that's why."[42] Lucy felt that by talking about it, it would help teach the community to open their minds. The frankness and openness of speaking out about gays and lesbians will inform people of our existence and force the issue in the open. In this way having parents come out will make others understand their experiences and allow for their validation and affirmation as well.

Although most of these parents have negative views about the acceptance level of friends and particularly with ethnic communities, some have taken steps to confide in people. One must also realize their opinion reflects their current situation and opinions which might change over time. Three of the parents have participated in panels and discussions on Asian American parents with lesbian and gay kids.

Advice to Other Parents

The mere fact these parents agreed to the interview has much to say about their feelings or attitudes towards lesbian and gay sexuality and their children. Although some parents might feel some unease and reservations, they had enough courage to speak to me and voice their opinions. Many of the parents did so out of love and concern for their children. A few thought that they did not have anything to say but agreed to talk to me. In the process of these interviews, some parents expressed appreciation and comfort in talking to someone about their experiences. Their struggle of coming to terms with their lesbian daughters and gay sons merits notice.

One of my last questions related to helping other parents. While some did not have an answer to the question, "What advice do you have for other parents with lesbian and gay kids?" a few responded with the following suggestions. For example,

Love them like a normal individual. Give all the compassion and understanding. Don't treat your child differently because the person is gay, because this is an individual…. I cannot understand why it is so hard for these parents to accept their child is gay. What makes them so different, because they are gay? The more you should support your kid, because as it is in society, it has not been accepted one hundred percent.[43]

I cannot throw them out. I love them so much. Even more now because they are more of a minority. They are American Asian, women and lesbian. Triple minority. I have to help fight for them…. Accept them as they are. Love them more. They will encounter problems. It will take years and years to overcome homophobia. Make them ambitious, well-educated, better than others so they can succeed.[44]

Tina Chan*, a fifty-eight-year-old Chinese immigrant, offers similar advice. Other parents concurred:

My advice is to accept them. They haven't changed at all. They're still the same person. The only thing different is their sexual orientation. They should really have the support from the family, so they would not have this battle like they're not even being accepted in the family. They should look at them like they have not changed. Parents can't do it. They think the whole person has changed and I think that's terrible because they haven't. I mean it's so stupid.[45]

Jack Chan* also leaves us with advice to take to heart:

Don't feel depressed that their parent [is] coming around so slow or not coming around at all. Remember when you come out to them, the parent generally go[es] into the closet themselves. However long it take you to come out, it'll probably take them longer to accept. It's a slow process. Don't give up.[46]

Concluding Remarks

George Tanaka* relates an incident where he and his wife told their coming out process in front of ten Asian American gay men and in the end found some of the men crying. "The tears surprised me.... We were representing the sadness that there could not be loving parents. Representing some hope their parents would likewise be able to become loving about it."[46] The belief that parents can change and go through a process where eventual acceptance and supportiveness appear to have a basis in reality, although a happy ending might not always be the case.

From these interviews one can sense some of the thoughts, actions, and experiences of Asian American parents. These stories are not the last word but signal the beginning of a more informed dialogue.

What would the stories of their daughters and sons look like against their parents' perceptions? It would be helpful to have the stories side by side to evaluate the differences. Moreover, gay and lesbian children might have perspectives that inform parents. Other issues such as socialization processes, religious, language and cultural issues, and spouses' opinions need further exploration. I did not include a discussion on the origins of lesbian and gay sexual identity. I hope these stories from the homefront can serve as an initial mapping of a complex sexual territory that is part of Asian American family dynamics.

Notes

1. Interview with Katherine Tanaka. Los Angeles, California, February 21, 1993.
2. The desire to work on this project came after listening to two Japanese American parents, George and Katherine Tanaka, talk about their lesbian daughter. They revealed a painful process of going through their own coming out while grappling with their daughter's sexual identity and their own values and beliefs. As members of Parents and Friends of Lesbians and Gays (PFLAG) they mentioned they were the only Asian Americans, the only parents of color, for that matter, in this organization. Despite being the Asian American contact Katherine has received less than ten calls during a two year time span and not one Asian American parent has ever come to PFLAG. She recounted her feelings and belief of being the only Asian parent with a gay child. That feeling of loneliness and alienation struck me deeply because as an Asian American lesbian I could identify with her feelings.
3. See Kitty Tsui, *the words of a woman who breathes fire* (San Francisco: Spinsters Ink, 1983). C. Chung, Alison Kim, and A.K. Lemshewsky, eds., *Between the Lines: An Anthology by Pacific/Asian Lesbians* (Santa Cruz: Dancing Bird Press, 1987). Rakesh Ratti, ed., *A Lotus of Another Color: The Unfolding of the South Asian Gay and Lesbian Experience* (Boston: Alyson Press, 1993). Silvera Makeda, ed., *A Piece of My Heart: A Lesbian of Colour Anthology* (Toronto: Sister Vision Press, 1993).
4. Mothers comprise the majority of the parents interviewed. Perhaps mothers are more apt to talk about their feelings and emotions about having a gay son or lesbian daugh-

ter than the father. Mothers might be more understanding and willing to discuss their emotions and experiences than the fathers who also know.

5. I did not interview parents who had a bisexual child. I believe a son or daughter who comes out as bisexual might encounter a different set of questions and reactions. Especially since the parent might hope and persuade the daughter or son to "choose" heterosexuality instead of homosexuality.

6. See Carolyn W. Griffin, Marian J. Wirth, and Arthur G. Wirth, *Beyond Acceptance: Parents of Lesbians and Gays Talk about their Experiences* (New York: St. Martin's Press, 1986).

7. Parents and Friends of Lesbians and Gays (PFlag) has chapters all around the United States. One couple and a father interviewed are involved with PFlag in their respective locales.

8. Ann Muller, *Parents Matter: Parents' Relationships with Lesbian Daughters and Gay Sons* (Tallahassee: The Naiad Press, Inc., 1987), 197.

9. Connie S. Chan "Issues of Identity Development among Asian-American Lesbians and Gay Men." *Journal of Counseling and Development,* 68 (September–October, 1989): 19.

10. Interview with Lucy Nguyen. Los Angeles, California, February 20, 1993.

11. Interview with Midori Asakura. Los Angeles, California, April 18, 1993.

12. Midori Asakura.

13. Ibid.

14. Mahu does not necessarily mean gay but defines a man who dresses and acts feminine. However, it common usage does denote a gay man.

15. Interview with Toni Barraquiel. Los Angeles, California, April 18, 1993.

16. Telephone interview Maria Santos. Portland, Oregon, May 9, 1993.

17. Lucy Nguyen.

18. Interview with Margaret Tsang. San Francisco, California, February 5, 1993.

19. Interview with Liz Lee. Los Angeles, California, May 11, 1993.

20. Liz based this respect on this particular woman's election to something similar to a city council and her standing in the community.

21. Liz Lee.

22. Midori Asakura.

23. Liz Lee.

24. Ibid.

25. Ibid.

26. Toni Barraquiel.

27. Ibid.

28. Katherine Tanaka.

29. Interview with George Tanaka. Los Angeles, California, February 21, 1993.

30. Katherine Tanaka.

31. Telephone interview with Nancy Shigekawa. Kaneohe, Hawaii, March 20, 1993.

32. Maria Santos.

33. Ibid.

34. Ibid.

35. Liz Lee.

36. Interview with MG Espiritu. Northern California, July 20, 1993.
37. Katherine Tanaka.
38. Nancy Shigekawa.
39. Liz Lee.
40. Ibid.
41. Interview with Jack Chan. Northern California, July 18, 1993.
42. Lucy Nguyen.
43. Toni Barraquiel.
44. Maria Santos.
45. Interview with Tina Chan. Northern California, July 18, 1993.
46. Jack Chan.
47. George Tanaka.

3

Searching for Community
Filipino Gay Men in New York City

Martin F. Manalansan IV

Introduction

In 1987, a Filipino gay man named Exotica was crowned Miss Fire Island. The Miss Fire Island beauty contest is an annual drag event on Fire Island (located off the coast of Long Island and considered to be the premier gay summer mecca in America.) It was interesting to note that a considerable number of the contestants who were not Caucasian were Filipinos. Furthermore, Exotica was not the first Filipino recipient of the crown, another Filipino was crowned earlier in the seventies. In 1992, a Filipino gay and lesbian group called Kambal sa Lusog marched in two separate parades in New York City, during Gay Pride Day and Philippine Independence Day. These iconic events suggest the strong presence of Filipinos in the American gay scene, particularly in New York City.

This paper delineates this presence by analyzing the issues of identity and community among fifty gay Filipino men in the city in their attempts to institutionalize or organize themselves. Through excerpts from life history interviews and field observations, I explore the ways in which being "gay" and being "Filipino" are continually being shaped by historical events.

I use the term community not as a static, closed, and unified system. Rather, I use the term strategically and conceptualize it as a fluid movement between subjectivity/identity and collective action.[1] Therefore, intrinsic to this use of the term "community" is a sense of dissent and contestation along with a sense of belonging to a group or cause. I also use Benedict Anderson's[2] notion of community as "imagined," which means symbols, language, and other cultural practices and products from songs to books are sites where people articulate their sense of belonging. The concept of identity is not a series or stages of development nor a given category, but a dynamic package of meanings contingent upon practices that are both individually and collectively reconfigured.[3]

The first section briefly explores the cleavages that give rise to a diversity of voices and outlines differences such as class, attitudes towards various homosexual practices, and ethnic/racial identity. In the next two sections, two pivotal moments, the *Miss Saigon* controversy and the AIDS pandemic, are discussed in terms of the patterns of cultural actions and countereactions. I focus on new or reconfigured collective discourses, specifically language and ritual. I also emphasize the organizing efforts of Filipinos to create a gay and lesbian group (Kambal sa Lusog) and an AIDS advocacy group. A specific activity called the Santacruzan by Kambal sa Lusog incorporates symbols from different national traditions and provides an example of the collective representation of community.

Divergent Voices

Ang sabi nila, iba't iba daw ang bakla, mayroon cheap, may pa-class, nandito yoong malandi at saka ang mayumi—kuno! (They say there are different kinds of bakla, those who are tacky, those who pretend they have class, then there are the whorish and the virginal—not!)

We are all gay. We are all Filipinos. We need to empower ourselves as a group.

Tigilan ako ng mga tsismosang bakla, wiz ko type maki-beso-beso sa mga baklang Pilipino—puro mga intrigera! [Get me away from those gossipy *bakla*, I don't want to socialize with those Filipino *bakla*, they are all gossip mongers!]

If we take these voices as indices of the opinions and stances of Filipino gay men, we will find a spectrum of similarities and differences. Most Filipino gay men consider place of birth as an important gauge of the attitudes and ideas of a gay individual. The dichotomy between U.S. born versus Philippine or native born Filipino gay men is actually used by many informants I have interviewed. This simplistic dichotomy is inadequate and erroneous. It does not begin to address the diversity among Filipino gay men.

Attitudes towards Homosexual Practices

In a group discussion I lead with a group of Filipino gay men and lesbians, one gay man pointed out that the culture in which one was raised in and more importantly the particular homosexual tradition one was socialized in mattered more than place of birth. This is particularly true in many of my informants who immigrated as young children or in their early teens. Many of them explored their sexual identities under the symbols and practices of American culture. Many of them were not exposed to the *bakla* traditions[4] and more frequently followed the idioms and practices of American gay culture. These men were usually concerned with issues of coming out and identified more with a hyper-masculine gay culture.

While almost all of my informants identified as gay, many of those who immigrated as adults and had some encounters in *bakla* practices and traditions, were emphatic in delineating major difference between American gay and Philippine *bakla* culture. Most of these differences centered on the issue of crossdressing and effeminacy.

However, there were some informants, including two American-born Filipinos, who through frequent visits to the Philippines as well as extended stays as students in Philippine schools, were exposed to and involved in the *bakla* tradition. This group of men were more familiar with the crossdressing traditions of homosexuality in the Philippines and usually spoke versions of Filipino swardspeak (a kind of gay argot).[5]

A case illustrates this point. One informant who was born and raised in California said that a turning point in his life was when he went to the Philippines at the age of sixteen and his uncle introduced him to crossdressing and other practices among homosexuals. That brief (month-and-a-half) visit was to become an important element in the way he now socialized in the gay community. He sought crossdressing opportunities not only with other transvestites but with other Filipinos. He said that Filipino gay men did not crossdress for shock value but for verisimilitude. He further mentioned that he was unlike those gay men who were into queer androgyny consciously looking midway between male and female. He and other gay men who crossdressed attempted to look like real women. More important, despite the fact that he was raised speaking English at home, his friendships with other Philippine-born gay men has encouraged him to attempt to speak at least some smattering of the Filipino gay argot.

Some informants felt that Filipino crossdressers had illusions (*ilusyonada*) and were internally homophobic or self-hating. These same informants were the ones who reported that they were part of the mainstream gay community. Some of them go to gyms and assume masculine ("straight-acting") mannerisms. They saw the crossdressing practices of other Filipinos to be either low-class, archaic/anachronous (meaning crossdressing belonged in the Philippines and not here in America).

On the other hand, the crossdressers would call these guys *pa-macho* (acting macho) or *pa-min* (acting like men). Filipino gay crossdressers accused these "masculine" men of mimicking white Americans and of having illusions of being "real" men. Exotica,[6] one of my informants, said that crossdressing for him was a way of getting men. He liked assuming more exotic identities and *nom de plumes* such as "Suzie Wong" or "Nancy Kwan." In the Philippines, he said he was able to get men for sex, but he had to pay them. In America, he said there was a "market" for his crossdressing talent and exotic beauty. He said that he could not compete in the hypermasculine, gym-oriented world of mainstream gay life in New York. He said, "With my slight build, who would even give me a second look if I was wearing a T-shirt." However, he said that there were men, particularly those who were not gay-identified who were attracted to "beautiful," "oriental" crossdressers. He said that here in America, he did not have to pay the man to have sex with him, it was the other way around. He complained, "Sometimes I feel so cheap because the man will insist on paying for everything including the pleasure of having sex with you. It is like everything goes on an opposite current here in America. I like it."

Conflicts between Filipino gay crossdressers and non-crossdressers are not dramatically played out in violent confrontations, but rather in avoidance. Furthermore, the differences are usually played down with a "live and let live" or "*yun ang type niya*" (that is his/her choice) attitude.

Social Class

Class is a more implicit boundary marker among gay Filipinos. Many of my informants denied noting any difference between themselves and other gay Filipinos. However, upon further probing, several of them (mostly those who were born and raised in the Philippines) will say, "Well, there are those who gossip a lot and just make bitchy remarks," or "Other Filipino gays are so tacky." Some Filipino gay men actually used terms as *baklang talipapa* (the *bakla* of the wet market), *baklang* cheap (tacky *bakla*), and *baklang kalye* (*bakla* of the streets), to designate gay Filipinos who they think are of a lower class standing or of lower "breeding." The indices of "low breeding" are myriad, but some informants agree that they include fluency in the English language, styles of dress, schools attended, and "bearing" or how a gay Filipino carries himself.

Family roots are said to be another marker of class. *De buena familia* (from a good family) is a term used by gay men to portray how someone has class and social standing. Another word used to describe somebody who has a lot of money as *datungera* (*datung* is swardspeak for money and the noun is given the feminine form). In most conversations between Filipinos that I have heard and observed, the typical insult hurled at other gay men apart from physical traits were the idioms derived from class or the lack thereof.

Despite these occurrences, many still assert that America has leveled off some of these distinctions. An informant said, "There are some Filipinos I would normally not have contact with back home in the Philippines, but here in

America we are thrown together in the bars, in the streets, some neighbor-hoods…you know."

The case of David, a gay Filipino in his forties, is particularly instructive. He was very proud of his aristocratic background in the Philippines. He said America was very funny because he was able to maintain relationships with people who were not of his class. Coming from a landed family in the Philippines, he said that he tried to create some distance from people who were not his equal. But this was not true in America. For a long time, his lover was a telephone linesman with a high school degree. He said there were times when the class disparity showed. For example, conflicts occurred in situations when their tastes for particular leisure activities were divided into, in his mind, the classy and the tasteless, between a concert and bowling.

He further reported that his first ten years of living in America were spent as an illegal alien. Despite having money and a good education, he started as a jan-itor or a busboy due to lack of legal papers. He said, "I guess living during those years and doing those kinds of jobs were exciting in a way…a different way of experiencing America." Indeed, David's own class-conscious ways have been tempered to a large extent by the immigration experience. He now has contacts with several Filipino gay men many of whom were of lower class origins.

Most of those who were born in America did not report any class distinc-tions among Filipinos. They were, however, more up front about their class origins. Two of my informants who were born and raised in California pref-aced their stories about childhood by stating that they were from working class families in the U.S. army.

Ethnic/Racial Identity

Most articles on Asian American gay men regard identity as a static given and construct ethnic identity as a polar opposite of gay identity.[7] Among the ques-tions I asked my fifty Filipino informants was how they identified ethnically or racially. All but one said that they identified as Filipino or Filipino American. When I asked about the category Asian/Pacific Islander, most of them said that while they assumed this category in official papers and functions, they per-ceived Asia or Asian only in geographic terms. When I asked the Filipino gay men how they differed from other Asian gay men, many Filipino informants said that they did not have the same kind of issues such as coming out and homophobia.

A majority of informants, mostly immigrants, felt that Philippine society was relatively tolerant of homosexuality. Some informants reported very good responses from families when they did "come out." Others felt that they didn't have to come out about being gay because they thought that their families knew about their identity without their having to verbally acknowledge it. Filipino informants felt that other Asian men, particularly those who have just immigrated to America did not speak English as well as they did. Important cultural differences, such as religion, were cited by informants as significant. Many felt that they had a closer cultural affinity with Latinos.

Among those who were born in the Philippines, regional ethno-linguistic differences became apparent in relation to other Filipinos. Some of the informants did not speak Pilipino or Tagalog and instead spoke a regional language such as Bisaya or Ilongo. However, differences in languages and region were usually displaced by the use of English or Filipino swardspeak, a gay argot used by many of the informants.

What I have presented above is a broad outline of the differences and similarities among Filipino gay men. This is to provide a kind of foundation in which to situate the succeeding discussions of Filipino men coming together and acting in a more collective manner. This section has shown how markers of difference such as class, cultural traditions, and practices of homosexuality are articulated in Filipino gay men's lives.

The *Miss Saigon* Interlude: Irony of a Different Kind

In the first full length article on Asian gays and lesbians in the now-defunct magazine *Outweek*,[8] Nina Reyes (a Filipino American lesbian) wrote how the controversy surrounding the Broadway show *Miss Saigon* acted as a catalyst in bringing together many Asian gay and straight political activists to the forefront. According to Reyes, apart from the controversy around hiring (specifically, the use of a Caucasian, Jonathan Price, to play a Eurasian pimp) and the allegedly racist Madame Butterfly inspired storyline, the opening night of *Miss Saigon* was the venue of protests by Asian gay and lesbian groups.

It is ironic that in the same article, Miss Reyes quoted a Filipino gay man who pointed out that not all Filipinos agreed with the protests since after all, the star of the show, Lea Salonga, was a Filipina. Indeed, many of my informants have seen the show and have reported how relatives and Filipino friends (both gay and straight), particularly those from other states and the Philippines, would include seeing the show as the highlight of their visits to the Big Apple. The issue here was not just a matter of taste but had important political underpinnings. Many Filipinos felt that their sentiments and thoughts about the show were not represented in the mass media.

This was not to be the end of this controversy. The Gay Asian Pacific Islander Men of New York (GAPIMNY), one of the most vociferous groups in the *Miss Saigon* protest, celebrated its anniversary with a variety show and dance at the Lesbian and Gay Community Center in Manhattan in the summer of 1992. One of the drag performers, a Filipino gay man, decided to participate with a lipsynch performance of one of Lea Salonga's songs in *Miss Saigon*. This caused a lot of ruckus. Before the performance, attempts were made by certain non-Filipinos to dissuade the drag performer from going through his intended repertoire even while the emcee was reading a disclaimer by GAPIMNY that stated that the group disavows any connection with the Broadway show. Furthermore, the disclaimer also stated that the audience should enjoy the performance and at the same time remember the racist underpinnings of the show's storyline and production practices.

It is important to note not only the effects of the *Miss Saigon* controversy on Asian American gay politics, but also how the representations and characters of this Broadway show have become icons of Filipino gay men. After each show, many Filipinos gathered backstage to talk to the actors and actresses (many of whom are Filipino or Filipino American). A good number of these fans are gay men.

Filipino gay men have appropriated many of the symbols and figures of this Broadway play. For Halloween in 1991, Leilani, a Filipino crossdresser, bought a cheongsam in Chinatown, had a friend pull his hair back into a bun and paraded around Greenwich Village with just a small woolen scarf to protect him from the blustery cold weather. He was extremely delighted to hear people scream "Miss Saigon" at him.

Several crossdressing Filipinos I interviewed have admitted to using either Kim (the main character in *Miss Saigon*) or Lea Salonga as drag names. In fact, they said that when they talk about another gay Filipino who is either in a moody sad state or is extremely despondent, they say that he is doing a *Miss Saigon* or he is playing the role of Kim (*nagmi—Miss Saigon* or *Kim ang drama niya ngayon*).

The issues surrounding the controversy and the reaction of Filipinos, particularly gay men, have to do with several factors. The first is that of immigration and the American dream. For many of these gay Filipinos, Lea Salonga represented their own aspirations regarding America. She initially had to be certified by Actor's Equity to enable her to work on Broadway since she was neither an American citizen/resident nor a member of the group. Her success in winning the Tony Award and her receiving the green card (permanent resident status) was very much seen as a collective triumph. An informant pointed to Miss Salonga's Tony acceptance speech as particularly meaningful. After receiving the award, she said, "Your dreams can come true."

Indeed for many Filipinos, gay or straight, these words seemed to be directed at them. Since a large number of my informants are immigrants, some of whom are illegally staying in the U.S., the play provided an alternative narrative to the frustrations of daily life as foreigner trying to attain the American dream. As one informant said, "*Mahirap dito sa Amerika pero kaunting tiyaga…biyuti ka na.*" [It is hard here in America, but with a little perseverance, you will succeed (beauty here is used as part of swardspeak, and connotes good luck or fate.)]

Race and racism, which were the central issues of the controversy, were less significant for many of my informants. Those who saw the play talked about the singing abilities of the actors and the magnificent stage design. When queried about the themes of the show, they said that the bar scenes reminded them of Olongapo and Angeles cities in the Philippines. These cities were sites of the two biggest U.S. military installations outside America. In these places, bars, prostitutes, and American servicemen were everyday scenes.

The discourse of race was not particularly meaningful for many of my informants, a majority of whom have immigrated in their twenties. Out of the fifty informants, four reported an incident of racial discrimination. Most reported never encountering it. This was not entirely fortuitous. These men may have encountered some kind of discriminatory practices, but interpreted it as part of the hardships of being an immigrant in America.

While many of them did not pick up on the Orientalist symbolisms of *Miss Saigon*, this should not be interpreted as a case of false consciousness, rather this kind of reaction is symptomatic in immigrant cultures. Immigrants constantly negotiate both dominant/hegemonic and subordinate (minority) cultural products and practices into meaningful arrangements that inform their lives.[9] In the case of *Miss Saigon*, the racial stereotypes are displaced and instead, the play is interpreted as a symbolic and literal vehicle for attaining success in America. Many of my informants felt that the crucial element of the play was that of getting to America and attaining the American dream.

In sum, with the *Miss Saigon* controversy, we have a historical moment which provided Filipinos in the U.S. a pool of collective symbols from which they could create discursive practices from crossdressing to swardspeak. For many gay Filipino men in New York City, *Miss Saigon* was the impetus for the generation of camp symbols and discourses about national/ethnic and immigrant identities and aspirations.

AIDS: Or the Aunt that Pulled Us Together

I remember that around 1986, I began to hear about some Filipino *bakla* dying of AIDS in the West Coast. Then soon after that I heard about a Filipino who died in New York City. Then, I heard about this famous Filipino hairdresser who died. Afterwards the first of my friends came down with pneumonia. It was of course, Tita Aida. She struck again and again.

Tita Aida or Auntie/Aunt Aida is the name Filipino gay men have coined for AIDS. I have explored this unique construction of AIDS by this group of men in an earlier paper,[10] but it is necessary to note that this construction is not idiosyncratic. It emanates from Philippine concepts of illness, gender, and sexuality. The personification of the disease by gay Filipinos reflects the growing number of AIDS cases among Filipino gay men in America.[11] During the period from 1986 to 1988, the rise of AIDS cases among Asians in San Francisco was first documented.[12]

It was the same period of time when many of my informants started to become aware of the devastation of the disease. Most of them thought that the disease only affected white men. One informant said, "I thought that only white men, *yung mga byuti* (the beautiful ones) who were having sex constantly, were the only ones getting it." Before 1986, there were rumors as well as some published articles both in Filipino publications here and back in the Philippines which talked about the natural immunity of Filipinos against the disease. Some articles talked about the diet (such as eating bagoong or salted shrimp paste) as the reason why there were no Filipinos with AIDS.

This was soon dispelled by the sudden onslaught of Filipino AIDS cases during the late eighties. An informant remembered how he took care of about five friends. He said,

> *Ang hirap…manash* [it was hard sister] I had to massage, clean, shop and do so many things. It was a horror watching them die slowly and painfully. And when they died…. My friends and I realized that there was no money for a burial or to send the bodies back to the Philippines. That was when we had some fundraising dinners. We just had dinner not the siyam-siyam (traditional Filipino prayer ritual held several days after a burial) but just a simple get-together at somebody's place and a hat is passed to get some money to defray some expenses.

Many of the informants who have had friends die of AIDS reported similar themes and situations. Many of their friends were alone and without family because they were the first in their families to settle here or because their families refused to have anything to do with them after the truth came out. Some families took these ailing gay Filipinos back and refused to acknowledge both these men's disease and sexual orientation. However, there were also a number of families who accepted them, their gay friends, and lovers. In cases where there was a lover (usually Caucasian), it was he who oftentimes took care of the ailing Filipino.

In cases when the Filipino was alone, going back home to the Philippines was not seen as a viable option. First, because there were no adequate medical facilities that could take care of a patient with AIDS. Second, there were horror stories going around about how some Filipino Americans with AIDS were deported from the Philippines. Third, coming down with the disease was seen by some as a failure on their part of attaining the American dream, particularly those who found out as part of their naturalization (citizenship) process. American immigration laws prohibit (despite high hopes for changes in the new Clinton administration) the immigration of people who either have AIDS or are HIV seropositive.

AIDS has created a common experience from which gay Filipinos in New York build and create new discourses and practices. *Abuloy* or alms for the dead have become institutionalized and have acquired a new dimension. Gay

Filipinos put on fashion shows and drag parties to help defray the burial or medical expenses of friends who have died. These collective efforts have become a regular occurrence.

Other collective efforts (most of whom are by gay and lesbian) include symposiums about AIDS in the Filipino community in New York. A group of gay Filipino men was formed to institutionalize efforts to help Filipinos with AIDS. This group, the Advocacy Group, got Filipinos with HIV/AIDS and formed to provide support services. There are still problems. Some Filipino gay men with AIDS are wary of other Filipino gay men helping them because of the interlocking network of gay Filipinos. There is a real possibility coming into contact with other Filipinos whom one knows. Other problems included Filipinos' inadequate access to services due to fear and lack of information.

Despite these difficulties, AIDS has provided a way of pulling Filipinos into some kind of collective action. While there are still sporadic attempts at solving some of the issues and problems many Filipino gay men face in the pandemic, there is a growing systematization of efforts.

Coming Together: Some Voices and (Re)Visions

In March 1991, an organization of Filipino gay men and lesbians called *Kambal sa Lusog* (which literally means "twins in health," but is interpreted to be "comrades in the struggle") was formed. Some informants who were members of this organization said that one of the impetuses for the formation of this group was the *Miss Saigon* controversy. However, after talking to one of the founders of the group, he said that there has been talk about such a group even before the *Miss Saigon* controversy. A large factor was that many Filipinos do not relate to other Asians or to an Asian identity.

This statement had been confirmed by my interviews with Filipino gay men. Many perceived Asia only in terms of geography; significant differences existed between other Asians and themselves. Furthermore, there was also a perception that Asian meant East Asians such as Japanese and Chinese. Due to these views, many felt that their interests as gay men would not be served by a group like GAPIMNY.

Kambal sa Lusog is a unique group because it includes gay men, lesbians, and bisexuals. It has a newsletter that usually comes out monthly. The group meets almost every month at the Lesbian and Gay Community Center in Manhattan. They have had numerous fundraisers and other group activities.

Among such fundraising activities was the *Santacruzan*. It was not only successful in attracting other Filipino gay men who were not members but more importantly, this particular production of the traditional Filipino ritual is perhaps the most evocative example of the kind of community and identity-formation that Filipino gay men in New York are struggling to achieve.

The *Santacruzan* is an important traditional Catholic celebration in the

Philippines held every May. It is a street procession that begins and ends in the church. The procession is essentially a symbolic reenactment of the finding of the cross of Christ by Queen Helena or Reyna Elena, the mother of Emperor Constantine of the Holy Roman Empire. The procession usually includes female personages, both mythical and historical. Among the usual figures are: Reyna Sentenciada (Justice), the three Virtues (Fe, Esperanza, and Caridad, or Faith, Hope, and Charity), Reina Banderada or Motherland (Queen of the Flag), Reina Elena, Rosa Mistica, Constantino (the young Emperor Constantine), and biblical characters such as Judith and Mary Magdalene.

In the Philippines, the important figures in the processions are usually portrayed by women with male escorts. Constantino is the only named male figure and is usually played by a child. However, in some areas, there have been cases when crossdressing men have participated in these processions. In fact one of these kinds of Santacruzans in Pasay City (one of the cities in the metropolitan Manila area) is famous for its crossdressing procession.

Kambal sa Lusog's *Santacruzan* is significant not only for its crossdressing personages, but because of the reconfiguration of the whole structure of the ritual. By describing the procession staged at the Lesbian and Gay Community Center in Manhattan in August, 1992, I am presenting what can be interpreted as a collective representation of identity and community. It is in this ritual where idioms of American and Philippine social symbolisms are selectively fused to provide structure to an implicit and subtle narrative of a community as well as a common cache of meanings and sentiments. This specific event locates the efforts of the organization at establishing a sense of collectivity.

First of all, this *Santacruzan* was not presented as a procession, but as a fashion show. The focal point of the show was the stage with a fashion runway. In the center of the stage, before the runway began was a floral arch which is reminiscent of the mobile arches of flowers that are carried in the procession for each mythical or historical personages.

The personages or figures were a combination of traditional *Santacruzan* figures as well as configurations of traditional figures and personages together with the creation of new ones. For example, while Reyna Sentenciada who is usually portrayed like the figure of Justice, carrying scales and in a blindfold, the "gay" Reyna Sentenciada is dressed in a leather (S & M) dominatrix garb. During the presentation, before he left the stage, Reyna Sentenciada, lifted his wig to show his bald pate. Reyna Libertad or Liberty was dressed also in a dominatrix garb complete with a whip. Liberty in this instance was construed to be sexual freedom. The three Virtues were the only figures who were portrayed by women (lesbians) dressed in denim shorts, combat boots and barong tagalog (the traditional Filipino male formal attire). Constantino who is usually portrayed by a child was a muscular Filipino in brief swimming trunks.

Other bolder representations were Reyna Banderada who usually carried the Philippine flag incorporated the symbols of the flag such as the stars and the red and blue strips in a slinky outfit. The three stars of the flag were strategically placed in each nipple and in the crotch area. A mask of the sun was carried by this new version of the motherland. Infanta Judith came out as a Greek goddess and instead of the head of Holofernes, the gay Judith revealed the head of George Bush. A new kind of queen was created for this presentation, Reyna Chismosa or Queen of Gossip. This queen came out in a tacky dressing gown and hair curlers, screaming on a cordless phone.

However, the finale was a return to tradition as Reyna Elena and the Emperatriz were dressed in traditional gowns and tiaras. The Reyna Elena carried an antique cross and flowers as all Reyna Elenas have done in the past.

The combination of secular/profane and religious imagery as well as Filipino and American gay icons provided an arena where symbols from the two countries were contested, dismantled, and reassembled in a dazzling series of statements. This *Santacruzan* therefore was built on shared experiences that juxtaposed such practices such as S & M and crossdressing with androgyny (the pulling off of the wig) with traditional Filipino ones like the *bakla* notion of drag.

Filipino gay men who participated in this presentation operated within the contours of the Santacruzan ritual while at the same time transgressing long-held beliefs and practices by injecting the culture and politics of the adopted country (i.e., George Bush's head). The *Santacruzan* can be seen as "a style of imagining" a community. In other words, the presentation can be seen as an attempt by Filipino gay men to negotiate and represent their collectivity to themselves and to others.

The Future of a Filipino Gay Community

The edges or borders of a Filipino gay community cannot be clearly demarcated as they traverse the edges of other communities of this diasporic world. However, despite the cleavages that run accross individuals and group interests, Filipino gay men, as I have shown, respond to various historical instances, such as the AIDS pandemic, anchored to shared cultural traditions that are continually renewed and reassembled. This kind of anchoring is never complete or final. There will always be oscillations between attachments or allegiances to particular groups, be it the Filipino gay community, the Asian gay community, or even the so-called "American" gay community.

While many observers and theorists of Asian American political movements see both the political necessity and historical inevitability of pan-Asian ethnic groupings, I argue that the path of the political evolution of Filipino gay men in America will not be unilinear. Filipinos as a group will not "mature" into a monolithic pan-Asian stage of development. Rather, there will emerge a multiplicity of identities and groupings.[13] Sentiments and allegiances to cultural traditions are continually strengthened and reshaped by the circular pattern of diasporas and migrations. The Filipino diaspora is continually replenished and altered by the changing flow of its migrants and exiles.

Such responses are reflected nationally in Filipino gay men's reactions to the *Miss Saigon* controversy and the AIDS pandemic. Especially with the *Santacruzan*, we find a vigorous and continued creation and reconstitution of cultural symbols and practices that go hand in hand with the revivification of a sense of belonging. These discourses will pave the way for a stronger future of a Filipino gay community in New York City and in America.

Notes

1. Terralee Bensinger, "Lesbian Pornography: The Re/Making of (a) Community." *Discourse* 15: 1 (1992): 69–93.
2. Benedict Anderson, *Imagined Communities: Reflections on the Origin and Spread of Nationalism* (London: Verso, 1983).
3. See Gillian Bottomley, *From Another Place: Migration and the Politics of Culture* (Melbourne: Cambridge University Press, 1992).
4. See William Whitam and Robin Mathy, *Homosexuality in Four Societies* (New York: Praeger, 1986), as well as my paper "Tolerance or Struggle: Male Homosexuality in the Philippines," which explored the tolerant and seemingly benign attitude of Filipinos as well as the cultural practices towards that *bakla*.

   I do not use the term *bakla* as the equivalent of gay. Rather I juxtapose the native term for homosexual/faggot as a way of portraying the different homosexual traditions, U.S. and Philippines. *Bakla* is socially constructed as a transvestic and/or effeminized being that occupies an interstitial position between men and women. In this paper therefore, I use the term gay only as a provisional term and do not imply a totally "gay" identified population. I also do not want to portray *bakla* traditions as static and unchanging, rather, as specifically demarcated practices continually being shaped and reshaped by both local and global influences and processes.
5. See Donn Hart and Harriet Hart, "Visayan Swardspeak: The Language of a Gay Community in the Philippines" *Crossroads* 5: 2 (1990): 27–49; and Manalansan, "Speaking of AIDS: Language and the Filipino Gay Experience in America" (in press).
6. All names of informants and other identifying statements have been changed to protect their identities.
7. Examples include Connie S. Chan, "Issues of Identity Development among Asian-American Lesbians and Gay Men," *Journal of Counseling & Development* 68 (1989): 16–20; and Terry Gock "Asian Pacific Islander Identity Issues: Identity Integration and Pride" in Betty Berzon, ed., *Positively Gay* (Los Angeles: Mediamix Association, 1984).
8. Nina Reyes, "Common Ground: Asians and Pacific Islanders look for unity in a queer world," *Outweek* 99 (1990).
9. See Bottomley, chapter 6.
10. Manalansan, Ibid.

11. While more than 85 percent of Filipino AIDS cases in America are gay and bisexual men, the opposite is true in the Philippines where more than half of the cases are women.

12. Jean M. Woo, George W. Rutherford, Susan F. Payne, J. Lowell Barnhardt, and George F. Lemp, "The Epidemiology of AIDS in Asian and Pacific Islander Population in San Francisco," *AIDS* 2 (1988):473–475.

13. See Yen Le Espiritu, *Asian American Panethnicity*, (Philadelphia: Temple University Press, 1992), chapter 7.

4

Breaking through the Chrysalis
Hanh Thi Pham

Erica L. H. Lee

In her piece, *Lesbian Precepts*, Hanh Thi Pham is seated naked in the center, regal and Buddha-like, with two shoes placed in front, on either side of her. One is a white ladies' pump, the other a black, heavy duty, combat boot. Unlike the usual mudras seen on Buddha statues, her hand gestures are her own; with her right hand raised, she makes the Vietnamese sign for "vagina," and with her other hand, she gestures as if ready to penetrate a lover during lesbian sex. By assuming this position, she reappropriates a powerful image for herself.

Upon reflecting on her life before coming out as a lesbian, she sees that,

> I was a very "good" and dutiful female before, in wanting to be someones else's
> wife, and eventually a mother; this following of Vietnamese wisdom of what it is
> to be a woman: this sacrifice through the bloodline of the family, the serving of
> patriarchal and familial wishes. I used to wear very feminine shoes that young
> women are supposed to wear, and had very long hair, and was married for twelve
> and a half years. So in that time I served the role of a formal wife, the genteel
> woman. I remember my marriage to a man, and living as a housewife, while try-
> ing to be a role model daughter in a family with three younger sisters. I tried

always to blend in with the expectations of family and femaleness.

But then after my divorce, I was more on my own, and was able to gain my own living. Which started to bring out the capacity that I have as a human being: taking charge of my own life, of not being controlled so much by what other people think what I should be. So for me, there was this new birth: bringing out the man within the woman.[1]

The shoes in the foreground are symbolic of her past and present state in life. For many Asian women, we know all too well about these fixed traditional ideals; while they are a part of our culture, it is also necessary and important to realize that the environment in which these conservative structures operate in has changed, and continues to change all the time. This notion of fixed identity and culture circulated among us has to be stopped; "As soon as we learn to be 'Asians in America'...we also recognize that we can't simply be Asians any longer."[2] As human beings, we continually grow and change everyday; to reject this notion of a constantly shifting, transitional process is debilitating and negates one's existence.

Raised with strong Buddhist teachings, Hanh had to rethink them in the different context America presents.

Lesbian Precepts. Photograph by Hanh Thi Pham.

All of a sudden, Buddha became smaller; before I respected him, but now the idea of him is too narrow for me, because in examining Buddhism I see that women have never been in leadership positions in the temple. You don't see goddesses teaching; the main events and rituals have always been headed by men, and followed through by monks. The truth is that the women have always been working behind the scenes: cooking the food, raising funds for the temple, etc. So I asked myself why it is that women are never listened to and silent. The men do everything. This bothered me, so that is why I had this idea of a Woman's Temple, a place where She can be revered and respected. Within me, there is this wanting to be larger than the Asian concept of largeness.[3]

It is upon this realization that pushes her to expand out the of the prescribed shell she once lived in. Difficult in task, again it is something she must do. In taking what she knows, and how she feels about Buddhism and feminism, she applied it to herself,

For a specific reason, I wanted to become Buddha. Not as Buddha the man, but Buddha as myself. I realized that, yes, my soul is evolved, and I am my own very dignified person. So, I wanted to have a temple, a pagoda, and be seated and teaching what it is for me to be a lesbian Buddha.

After staring at myself at eye level for a long time, I realized that the Self is beyond uniqueness, and Buddha, in my mind, was beyond one thought. So there is the urge of wanting to have all these different spirits in the world manifest through and channeled through the body. And it was at that moment that I thought I had the clearest thinking about existence. And it was sort of like, you're in a trance, many other lives went through you. Also it was like a fast film, where your life rolled by, and there's a review of your past history and your present.[4]

With this revelation, she saw within herself the possibilities and the power of being a Woman; this concept of being a woman which stretches farther than the one that society has set out for us. For Hanh, she manages to take such ideas and rework them; or rather, make them work for her, thereby, celebrating herself, women, and our strength, "because we are women and not in spite of it."[5]

This piece belongs to a larger work that was composed of composites, text, installation and sculpture. The title, *Lesbian Precepts*, draws from the five important and strict Buddhist Precepts: not to kill, not to lie, no alcohol consumption, no extramarital sexual involvement, and an adherence to a vegetarian diet. In finding more about lesbians and lesbianism, she discovered that there are many different levels of lesbianism, and different sorts of concepts lesbians have of their existence and their practices. "The politics of lesbians is something I'm very interested in exploring, in studying. Not only of my own, but also what I've learned from life. This is just a small step to a larger study of life."[6] Existing is this inability to extricate living her life with the same issues that cross her path, into her art; the inability of Asian American women to extricate the politics of living with our ethnocultural identity, gender, and sexuality.

In reaction to the 1992 Los Angeles uprisings, Hanh produced *Misbegotten No More*, a piece that includes color xeroxes on transparencies, handwriting, poems in Vietnamese, and other college newspaper photographs collected about the Vietnamese experience, both in Vietnam and the United States.

The detailed close up of the work shows a picture of Hanh, fist raised, over a crossed out, upside-down image of Buffalo Bill Cody on a horse, symbolic of America. Her gesture is one of defiance, a very definite "Fuck You" pose. Cody, one of America's celebrated heroes of the Wild West, figured prominently during the white man's expansion westward; regardless of the amount of lauding history books give him, it must be known that he was infamously responsible, not only for the killing of buffalo, but also for the countless deaths of Native American Indians. However, in this piece, it is crucial to note the positioning: not only is Hanh dominate over him, but she is much larger than Cody. "The close up photograph refers to my decision and anger in not wanting to participate in white mainstream tokenism about art and artists, Asians and women. It's an attempt to revolt against the American system."[7]

At the end of 1992, the subject of family values and the presidential campaign inundated the television, newspapers, and day-to-day living. Used as a campaign tactic, it might as well have been called the "white, heterosexual, patriarchal, conservative family values," because the candidates nevertheless failed in addressing the differences that occur within the family unit. What does it mean for a lesbian couple who want to raise a child? What does it mean for a single black mother in this country? Even though it was an attempt to alleviate people's minds and assuage the anxiety over the country's economic situation (essentially: turning back to the "good old days" [good for whom?] and implying that if all men and women married and had children, jobs would magically appear, which would solve all the crises, and this country would be a better place), the campaign tactic raised more questions and alienated more people than it gave answers. In reaction, Hanh wanted to let her family, the people around her, and the audience know how enraged she is in being a citizen in the United States, and forced to play a participatory role in a sexist, racist, classist, homophobic, capitalistic system.

I was angry about [the plight of] Asians, especially the Vietnamese people, being ignored [by the media], because we were also the ones affected by the uprising; Vietnamese stores were vandalized, and we were hated by the Blacks. It still happens in daily life today. I know, because I experience the hatred on the streets, in situations where I didn't do anything and was innocent but was hated by Blacks just the same. They are people I've thought a lot about—about the hard life they have. But I am also very aware of the extreme situation many Vietnamese people are in, where many of my family members have been in—being paid forty-nine cents an hour, working long, hard hours in the sweat shops. And I have to help them. So this American system does not really help the minorities or the poor people. These people have always been taken advantage of, as have teachers, Asian teachers, and Asian artists.[8]

Once again, the media was biased, failing to even distinguish between the different Asian ethnicities. They either showed Koreans as gun-toting, territorial, crazed people that we were supposed to hate, misunderstand, and feel sorry for, or they did not bother showing Asian American experiences at all. But these things must be exposed, and the public must take action to understand our realities. There are too many atrocities and injustices that happen everyday—too many to count or even recount, but which we live through. In a city such as Los Angeles, where so many things are hidden or avoided, it is even more of a struggle to make our views known.

So therefore, in the picture, I no longer want to be a servant of the system, and I can be my own Self. I'm a lesbian. I'm very proud of myself as a woman. I'm very proud of my body, the muscles of my body, and my intentions as a person. [This is] my empowerment, given to me by myself.[9]

This art piece is significant in that "it's sort of a new birth, a beginning of something more substantial."[10] Like a pupa, Hanh continually breaks through each chrysalis that society wraps her in.

Notes

1. Hanh Thi Pham, personal interview, October 8, 1993.
2. Quote from Trinh T. Minh-ha, in Russell Leong, ed., *Moving the Image* (Seattle: University of Washington Press, 1991), 87.
3. Hanh Thi Pham interview.
4. Ibid.
5. Velina Hasu Houston, *The Politics of Life* (Philadelphia: Temple University Press, 1993), 13.
6. Hanh Thi Pham interview.
7. Ibid.
8. Ibid.
9. Ibid.
10. Ibid.

Preserving the Paradox
Stories from a *Gay-Loh*

Eric C. Wat

I. Gazes and Grins

> When race and ethnicity become commodified as resources for pleasure, the culture of specific groups, as well as the bodies of individuals, can be seen as constituting an alternative playground where members of dominating races, genders, sexual practices affirm their power over in intimate relations with the Other.
>
> bell hooks, "Eating the Other"[1]

We were glad to see two Asian Pacific Islanders crossing the street in our direction. It is not too often when you see Asian Pacific Islanders in West Hollywood. We'd been there for almost an hour; yet none of us had filled up the eight entries in our survey sheet. So when they finally reached the sidewalk, my friend Steven stopped one of them and I the other. We wanted to find out how much Asians and Pacific Islanders like them know about AIDS.

I approached him in the usual way. I told him that we were conducting the survey on behalf of Asian Pacific AIDS Intervention Team (APAIT) and asked if he could spare a minute of his time to answer some questions. He hesitated at first. Then I felt this white man creep up behind me.

"What are you doing?" he asked.

I turned to look at him. He was tall, middle-aged, with thinning white hair. He had a grin on his face that reminded me of another white man who came up to me at a party once to caress my elbow—all because I was "the only Oriental there and he just had to come across from the other corner to say hi." This gangling man before me had the same grin as if he had just stumbled on some treasure chest in the deep sea. I wasn't flattered. Rudely interrupted, I tried to give him an eye that would send him back to the corner from whence he came.

That didn't work.

"He is my wife," he explained, pointing at the person I was about to interview.

Ignoring his comment, I explained to him what I was doing instead.

"Go ahead," he encouraged his lover, who reluctantly nodded his consent.

I asked about his ethnicity.

"Filipino," the white man interrupted again. "Or he prefers Filipina." He laughed.

I ignored him and proceeded to ask my subject to name three ways HIV can be transmitted. He didn't come up with an answer right away.

"Come now, don't upset your lover," the white man said. When that, too, failed to produce a response, he started to paraphrase the question by yelling, "How do you get AIDS? You get it by doing what?" I was shocked by his loud voice. I was going to tell him that it was all right. The reason I was there was to educate, not to admonish. But I couldn't get a word in edgewise. "Sex! You get it through sex. And what else? Drugs!" he yelled out the answers (which, by the way, were not entirely correct). His lover repeated his responses in a whisper.

I finally gave him a safe sex packet and thanked him for his participation. He was well on his way out of there, but not his lover.

"So where did your great-grandmother live?" the white man asked me.

I was surprised by the question and responded awkwardly. "Which great-grandmother? I have four. Do you mean the mother of my grandmother on my mother's side, or...."

All the while he kept the grin on his face. I was thinking: shouldn't he be going with his lover, who was half a block away by now?

"I mean, what are you?"

In retrospect, I should have told him that I came from some exotic island in the South Pacific where people are so Asian that they use three chopsticks—you know, just to see him drool.

But I complied stupidly.

"Chinese," I said.

Then the most offensive thing happened. He started speaking to me in

Mandarin, with phrases that I vaguely recognized and accents that didn't sound at all like those my Taiwanese uncle had. I felt myself walking away, shocked. Yet he insisted in speaking that way, as if I would find it attractive. His voice grew fainter and fainter as I crossed the street and finally reached the other side, safe from his touch.

I hated his gaze; I hated his grin; I hated his assumptions. When he asked me where I was from, a question often asked of Asians, he was less concerned with my roots than with his own fascination about my (racial) difference.

"The commodification of Otherness," bell hooks writes, "has been so successful because it is offered as a new delight, more intense, more satisfying than normal ways of doing and feeling. Within commodity culture, ethnicity becomes spice, seasoning that can liven up the dull dish that is mainstream white culture."[2] In the fantasies of gay, white, male culture, the role of servitude is more often than not assigned to Asian men (for an analysis of this, see Richard Fung's "Looking For My Penis").[3]

These fantasies are unfortunately manifested in reality. When a friend of mine finally convinced a drunken white man who had been forcing himself on him that he did not like playing the submissive role, the white man became disgusted and said, "You have completely turned Americanized. Go back to Asia and learn how to be Asian." This white man and others like him, sober or inebriated, have no way of relating to my Asian brothers except from atop.

What troubled me just as much, however, is how many white men perceive this fascination with our Otherness as a confirmation of their progressive politics. They are not aware that their desire, when based on fantasies and stereotypes, shares the same source of a bigot's hatred, and both reaffirm the racial hegemony that is imposed on all people of color. It is still they who define and control the terms of our relationships with them.

The white man who insisted on speaking to me in Mandarin— and it mattered little to him that I don't speak Mandarin—may pride himself on his knowledge of a foreign language, an indication, he believes, of his open-mindedness to other cultures. But to what purpose is he directing this knowledge? To ensnare another exotic trophy while his lover was still within sight?

But I also hated myself for allowing him to look at me that way; I hated myself for answering his questions like a submissive, demure, Asian "house boy" should, a stereotype that probably encouraged him more than anything else. This self-hate, though irrational in retrospect, reflects the limitation of the power and presence of people of color in the mainstream gay communities. The fact that he and others like him can openly and publicly approach Asian men in such an offensive manner is a testimony to the imbalanced power dynamics existing in gay communities. As Richard Fung, queer Asian filmmaker, once stated, "the mainstream gay movement can be a place of freedom and sexual identity. But it is also a site of racial, cultural, and sexual alienation sometimes more pronounced than that in a straight society."[4] It is not until that night at the corner of San Vicente and Santa Monica Boulevard did I feel so far from home, exiled by a white man's fetish.

But I felt sorry most for the lover; he is the one who has to live with that white man day after day. In a community that is sometimes shallow and ageist, older white men have problems finding their "ideal" mate. People who are more exploitable become easy targets for them; economics becomes a venue for sexual expression. Some of these young Asian lovers are recent immigrants who cannot speak English, fluently or at all, and who have a hard time in the job market. Some of them have inferred their "inferiority" from the lack of substantive images of Asian gay men in the media. Some of them have suffered ostracism from their own ethnic communities and have turned "outward." This cultural exile evokes in them distrust, fear, and even hatred of anyone of the same racial identity. A young Taiwanese friend of mine, threatened with exorcism by his zealous family, once called me up in the middle of the night just to warn me not to ever date Asians. Faced with these adversities, classism, racism, and homophobia sadly become acceptable foundation for their relationships.

I made up my mind that for the rest of that night I would only interview Asians who were not with a white man. The sad thing is, I didn't find any.

II. Blood, Thick and Thin

You must not tell anyone…what I am about to tell you.
—Maxine Hong Kingston, *The Woman Warrior*[5]

It was a small point of contention. To my parents at least. But I insisted that they hated me. In an argument I once had with my mother not so long ago, the insanity of this truth baffled me so much that it came out the wrong way.

"What do you mean I don't love you?" She asked. Then she gave a list of things that she had done to show her love for me. I tried to explain to her that that was not what I meant.

"You said that I don't love you," she replied. That was the truth I could not deny. She continued, sprinkling English words in the few broken gaps of Cantonese, "I could say that you don't love me. You always took your grandma to lunch; you have never done that with me once. You have never told me anything. Every time I ask you a question, you act like I am going to eat you. But you are so different with your friends. You tell them everything. You give them…advices. With me you don't say a word. I didn't know you have gotten a job until I asked you. So who doesn't love whom?"

I tried to say something in my defense, but she seemed to have torn down a wall that had been erected between us, and, like a furious battle ram in its full momentum, she could not stop.

"How can you say I don't love you? Why am I in America?… For you and your brother…Daddy and I had to start all over." The veins in her forehead, blue and strong, overshadowed the testament of years of hard work that is her wrinkles.

"And I couldn't pass this damn nursing test. Something always happens before the test. If it's not fighting with your father, then it's you. I was a registered nurse in Hong Kong; I had seniority. Now I am working under some twenty-some-year-old who doesn't know one end of a needle from the other. It's enough to upset a saint, but you don't hear me complain when I come home. No, I just drop everything and start making dinner for you all. And I wash the dishes, clean the stove without saying a word. Why do I make all these sacrifices? For you and your brother. And you say I don't love you. It hurts me when I hear that…."

She finally dropped to the floor. Any place she could sit in her room would be too close to me; so she finally dropped to the floor.

Years of silence. That was years of silence, prompted only by one sentence I uttered: "You don't love me." But it wasn't that my parents "don't love" me; what I meant to say, but did not in the heat of the argument, was that they "hate" me.

"We don't hate you," Father, heretofore silent and standing by the door, decided to jump in. And as I learned when I was little, when Father jumps in, it's time to prepare yourself, especially when his voice, calm and patient, bears the shield of "rationality." The same rationality that is reflected in his glasses, distorting his eyes. "We are father and son. I never said I hated you."

"You are corrupting the world, and I am corrupting the world by having you," I quoted him—verbatim.

He said, shaking his head, "And to this day I still maintain what I said. I have to be honest; I still disapprove of this."

This being homosexuality.

He continued, "But this is only a disagreement in our moral systems. We already agreed that it is all right for two people to disagree on that."

"I don't mind your moral system. But the truth is, you hate me because I'm gay."

"No, I hate homosexuality. That's not the same thing. Cannot two friends disagree on that?"

"I don't have friends who hate me," I retorted.

"I think you are taking it the wrong way. I don't see any contradiction. Just because I cannot morally accept this…."

This being homosexuality.

I interjected, "We are not talking about philosophy. I am not an abstraction. I hurt, and I get hurt, too."

He came closer to me, passing Mother who was still choking on her own tears on the floor. Pain wrought by years of silence—I know thy face only too well. But even Father, a weathered frame of five-feet-four, just passed you by with ease.

"I think you took it the wrong way," he said, his voice more tender than before. "I used to think, out of all the kids in the family, you would turn out the best. And I was not measuring that in terms of money. Your cousins might be doctors, businessmen, accountants, but you are different. You are a thinking man, and you want to spend the rest of your life thinking, helping other people. But now, you have this thing corrupting your mind…."

This thing, again, being homosexuality.

The irony killed me. Almost everything I had done, I had been able to do because I am gay, because I had the burden of proof. And I had been too successful in proving that I was a good person, that this family needed me as much as I did them. This was why they were having such a hard time dealing with my sexuality, accepting it. It went against everything they knew about being gay. And now my own father was using the source of my strength against me.

My parents' paradox—they hate queers, but they love me, even though I am gay—can be achieved by separating my gayness from my other identities, familial and cultural. This is easily done, since, for most Asian parents, being Asian and being gay are mutually exclusive. It is not only that homosexuality is a forbidden topic in most Asian communities. More significant, there is not a need to talk about "it" because it is only a problem for white people: "it" is a white disease. For example, in Hong Kong, a Westernized colony where a gay community has become more visible in the last few years, the colloquial word for a gay man is simply gay-loh (gay fellow).

The concept that all queers are white is well collaborated by the media, where queers of color are nearly nonexistent. This is distressful for many Asian queers, especially those families where English is seldom or never spoken. To introduce dialogue will be difficult when homosexuality is not in one's verbal or conceptual lexicon. Even if it can be initiated, understanding would take tremendous time and effort.

The implication that homosexuality is a Western phenomenon reaches deeper into the lives of many queer Asians. To occupy an identity that tradition has not allowed room for is, for many Asian parents, to reject the validity of that tradition and, by extension, of the family whose foundation rests on that very tradition itself. If a language barrier has made coming out difficult, possible charges of betrayal and of disgraces to the family have kept many of us, as well as our parents, in the closet. After I came out to my parents, they immediately asked me not to repeat the revelation to other relatives, some of whom we live with. We made sure our eyes were dry before we left my room that night. In *Making Waves*, Pamela H. relates a similar pressure among Asian American lesbians: "Concern that family honor will be tarnished motivates many women to hide their lesbianism. This family shame factor reflects the tightness of many Asian communities…. In fact the general Asian American community may be too close-knit for the closeted lesbian[s]."[6]

Before I came out to my parents, my silence about my sexuality had permeated the rest of our relationship, building a wall between us, making communciation nearly impossible and conflicts inevitable. I did not want to depend too much on them for either emotional and financial support. Sometimes I was wary that when that day would eventually come, they would use that support as "debts," as "bargaining chips." Other times I was afraid that if they played a part any more larger in my life than they already had, their possible rejection later would be that much harder to take. This silence, driven by fear of stigmatization and rejection from one's family, becomes more of a burden than the intolerance of the larger society. And many of us, though active in the gay community, remain closeted to our families.

However, that does not mean that a queer identity can never be developed among Asians. Tragically, the perceived conservatism of Asian communities has often led queer Asians to turn their backs on their ethnic and cultural identities. The separation is hereby complete, and the paradox preserved.

The paradox survives when we refuse to talk about being Asian and being gay at the same time, when one is abandoned for the sake of another. After many arguments, my father said to me eventually, "No matter what you do outside, you are still my son. You can always come home; you will always have a shelter." This was his compromise, his "acceptance." This is something I should feel good about, and I did.

And I did, until I remembered that this was essentially his philosophy about Ralph—our family dog. "If he runs away, he runs away. But as long as he stays with us, he is our responsibility." This compromise was not good enough. And it will never be, as long as my gayness is something I do outside, as long as our love for each other is only bound by blood, which, no matter how thick it is, cannot wash away twenty-some years of our lives.

III. Sex, Lies, and Newspapers

At some point, on our way to a new consciousness, we will have to leave the opposite bank, the split between the mortal combatants somehow healed so that we are on both shores at once and, at once, see through serpent and eagle eyes.

—Gloria Anzaldúa, *Borderlands/La Frontera*[7]

The *Los Angeles Times* did not lie; neither did the Chinese-language newspaper that serves the local communities.[8] Truong Loc Minh, a Vietnamese immigrant, was walking along a coastal strip in Laguna Beach at 1:30 A.M., technically January 10, 1993, a Sunday. But as far as the three gay bars nearby were concerned, Saturday night was just beginning to wind down. Truong encountered a group of young, white, (presumably) straight men, who proceeded to beat him to a pulp. When the police arrived, Truong was so disfigured that they could hardly determine his race. It was a hate crime, the police suggested.

The two articles run parallel up to that point: the what, the who, the when, and the where are duly recorded. But, after all, an eagle cannot see with serpent eyes. Once confronted by the complex intersection of racial and sexual oppressions, one keeps going straight—so to speak—and the other makes a turn so sharp that no traces remain of where it has taken us before.

Resting snugly in the cushion of its mainstream vehicle, the *Times* article tells us Truong's ethnicity once in its lead-in paragraph, but there is no more mention of it thereafter as if it is completely irrelevant: It was gay-bashing and not much more. In fact, so convinced were its editors about the nature of the beating that they ran an editorial on the same day, linking the crime conveniently (but with good intentions, of course) to the need of "improving" "the climate against [?] gays."

The Chinese article, on the other hand, assuages its readers by assuring them—in the headline—that the victim is not gay, that the hate crime, thank goodness, was motivated by race. The family, it is reported here as in the *Times* article, denied the unspeakable while Truong lay in critical condition in a hospital bed, unconscious. But our local boys have one-upped the giant establishment and gotten an exclusive: When Truong came to, he denied it, too. All the while, the article neglects to mention that Truong was arrested several years ago at the same beach where he was bashed for lewd conduct with another man, a charge to which he eventually pleaded guilty.

Disfigured faces, denied identities—such is the plight that afflicts us Asian gay men, and to a larger degree, our lesbian sisters. In the "liberal" white media, be it gay or straight, our race is marginalized; it is handy for identification purposes only. In our own Asian communities, our sexualities are invisible. If mentioned sometimes, it is only done so to be knocked down, dismissed, and sent back to the hell of silence and nonentity.

We are nobody's children. We can scream and yell, but the editors of both papers can sleep easy at night on the other side, as if our sound waves are intercepted by a thick wall of glass called the "truth," which they can record faithfully. That they did, but the thick glass inevitably distorts. So, as I said before, the papers did not exactly lie. Theirs is a sin of omission, not one of commission; but as any good Catholic can tell you, one is just as bad as the other. In the end, they are not so different.

I don't mean to cast aspersions on a simple hate crime, as one friend suggested. But I doubt that a hate crime can ever be simple, especially when it comes to what I call a hyphenated Other. In the history of oppression, few things happened by chance.

For example, why Truong?

Let me put it another way: three gay bars, Saturday night, Orange County. Why a fifty-five-year old Vietnamese man if it is just gay bashing?

Truong does not exactly epitomize the "faggot" stereotype, which tends to be younger and white. This contention is not without merit. Too many times have I heard from my gay Asian friends that before they came out, each thought he was the only gay Asian man on the face of the earth. There had not been too many Asian queers in the media to prove us wrong.

The media is where our stereotypes become complicated, even contradictory. As gay men, we are "hypersexual"; as Asian men, we are "asexual." One is not compatible with the other; we can't be both. All the Asians are straight, all the queers are white, but it was a while before we found out that some of us are brave.[9] Hypersexual or asexual, these are, of course, only stereotypes, but bashers operate on stereotypes. So, I ask again, why Truong?

I know that one of the bashers stalking Truong referred to him as a "faggot," but one must not take a bigot's vocabulary of epithets too literally. I remember one Chinese New Year I was donning a traditional cap that looks like a black dome with a button sewn at the apex. I had found it as I was rummaging the many cardboard boxes in my closet, and I was trying it on only to see how one does look with it over the head. When my cousin saw me, he immediately remarked, "That's so gay." Now, I don't think he meant that, were I to sport such a cap in the same way Hester Prynne wears her scarlet letter, I am displaying to the whole world my sexual "transgression." He merely didn't like the cap, and he associated it with other things that he didn't like (maybe about himself). So, the young basher, too, might have seen something displeasing about Truong's appearance but was unable to articulate it precisely. All I am saying is, it doesn't have to be either gay or Asian. It could be both.

Meanwhile, I am still left wondering about what side of the hate crime statistics Truong would find himself under. Would he be a different person if he were not beaten outside of three gay bars, but three Vietnamese cafés? Oppression is very tricky sometimes, not at all what the two newspapers have made it out to be. We can't add it up like numbers, and we can't wear it like a cap. No one can say the bashers did what they did, 70 percent because Truong looks gay and 30 percent because he is Asian. And no one has the right to forsake one of his identities at the expense of another (especially in order to further one's own agenda). Failing to reflect the complexity of oppression, the papers are not much different from the bashers. Their words, like the bashers' clenched fists, have distorted Truong's face so that they won't have to see what they don't want to see.

Like Truong, many gay Asian men are run over at the intersection of racism and homophobia. When each part of ourselves is not acknowledged at one time or another, it becomes difficult to define who we are. We are forever left in the middle of the road, unacceptable to those at either side of the street. But we know who we are not: We are neither corrupt, assimilated perverts nor submissive, domesticated "house boys." And we refuse, for the sake of safety, to stand with those for whom either of these assumptions is the foundation on which they relate to us. This is not to negate their love; this is to acknowledge our hurt. Somehow, sometime, somewhere, gay Asian men must find that third side of the street where we can grow, find our voices, learn about ourselves, and educate others about who we are, so that eventually we can join them at both sides of the street.

Notes

1. bell hooks, "Eating the Other," *Black Looks: Race and Representation* (Boston: South End Press, 1992), 23.
2. Ibid., 21.
3. Richard Fung, "Looking for my Penis: The Eroticized Asian in Gay Video Porn," *How Do I Look?* ed. Bad Object-Choices (Seattle: Bay Press, 1991), 145–68.
4. Ibid., 4.
5. Maxine Hong Kingston, *The Woman Warrior* (New York: Vintage Books, 1975), 3.
6. Pamela H., "Asian American Lesbians: An Emerging Voice in the Asian American Community," *Making Waves*, ed. Asian Women United (Boston: Beacon Press, 1989), 282–90.
7. Gloria Anzaldúa, *Borderlands/La Frontera* (San Francisco: Spinsters/Aunt Lute, 1987), 79.
8. "Asian man bashed at Laguna Beach" (my translation) *International Daily*, 12 January 1993; Gregory Crouch, "Two More Arrested in Laguna Beach," *Los Angeles Times*, 12 January 1993; and "A Shocking Hate Crime: In Orange County an Incident of Gay-Bashing at Its Worst," editorial, *Los Angeles Times*, 12 January 1993.
9. With apologies to Barbara Smith.

y, the quiet, passive, exotic
match our 'slanted' eyes or ·
ll size. But we are not."

—Michiyo Cornell

The Body Politic

6

Living in Asian America

An Asian American Lesbian's Address before the Washington Monument (1979)

Michiyo Cornell

Sisters and Brothers,

I am here to represent the Lesbian and Gay Asian Collective, which was formed at the first National Third World Lesbian and Gay Conference (Oct. 12-15, 1979) this weekend. I don't know if any non-Asian American lesbian and gay men know how important this moment is. This is the first time in the history of the American hemisphere that Asian American lesbians and gay men have joined to form a network of support of, by, and for Asian American lesbians and gay men. I must interject a little comment here. I am being careful to use the phrase Asian American because we are not hyphenated Americans nor are we always foreign born women and men of Asia. We have been in this country for over 150 years! We live in *Asian America*. It is a statement of our experiences and a statement of racism in America.

I am in awe of this moment and what it can mean for Asian American Lesbians and gay men. America has called us the model minority and has claimed we are 200% Americans. The truth is that because we are less than 1% of the population of this country and because of the lies that the American media perpetuates about us, we have difficulty in impacting even Third World lesbians and gay men. We are called the model minority, the quiet, passive, exotic erotics with the slanted cunt to match our slanted eyes or the small dick to match our small size. But we are not.

For years Asian Americans have organized against our oppression. We protested and were lynched, deported, and put into concentration camps during World War II. We must not forget that the United States of America has bombed, napalmed, and colonized Asian countries for decades. Thus it was possible for America to bomb Hiroshima and Nagasaki and to continue to economically colonize and rape Asian countries. It could rape and murder Vietnamese women, children, and men, then claim that Asians don't value human life.

I am an Asian American woman, a mother and a lesbian. Because these things are difficult to put into a neat package, because I am genuinely different—I know that I live in the face of this country's determination to destroy me, to negate me, to render me invisible. And the reality is that non-Asian Americans are ignorant of our existence. We share the same problems that other Third World lesbians and gay men share. Because of fear of deportation, because of Asian American dependence on our families and Asian American communities for support, it is very difficult for us to be out of the closet. But we need to come out of the closet for not to do so would be living a lie, and the great lie, which is America, can use that weakness not only to destroy Asian American lesbians and gay men, but also our Third World lesbian and gay sisters and brothers.

We have a right to our sexuality, to our love, and to our racial identities. This is something that sets us apart from and challenges white lesbians and gay men. We demand that you white lesbians and gay men begin to think of how you repress and oppress your Asian American lesbian and gay sisters and brothers. You share oppression from homophobia with us but unless you begin to address your white skin privilege and actively support Asian American lesbian and gay men, you will not have our support and you will lose out on a chance to build the kind of world we all need, to live decently, and lead full productive lives.

We must realize the capitalist system uses not just sexual preference but race and class as well to divide us. To our Third World sisters and brothers, gay and straight, I would like to say we all share the same oppression as Third World people, and for that reason we must stand together or be hanged separately by what Audre Lorde calls the noose of conformity.

To our closeted Asian American lesbians and gay men, I would like you to consider how we become accomplices to our own sexual and racial oppression when we fail to claim our true identities.

I have a three-year-old daughter and any risk that I must take to build a free future for myself and my daughter is worth it. It is as concrete and as abstract as that.

Notes

From *Gay Insurgent*, 6 (Summer 1980): 16. © 1995, published with permission of Daniel C. Tsang, editor.

7

Strategies for Queer Asian and Pacific Islander Spaces

Eric Estuar Reyes

March 7, 1995

Michiyo Cornell wrote "Living in Asian America" for the first March on Washington in 1979.[1] Unlike her, I am not writing to present these thoughts in front of a monument. Nor do I represent a collective body of Queer Asian Americans. However, I am discussing some issues that she raised then and that today are still sites of struggle for Asian and Pacific Islander (API) lesbians, gay, bisexual and transgendered individuals. These are the issues that form the basis of our struggle for our cultural and political citizenship as members of sexually and racially marginalized cultures.

Cornell writes of the great lie, which is America. Fifteen years later, I can only imagine the America she lived in, but in 1995 I ask *which* America should I call a lie. Is it the eurocentric and heterosexual male-dominated America, the white gay male-centered Queer America, the marginalized People of Color (POC) America, or our often-romanticized Asian America? As a Queer API, I ask *where* is this truth situated that betrays our belief that we have a space here in this place called America? Locating this space from which we draw our strength and our meaning is the part of coming out that never ends. Coming out as Cornell notes is very difficult, but it is the personal truth that shatters the lie of individual and collective invisibility. This invisibility, both as sexually and racially persecuted individuals, conflicts with our notions of cultural and political citizenship in this society. The expression of our citizenship, as rights and responsibilities, relies on an assumed access to a certain public space. The public space I refer to here is America and the denial of access to this space is the negation of our rights and responsibilities to be who we are and to live our lives with fullness and productivity.

March on Washington, 1993. Two participants embrace on the mall.
Photograph © 1993 Daniel C. Tsang.

Fifteen years later, we still are combating representational hyphenization and stereotypes as a model minority with exotic (a)sexualities. To this list of issues, we must add the challenges of HIV/AIDS, the related battles for control over our bodies exemplified by debates on breast cancer and abortion, and the multiplicity of our differences rather than the dualisms of homo/het, in/out, female/male, private/public, old/young, and citizen/alien.[2] Fifteen years ago, Cornell's central call for coming out as a political act still stands as a primary strategy for Queer APIs. However, in 1995 our historical context requires us to deploy additional tactics, both subtle and overt.

I remember marching in the Asian and Pacific Islander contingent in the 1993 March on Washington. The streets were filled with thousands of visible and vocal APIs in many contingents amid hundreds of thousands of other queers. It was Sunday and besides us (and the press), the streets were trafficless and the buildings empty. Is this really an intervention into the national public space of the capital city? If so, besides the media, which public are we disrupting? This was a demonstration, wasn't it?! Still, I looked at the handwritten signs that many carried in our contingent and saw how these slogans reflected the complexity of our work as Queer Asians and Pacific Islanders and as Queer Americans. We are visible. We are sexual. We are not all one Asian or Pacific Islander ethnicity, or one gender. We are not the other. We are who we are—complex human beings! It felt good to march with so many APIs. It did feel powerful and prideful. It was fun!

Two years after our March on Washington in 1993, I recall these events as I read Cornell's address and realize our efforts at creating an ideal culture cannot end with a simplified call to come out. Cornell refers to our shared oppressions with our Third World sisters and brothers in 1979, and this is still true today. As APIs and POC, coming out in different places incites different possibilities and risks. Our political citizenship is confined to a physical territory. Yet, as Queer POC, we access different types of territories that demand different forms of cultural citizenships. We have a right to our sexualities, our desires, and our racial and ethnic identities. We also have responsibilities not only to ourselves, but to our families, our communities, and our cultures. The spectacle of thousands is a strategy that Queer America has deployed along with other groups in search of establishing presence in the *national* political landscape. Yet I suggest we consider the *local* struggle, and I believe, the responsibility to incorporate our daily life experiences as bisexuals, homosexuals, and transgendered individuals, as well as members of specific Asian and Pacific Islander cultures into our various local and particular landscapes.

These cultural practices include creating presence through overt visibility or subtle shifts such as de-/re-gendering our discussions about our loves. *Bring your lover to your cousin's wedding banquet.* The shattering of API stereotypes within our workplaces, cultural productions, and our social gatherings—API or non-API—erodes the basis of the dominant culture's xenophobic ignorance. *Have your butch dyke lust interest deliver flowers to you at your office.* Confronting the ownership, content, scale, and process of our economic modes of production that commodify and fetishize difference resists the convenient detachment of social discriminations from material divisions. *Consider which do you really want—rice queen fantasies at your bookstore or freedom rings at the checkout stand of your local Asian market?* Meeting the challenge of HIV/AIDS by not only promoting but practicing and expecting safer sex, and supporting HIV-affected, infected, or AIDS diagnosed APIs creates altered values and behaviors. *Using latex is not a reflection of mistrust, but of responsibility.*

I raise these issues to call not only for coming out and generating Queer API spaces, but to urge us to transgress or open up the different closets of scale we cross every day. Whether it is the closet of one, the closet of a gay or ethnic ghetto, or the closet of the weekly family gathering, we travel and in each place we can carry a space for ourselves.[3] Let us not only paint the surface with our visibilities, but unfold these spaces within our lives for us and others. The strategy of transgression must be added to our strategy of visibility for a silhoüette is only another name for a shadow. Our lives are full of light and depth and within this brightness we can create a new public space from which we can draw strength and meaning.

Cornell is right in acknowledging the hostility of the dominant culture within dominant Queer communities, but I would also extend this to other people of color queers, people of color communities, Asian and Pacific Islander communities, and ourselves. We can't just fight xenophobia, oppression and discrimination with the same tools of dominance.[4] Slogans are for signs, and if we carry the signs of our identities, we should follow through on our positions. Focusing on specific issues and practical action provides the basis for collaborative efforts across ethnicity, sexuality, residency status, and other differences. Whether the issue or action is to increase HIV/AIDS funding or to protest exploitive labor practices, we can work together on local levels with tangible results.

Whether we draw our strength and meaning from one or many of the Asian and Pacific Islander, People of Color, Dominant Culture, Queer, or Queer People of Color Communities, we must also consider the strength of traveling across these communities. Creating and locating our home spaces has consumed our activism as Queer and/or APIs. These home spaces are still very important, but with a strategy of transgression we deploy *a politics of location* on different *scales of struggle.*[5] We can consider positions such as bisexuality, transgender, and multiracial issues that span traditional categories. We can access different Americas in other ways besides grand national displays of presence. In this time of the continuing challenges of HIV/AIDS, a conservative U.S. Congress, efforts to legitimize xenophobia through legislature such as Proposition 187, and challenges to affirmative action, we must exercise our rights and we must fulfill our responsibilities.[6]

Finally, we need to take seriously our responsibility to each other whether as lovers, friends, families, colleagues, communities, or cultures. Whether through safer sex or political action groups, we should continue to build upon our individual and collective knowledges, consciousness, and actions. To paraphrase Cornel West, we should endeavor to respect ourselves and each other with humor, vision, dignity, courage, and style.[7] Make the abstract concrete.

Notes

Thanks to David L. Eng, Alice Y. Hom, Russell C. Leong, and Steven Shum for their suggestions and support in writing this essay.

1. Margaret Noshiko Cornell, "Living in Asian America: An Asian American Lesbian's Address before the Washington Monument." *The Gay Insurgent* 6 (Summer 1980): 16.

2. For more on breast cancer and women s health issues see Merle Woo, "The Politics of Breast Cancer," in *The Very Inside, An Anthology of Writing by Asian and Pacific Islander Lesbian and Bisexual Women,* ed. Sharon Lim-Hing (Toronto: Sister Vision Press, 1994), 416–25. For more historical context, also in *The Very Inside,* see Trinity A. Ordona's "The Challenges Facing Asian and Pacific Islander Lesbian and Bisexual Women in the U.S.," 384–90. Also, see Alice Y. Hom and Ming-Yuen S. Ma's "Premature Gestures: A Speculative Dialogue on Asian Pacific Islander Lesbian and Gay Writing," in *Critical Essays: Gay and Lesbian Writers of Color,* ed. Emmanuel S. Nelson (New York: Harrington Park Press, 1993), 21–52. For current issues see Karin Aguilar-San Juan's "Linking the Issues, From Identity to Activism," 1–15, and Yoko Yoshikawa's "The Heat is On *Miss Saigon* Coalition: Organizing Across Race and Sexuality," 275–94, both in *The State of Asian America—Activism and Resistance in the 1990s* (Boston: South End Press, 1993).

3. I discuss issues of *closets of scale* for Queer API communities in "Queer Asian Pacific Space" in *Privileging Positions, The Sites of Asian American Studies,* ed. Gary Y. Okihiro, et al. (Pullman, WA: Washington State University Press, Forthcoming).

4. Paraphrased from Audre Lorde's "Age, Race, Class, and Sex: Woman Redefining Difference," in *Out There—Marginalization and Contemporary Cultures,* ed. Russell Ferguson, Martha Gever, Trinh T. Minh-ha, and Cornel West (Cambridge, MA: The New Museum of Contemporary Art and MIT Press, 1990), 281–88.

5. bell hooks discusses notions of a *politic of location* in her essay, "Choosing the Margin as a Space of Radical Openness," in her book of essays, *Yearning—Race, Gender, and Cultural Politics* (Boston: South End Press, 1990), 145–53. I discuss spatial dimensions of activism for Queer People of Color communities in "Queer Spaces, The Spaces of Lesbians and Gay Men of Color in Los Angeles." (Master's Thesis in Urban Planning, UCLA, 1993.

6. Proposition 187 in California was passed in the 1994 November elections. This legislation would restrict the provision of publicly funded services only to legitimate California citizens and would require all publicly funded programs to demand documentation of such legitimate residency status from those seeking services. As of March 1995, the implementation of the legislation has been blocked pending constitutional review.

7. From Cornel West's "The New Cultural Politics of Difference," in *Out There — Marginalization and Contemporary Cultures,* ed. Russell Ferguson, Martha Gever, Trinh T. Minh-ha, and Cornel West (Cambridge, MA: The New Museum of Contemporary Art and MIT Press, 1990), 19–37.

8

In Our Own Way

A Roundtable Discussion

Cristy Chung, Aly Kim, Zoon Nguyen,
and Trinity Ordona, with Arlene Stein

During the past decade, Asian lesbians began to form cultural, social, and political networks in major cities across the country. In May 1987 the first West Coast Asian/Pacific Lesbian Retreat, "Coming Out and Coming Together," drew about eighty women, mostly from the San Francisco Bay Area. The following October, a group of sixty Asian lesbians and gay men from across the country formed an Asian contingent at the 1987 March on Washington for Gay Rights in Washington, D.C. This organizing had ripple effects. In 1988, the Asian/Pacific Lesbian Network formed and sponsored the first national retreat in September 1989, bringing together over one hundred forty Asian and Pacific Islander lesbians from the U.S., Canada, and England. That same year, the Asia-based international organization of lesbians, the Asian Lesbian Network, held its first conference in December 1989 in Bangkok, Thailand. Networks of Asian and Pacific Islander lesbians continue to build in North America, Europe, Australia, Asia, and the Pacific Basin.

The following is a discussion among Arlene Stein, lesbian cultural critic and editor of the recently-published book, *Sisters, Sexperts, Queers* (Plume, 1993), and four Asian-American lesbian activists in San Francisco, November 1990.

Cristy and Aly are San Francisco Bay Area writers and editors who recently served on the Editorial Board for *Sinister Wisdom*'s 1992 Lesbian of Color issue (#47), *Tellin' It Like It 'Tis*. Trinity is a community activist and graduate student conducting the first ethnography of Asian lesbian and bisexual women in the U.S. Zoon works in Washington, D.C., as Executive Assistant to Roberta Achtenberg, Assistant Secretary, Office of Fair Housing and Equal Employment and the highest political appointee from the gay community by the Clinton Administration.

ARLENE: Let's start with the question of your relationship to the "larger" lesbian community. How do you see that relationship?

ZOON: In terms of politics, I feel like I'm right in the middle of things. This whole idea of inclusion is wonderful, but I'm tired of just being included. I want people to ask for my input, for my input to be on paper, and to turn into policy. I can sit here and say this and that, but if none of it gets taken seriously and implemented, then it's a waste of time, my time and your time.

ARLENE: What would be an example of this?

ZOON: Proposition K in 1989 (a San Francisco legislation to recognize domestic partners) is an example. One of my criticisms then was that people of color were not part of the campaign. The press also pitted the Asian community against the gay community as being very homophobic. One of the things I did the next time was to say: "What about the communities of color?" I went to some community meetings, which were mostly attended by white gay men, and no one heard me. So I just split the scene. Much later on, the Prop K campaign people started up a People of Color Task Force, and I was asked to sit on it. It felt like a slap in the face. It was tokenism. "Why are you asking me now instead of at the very beginning when I was very loud and clear about it?"

ARLENE: Why do you think they didn't hear you?

ZOON: As with most things, white gay and lesbian folks have a certain agenda, and in my experience, anybody that tries to bring awareness of racial issues is often seen as "us" trying to sabotage "them." That is just not the case. In the gay community, we need to be more aware of how to incorporate the non-gay community. Domestic partnership is not just about gayness, it's about more that… [otherwise, it comes out as] pitting the gay community against the minority community. Those of us who are gay people of color are often forced to choose between the gay culture and people of color culture.

CRISTY: Which we do every day. If you work in social services, do you work in your community in the Asian community social services and remain invisible as a lesbian? Do you work in the lesbian and gay community and remain invisible as a person of color and your issues never get heard? People of color issues are always a tag on the end.

ZOON: We're always an afterthought.

TRINITY: Let me give you a good example. In the Asian community, immigration is a big concern; the majority of our community have immigrated since 1965. There is a prevailing anti-immigrant prejudice—"they're taking our jobs"—and inequities in the way immigration law is implemented. For immigrants, though, if you're homosexual, you're an "undesirable alien" and subject to forced deportation. Prop K was a good thing in that it recognizes domestic partners; on the other hand if you are an immigrant and register your relationship, the INS has documented proof that you are an "undesirable alien." Was there any discussion about this in the gay community? The only time immigration is seen as a "gay community" problem is when HIV-status persons can't get into the country to attend a conference.

ZOON: It was brought up but it wasn't dealt with; again, they felt "we" were trying to sabotage "them."

TRINITY: Current immigration law has unadulterated homophobia right in the middle of it, yet the gay community isn't fighting it. Yet, who are the people being affected by anti-gay immigration law? Large numbers of new immigrant gays, mostly from Asia and Latin America, who are living here already.

ZOON: The point is that we have to choose, and we just can't be who we are.

TRINITY: This is also an example of how we live in the "twilight zone" of both worlds, because we don't have the Asian community trying to change the anti-gay immigration parts of the law, either. We have to do double time on both ends. I believe that if you want to fight for gay rights, straight people must also fight too. If you want to fight racism, white people, including white gay people, have to take up the struggle because it affects their brothers and sisters on the other side of the color line. The gay community fights the right wing; there's political organizing and creative work, like "The Quilt," …so it's the lack of effort [to fight racism] that makes me upset.

CRISTY: That's why it makes it hard to feel a part of the larger lesbian community. You're not a part of it. They don't hear your issues.

ARLENE: What are some other issues that aren't being addressed?

TRINITY: Besides immigration, which is a big one. (laughter)

CRISTY: There's tokenism, and racism, not hearing what our issues are or what we have to say, not taking into consideration what our scope, and where we're coming from as a culture as a diverse group of communities…. Asian Pacific lesbians participate in the AIDS movement, social service programs, work against hate crimes, domestic violence, and rape. It's not like we don't participate in the larger communities because there's racism; but we participate with a knowledge of what we're going to be faced with. For example, I'm on the board of a San Francisco women's anti-rape organization; but I know I have to do a lot of work to educate them about women of color and lesbian of color needs.

CRISTY: If you're gonna have a crisis line, it has to be language accessible. However, the Asian community doesn't reach out through crisis lines. I work at an Asian women's shelter, and we don't get a lot of calls directly from women; we get them from social service agencies.

ZOON: As referrals....

CRISTY: Yes, as referrals. The Asian women will first go to someone they feel safe to talk to. They're not going to pick up a phone when there's other family members in the house who can hear, much less, talk to a total stranger on the other line who's gonna be someone who speaks English, and not their native language.

ZOON: So, if you were in tune with our language and cultural barriers, you would, do a [multilingual] brochure....

CRISTY: Or you would start doing more volunteer recruitment in the Asian community. Not because you need more Asians to look more racially balanced, but because you really want to work with the Asian community; you want to outreach and provide services for and need help because you can't otherwise do it yourself. Be honest.

ZOON: But don't assume that you are the almighty who's doing me the favor...that I'm on my knees bowing down to you. Be honest when you don't know something. I respect people who do that.

CRISTY: You also need to look deeper. You can't assume that the services that you provide to American English speakers are going to work for the Asian community. You have to do some extra work. You're going to have to go that extra mile, that extra time and energy to find what will really work.

ALY: Unfortunately, I don't think that [Cristy's and Zoon's approach] exists in the broader gay and lesbian movement. They say—we're having a hard enough time getting gay rights, how can we break off and work for gay and lesbian rights for people of color or deal with racism. When I first came out, I was involved in a lesbian movement, but I was the only lesbian of color. I had to work on the issues of racism, otherwise it wouldn't happen. But I got tired of having to do it that way. For myself I had to pull out. I'm glad that we have gay pride marches and this overall gay and lesbian community. But my energy is put into Pacific Asian lesbians. I want us to be the focus, to work on documenting who we are and show every part of us.

TRINITY: I've been out for twenty years. I've spent most of my political life in the Filipino and anti-racist movement, fighting the Klan and fighting on different issues. During that time, I'd never found the gay/lesbian community inviting. Later, at a certain junction in my political and personal life, I turned to the gay and lesbian community. I found it very open and progressive, but I also found myself personally at a loss. I liked the talk about changing and fighting for gay rights, but very little around me reflected my own life experiences. It was very disheartening. So I found other gay people of color, specifically other Asian/Pacific Islander lesbians and Filipino lesbians, especially. I did not grow up as a "generic Asian," I grew up Filipino…we ate pinakbet and my parents spoke Tagalog—a particular language, a particular culture.

ARLENE: And yet there are "Asian" lesbian organizations that cross ethnic lines.

CRISTY: That's why our community also struggles with unity in diversity. Sometimes, we're all feeling like we should all be the same—we're all Asians or Pacific Islanders— yet that's not our experience at all. For me, as someone who's fourth generation biracial, I grew up in a very white area; my experience is so different, my foods are different. They're mixed. I have both Chinese and Japanese and American food, mixed.

TRINITY: Yet if someone tries to put you down with a racist slur and call you "Jap" instead of "Chink," it doesn't make any difference. Because it means the same thing. You can't say, excuse me….

ZOON: …I'm not a "Jap," I'm a "Gook" (everyone laughs).

TRINITY: …Racism is the equalizer.

ZOON: In terms of diversity, there's language too. For the Southeast Asians, we have Chinese, Vietnamese, Laotian, Cambodian language differences. So even while Asian lesbians were starting to gather, I was one of the first to start a Vietnamese gay and lesbian support group. I felt that I needed to be in my own space talking about our issues. As a first-generation immigrant, how do we deal with coming out? We have examined the concept of coming out. Is it a Western concept? Do you really have to come out? Is it something that is understood by your family without having to say, "Mom, I'm a dyke?"

ARLENE: Can others address this? Is coming out different in your families? Does the "white" model of coming out apply to your experiences?

CRISTY: For me it's split really clearly. My mom is white, and my dad is Chinese. My Mom is also a lesbian, so it was easy for me to tell her in a standard American way, "Mom, I have something to tell you." We came out to each other at the same time. Forget it when it comes to my Dad's side of the family. We don't talk about it. I just don't bring it up. He'll love me forever, and he knows, even though every now and then he'll try to set me up with a business buddy's son. He basically gets it but we don't talk about it. We don't talk about my work in the community, about anything that I might write. It's understood. I would never tell anyone on his side of the family.

TRINITY: That's his right. You can't infringe on that.

CRISTY: It's out of respect for his family, his position in the family.

ZOON: He's the elder.

CRISTY: He maintains a certain position in the family. I don't feel like it's my place to upset that balance. And I don't feel I need to.

ARLENE: How do you talk about what you do?

CRISTY: He knows. We've been together long enough for him to know.

ALY: You just say so-and-so and I, and you say her name over and over and over till they get it.

ARLENE: Well, that's exactly what I do....

CRISTY: I never directly came out to him. I never said to him, "Dad I'm a lesbian."

TRINITY: The words I used with my Mom were: "We are together." That's all I said. I never used the "L" word. Then Mom told me a story as her way to telling me she understood. She said that when she was in the Philippines, she had a best girlfriend and they went everywhere together, and one day her girlfriend came in with a different girlfriend. Now in the Philippines, and in most Asian countries, girl-girl/boy-boy relationships are encouraged because they don't want you to go out and have babies too early. That's discouraged throughout puberty. So young men and women easily form close, intimate friendships with people of the same sex. So, Mom related her emotional experiences to mine, and hit it right on the nose. That's how we talked about it.

ZOON: That brings me back to what I said earlier. The gay/lesbian community oftentimes views Asian/Pacific gays and our community as homophobic. I don't think any group of people is more or less homophobic than the other. Asian friends of mine have come out, like Cristy said, and their folks just kind of know. They might not talk about it, but they're not denying your right to live. They will love you. Mom and Dad will not disown you, though there are some who do; but then, there are lots of white families who have also disowned their gay kids. But somehow, it's a bigger deal when a family of color disowns their gay son or daughter. Because of racism, it is an especially painful loss, to lose your connection to your family. But it still does not mean that our community is "more homophobic" than any other.

TRINITY: Besides, over time, the more Asian lesbians and gay men come out, the more parents have to deal with the issue.

ARLENE: Is there a great deal more visibility now, more than there has been over the last ten years?

ZOON: Even though we're not "huggy kissy united," we are much more visible. During the gay parade we're out there marching.

ALY: You can't generalize across the country. Because we're really talking cities and visibility.

TRINITY: And it's also relative to the size of the Asian population in these cities, too. Where the Asian community is only a handful, then we're in smaller numbers. That's why we gather on a regional and national basis, because the community is so spread out across the country.... Just to be able to see (other Asian and Pacific Islander lesbians) is very invigorating, it's an experience that we give each other just by our numbers and sharing with each other.

ALY: I remember the first Asian/Pacific lesbian dance I went to in 1980. I walked into the room and my mouth just fell open. (heavy inhales and laughter)

ARLENE: How do you account for the fact that the Asian lesbian movement is finally taking off now?

TRINITY: I think population is one [reason], Asian population.

CRISTY: Maybe migration to this area.

ALY: The greater gay and lesbian community is becoming more visible. So as that becomes more visible, it affects our visibility too. Everything is growing. I came out and migrated up this way. I also think coming from isolated areas, we search each other out more. At the First West Coast Music Festival, I went around to every Pacific Asian lesbian. You gotta get up the guts to go over and introduce yourself and say, "How'd you like to just meet together?" There were six of us and for all those women, that was the first time they had been with that many other Asian lesbians. So, it's coming from a place of not having any, and you want to build a community.

ARLENE: When you came out, did you come out through/to the white lesbian community?

ALY: I was really isolated for years, six years, before I came out into a lesbian community [and] to my parents, although they knew by the time I told them. The whole thing about family, about respect for the culture and the parents...well, my lovers at the time were Asian and they didn't want to be out to their families. My brothers were coming on to them at the time, and I was tripping out; but I couldn't say anything because they didn't want to be out and I had to respect that I couldn't come out for them. I wanted to desperately come out for myself (laughter) but I couldn't because that was their life. But when I did, I was ecstatic. I went back East to a music festival. I had bought one of those belts that said "Women Loving Women" on it... (laughter). But I came home wearing it and pulling down my shirt so no one could see it. No one ever said anything about it, but they made comments, like "I've never seen her look so happy before, so whatever she's doing is good."

TRINITY: After I came out to my Mom, which was about 16 years ago, I never beat it down her throat after that. When I had a lover at the time, I would introduce her and just do it in a way that she could understand. There was one occasion when my lover's mother was down in San Diego, where my family lives, at the holidays. We managed to get the two mothers to meet, and Mom could relate to that. I never used lesbian language to talk about it.

ALY: You can't....

TRINITY: It doesn't make sense to them. But they can understand commitment and love, feelings, emotions, happiness, security, and good things like that, so....

ZOON: There's a certain level of respect, too...understanding the style in which you have to approach your parents and leave it at that; and not try to force the issue in a way....

TRINITY: ...That's supposed to be politically correct. Saying, "Mom, we are together," is just as good as saying, "I'm a lesbian."

ZOON: Yeah, we fuck each other every night, man! ...(laughter)

ARLENE: Well, I think the white, middle class model of coming out suggests that if you need to move far away from your family, even cut them out in order to be a lesbian or gay person, you do that. This sounds very different.

ZOON: Our families are so important. I could never cut them out of my life. That's me, I am an extension of my family.

CRISTY: Family obligation too. My lover's family—her parents are immigrants, and they are very traditional; and they don't speak a lot of English. If she were to even think about not going home once a week and to not be there for them, and to not help out at home.... Those are her family obligations; her first priority, even though I'm a priority, they are also as much a priority.

TRINITY: That's understood between Cristy and Lancy.

CRISTY: Right—sometimes. (laughter)

ZOON: My lover now is biracial, half-Japanese. And it's understood a lot easier than when I was going out with white women. 'Cause I think a lot of the white experience has been, oh, when you come out you sort of have to denounce the family, they're not a part of you anymore, you are a separate person, independence, you know, at age eighteen, you're free to do whatever. And I feel like sometimes when I tell my non-Asian friends, I have to defend myself, "Oh no, they really love me, they do." I think they see it that you're not strong enough, you didn't make a statement by "coming out" to your family. And it's "out" by whose standard? It's a very white model, a very non-Asian or Pacific Islander standard.

CRISTY: And it makes you question yourself; maybe I should be saying more or pushing him on this issue so he really can get it.

ZOON: I also think our issues are not always gay issues; who we are as people of color just can't be separated.

ARLENE: It's my sense that lesbians and gay men of color have been broadening the gay political agenda. I can see that in the AIDS movement. It has often been black lesbians who have made the argument that AIDS is not just a "gay disease."

TRINITY: I think it will be interesting as the years unfold ahead of us. The more we deal with our individual and collective experience (as Asian/Pacific lesbians), the more we're able to work side by side with other people of color because we feel strong within ourselves.... I'm very optimistic. We may be scrapping and fighting with each other, but we're not turning away. We might not always like each other, but we're still not turning away. We still recognize that we're part of the same struggle. We just have to learn to tolerate differences and accept individuality and accept conflict as a part of being together. (The old definition) of unity has always been the absence of conflict.

CRISTY: And a safe place, whatever "safe" means. It's never same for a women of color, a person of color, in the world. Everyday, you go through pain and painful experiences. So to try to create a space that's safe and unified is false.

TRINITY: We're trying to change the world, and we have to go out and change it every place we can. But we can't go out there and fight all the time. We need each other.

ZOON: Besides, we're getting old too. (laughter)

9

From the 1970s to the 1990s
Perspective of a Gay
Filipino American Activist

Gil Mangaoang

It was an early March evening in 1975 in Oakland, California. I was in a meeting listening to my ex-fiancée Arlene and other women point out how the men were guilty of sexist attitudes towards women in our organization. I had just broken up with Arlene; I thought everyone knew why I left her—but no one asked me directly, and I offered no explanation. I felt trapped in the discussion. On the one hand, I wanted to escape from the degrading experience, yet I felt that perhaps they're right and that I had to correct my behavior. But I knew instinctively that wasn't the issue. I was disoriented; the only thing that I knew was that I could no longer endure the pressure of maintaining a straight male facade.

The Roots of 1970s Activism

Being gay in the early 70s should have been easy, but being Filipino American and a political activist complicated the process. As a Filipino it was difficult to tap into the exhilarating feeling of being openly gay and to become an integral part of that 70s generation of gay activists. The dominant attitude among Filipinos was to assimilate into U.S. society and not rock the boat. To be openly gay was the least of our problems, while racism against minorities including Filipinos continued.

In response to these conditions, I chose to be an activist. This decision reflected the influence of social activism I was exposed to as part of my strong religious fundamentalist family upbringing that stressed principles of helping society's disenfranchised. The push for social activism may not have been a popular position to hold within the Filipino community; I was just one of many individuals who chose to resist racism and discriminatory practices. But simultaneously on a personal level, I was faced with the internal dilemma of striking a balance of what it meant to be a Filipino, a political activist and a gay man.

My Filipino American Heritage

For the first twenty-three years of my life, being Filipino was identifying merely with the fact that my family was from the Philippines. I considered myself to be a Filipino American. I had been raised with little knowledge of my heritage.

I found it difficult to be a Filipino in the United States because I had no idea what that meant. However, after I was discharged from the U. S. Air Force in 1970, I continued my education at the City College of San Francisco. There I began to learn about my people through Philippine history courses and by attending off-campus programs and conferences that provided a forum for the exchange of ideas about Filipino Americans. I began to understand that Filipinos had been part of the U.S. labor force since the early 1900s, primarily in the agricultural fields of the West Coast, the plantations of Hawaii, and in the canneries of Alaska. I learned that Filipinos were attacked by Whites solely because we were socializing with white women. Miscegenation laws prevented Filipinos from marrying white women. Understanding history led me to reflect on my own family's coming to the United States.

I was part of the second generation of Filipinos to be born and raised here. The first twentieth-century immigration of Filipinos that came here from before 1910 through the 1920s was primarily single men contracted to work in the agricultural fields of California and Hawaii. However, there was a small percentage of Filipinos who migrated as entire family units, including my family.

The Hawaiian Sugar Plantation Association (HSPA) went to the Ilocos provinces of Northern Luzon to recruit a new labor force to work the plantation fields of Hawaii to replace the Japanese and Chinese laborers. The image of "streets paved with gold" coupled with the lure of a regular salary dangled by the HSPA, created an opportunity for my great-grandfather Villanueva. Thus, he accepted the offer to work in Hawaii and became a contract laborer. It was through this recruitment channel that my great-grandparents and their children became one of the first families brought to Hawaii from the Philippines and eventually to California.

As subsequent generations of my family became more acculturated, the less Filipino they became in their values and attitudes. I was only able to recapture my identity as a Filipino through the re-education process I was exposed to at City College. In so doing, I became one of hundreds of Filipino Americans at the beginning of the 1970s, who along with thousands of other ethnic minority activists, placed key emphasis on the assertion of one's ethnic identity in a white-dominated society.

At the City College of San Francisco, I was on the Student Council and a member of the Filipino Club. I worked side by side with other student activists and minority organizations in the efforts to establish an ethnic studies program. We negotiated with the administration to ensure that Philippine history and Tagalog courses were included in the curricula. The issue of parity in the hiring of faculty and counselors on campus was emphasized to match the sizable minority student enrollment. However, in the quest for defining my Filipino American identity, I also began to question the political and social structure of the United States.

"To Serve the People"

I had become restless and impatient with the City College administration. The issues still seemed to be confined to the "ivory tower," remote from the concerns of daily survival for Filipinos and other minorities. Dissatisfied with the elite political structure of the U.S. and its exploitative social characteristics, I was searching for alternatives. My youthful impetuosity of the time demanded that changes in society must occur immediately.

Coincidentally, an informal study group of minority students—Jane, Joyce, Fern, Jim, and James—developed on campus. The group studied the works of Mao Tse-Tung. I found myself attracted to the philosophical viewpoints raised, particularly the concept of "Serve the People." Bolstered with this theoretical insight, I searched for a tangible way to work in the Filipino community. Some members of the study group were doing volunteer work at the International Hotel (IH). The IH was a low-income residential hotel located on the fringes of San Francisco's burgeoning financial district and adjacent to Chinatown. The hotel's tenants were mostly single elderly Filipino men. This neighborhood was known in the community as "Manilatown."

Many retired single Filipino men lived in residential hotels such as the IH. Nearby were numerous restaurants, pool halls, and barber shops. From the 1920s through the late 1960s, "Manilatown" spanned a three-block corridor along Kearny Street. The International Hotel represented the last bastion of Manilatown. The master plan for redevelopment of the San Francisco financial district included the destruction of many older hotels such as the International Hotel. Residents of the IH were fighting an eviction by the owner on the principle that if they were to be evicted, there were no other low-income single room

Gil Mangaoang, Union Square anti-Marcos rally,
San Francisco, 1960s. Photograph courtesy of Gil
Mangaoang.

occupancy units available to them in the surrounding community where they
chose to live. Other residential hotels in the areas had already been demolished.

Through this study group I came into contact with other Asians and Filipino
American leftists—Burl, Brent, Ernie, and Sally—who were working at the
International Hotel. Many of these individuals were current or former stu-
dents from the University of California, Berkeley; California State University,
San Francisco; or the City College of San Francisco.

These individuals recognized that minorities and working people in the
United States were oppressed as a direct result of the inequalities of society
structured on a capitalist economic and social foundation. This commonality
of world view led these individuals to found the Kalayaan (freedom) Collective,
as a community-based organization in the Filipino community comprised of
both Filipinos born in the United States and in the Philippines.

Working together at the IH provided me opportunities to discuss the inaccessibility of affordable health care or quality low-cost housing and the inequity of depressed wages as compared to increased corporate dividends in the U.S. As I began to understand their viewpoints, I recognized that the essence of their positions represented the classic communist orientation. At first I was shocked and felt that I had been deceived by the hidden agenda of these people with whom I had worked with side by side. However, I believed that if the good work they did for the community reflected their political viewpoints, then I could adopt those same political viewpoints. In 1971 I was invited to become a Kalayaan member, and I willingly joined the collective.

Theoretically, the Kalayaan was influenced by the teachings of Mao Tse-Tung and Jo Ma Sison, the Chairman of the Communist Party of the Philippines. Since the Kalayaan membership included Philippine nationals as well as Filipino Americans, its political focus was two-fold. First, this translated into the necessity to replace the capitalist mode of production in the United States with a socialist society. Second, the Kalayaan also recognized the importance of supporting the revolutionary struggle in the Philippines.

In regards to its first objective, Kalayaan members were committed to provide the Filipino community with educational information about the historical role Filipinos had played in contributing to the economic growth of the U.S. particularly since the 1920s and 1930s as agricultural workers. The contradiction was that while Filipinos had contributed to the economic growth of the U.S., they had been discriminated against as second-class citizens and not advanced economically and socially. The Kalayaan Collective put its philosophical views into action by organizing around the social conditions of the Filipino American community. In this context, members were involved in the International Hotel, ethnic studies programs on college and university campuses, and in labor union organizing activities. For the Kayalaan, social injustices could only be rectified by replacing the capitalist system with a socialist order.

The Kalayaan Collective demonstrated its second political objective during the initial imposition of martial law in the Philippines by Ferdinand Marcos. The Kalayaan along with other groups throughout the U.S. which supported genuine national democracy in the Philippines was part of the critical voice that provided uncensored information to the Filipino community and general public. This was done through public rallies and demonstrations denouncing the repressive activities conducted by the Marcos regime. In addition, the Kalayaan newspaper, published by the Collective, contained articles exposing the atrocities perpetuated against the Filipino people in the name of democracy.

Through these anti-Marcos resistance efforts, nationwide contact increased between the Kalayaan Collective and other progressive Philippine nationals and Filipino Americans working as individuals or organized groups. As consistent work relationships began to emerge among these groups, it became necessary to coordinate these efforts nationwide. This led to the demise of the Kalayaan and the formation of the Union of Democratic Filipinos—Katipunan ng mga Demokratikong Pilipino (KDP) in 1972. As a leftist nationwide Filipino organization, its principles were similar to those of the Kalayaan. It emphasized the need to challenge and correct the racial discrimination and social injustices perpetrated against Filipinos through the establishment of socialism in the United States, while simultaneously supporting the genuine democratic rights movement of patriotic forces in the Philippines.

It was difficult being a radical leftist in the Filipino community since the KDP members were often regarded by mainstream Filipinos as young, sloganeering idealists incapable of changing society. Yet the KDP was to remain an active force in the Filipino community for over fifteen years. Among the KDP's more notable accomplishments were the reversal of unjust federal immigration policies regarding Foreign Medical Graduates in 1975 and Foreign Nurse Graduates in 1977; the formation of a national immigrant rights organization; the release of two nurses framed in Chicago for murder charges in 1976; the organization of regional conventions on the West Coast between 1971 and 1978 that annually brought together hundreds of Filipinos to discuss concerns of the community at large; the expulsion of corrupt union officials among Alaska cannery workers and their replacement with a union leadership team that was sensitive to the rank and file needs; the reform of the portrayal of Filipinos in California textbooks in 1979; and, the establishment of an effective national anti-martial law grassroots lobbying movement that consistently curtailed the annual United States Congressional military financial aid appropriations to the Philippines during the entire reign of the Marcos regime.

Sexual Identity

While I was discovering my Filipino-American identity and was immersed in the political struggle of social justice for Filipinos both in the U.S. and the Philippines, I was struggling with my sexual identity. I wanted to understand not only what it meant to be gay, but also to participate as an openly gay male in society. Initially, I felt that these two identities—Filipino and gay—were contradictory and irreconcilable.

To come out in the Filipino community would be double jeopardy. My first concern was that being openly gay would further jeopardize the serious consideration my political viewpoints would be given in the Filipino community. Secondly, to come out in mainstream society would force me to confront the homophobic attitudes of society at large in addition to the racial discrimination that I was already subjected to as an ethnic minority.

Gradually I began to understand that the discrimination and homophobia I perceived were two sides of the same coin and, that in fact, there were similarities of oppression. As a Filipino, I experienced the racial discrimination any minority living in America encounters. But as a gay male, the parameters were even more complex.

I recognized that being a self-proclaimed gay man would put me at odds not only with mainstream society but also with the Filipino community. Yet I saw that being gay automatically aligned me with other gay men of all nationalities. Later I would recognize that racism as a social dynamic also permeates the gay subculture.

How to resolve this dual identity? I resolved that my primary orientation and approach to society was first as a political activist motivated to improve the discriminatory conditions experienced by Filipino Americans. As a community organizer, my primary interaction with people focused principally on the organizing issue or campaign at hand. Those political organizing relationships seldom provided the opportunity to discuss my sexual orientation. I did not flaunt the fact that I was gay or feel compelled to tell others of my orientation. This is not to say that I was totally "closeted"; my openness depended on the situation and the individuals involved. Being a single male, I often worked closely with single females. I was invariably asked if I was married and did I have a family. My response was usually "I'm single now, but I was married before; I like being single." I was careful not to reveal that I was gay for fear of creating any unnecessary alienation between myself and those individuals I was working with and thus jeopardize the organizing efforts.

However, my relationship with KDP members was much more candid. Before I came out, I was influenced to a certain extent by Filipino gay and lesbian activists from the Philippines who were very open about their sexual orientation. On the one hand, I saw them as a threat to me; I avoided any contact with them socially for fear of being identified as "one of them." This was particularly true during the days of the Kalayaan when the identifiable gay activist men from the Philippines—Jason and Ned who were on the periphery of the collective—exhibited mannerisms that were effeminate. Perhaps this was due to the fact that in the Philippines their families were part of the elite upper-class strata, which enabled them to lead any lifestyle they chose, be it homosexual or heterosexual, without social constraints and fear of economic repercussion, i.e. discrimination in employment.

There were only a couple of Filipina American lesbians—Jane and Sally— that were politically active and with whom I more readily identified since our ideological perspectives were similar. Nevertheless, these were the only gay Filipinos I knew. In retrospect, they were role models of how it was possible to be uninhibited and positive about being gay and yet be politically active in the Filipino community.

When I decided to come out in KDP, I felt liberated and knew that I could be myself with these comrades with whom I had worked closely over the years on many political issues. Although there was not explicit support for my lifestyle, there was no opposition to it. In the course of my political work, I often came in contact with men to whom I was sexually attracted. It was difficult to keep my emotions in control and not let them run away, especially with the high sexual libido of a male in his early twenties influenced by the dominant gay liberation lifestyle. I enjoyed the game of flirting with the straight political guys. In fact, there was a period of time when I just came out, that I went out of my way to be outrageous in how I expressed my declaration about being "gay and proud." Most of the time it just meant wearing an earring and lots of body jewelry. I felt that the shock value of outrageous behavior was a positive way of asserting my sexual identity. These youthful actions were a passive-aggressive way of seeking recognition without the responsibility of having to justify my actions. One situation in particular comes to mind.

In 1975, I had been out no more than a couple of months and was just developing my network of gay friends. I had seen Ben at numerous community events, but it was not until we were both involved in a recording album project geared towards popularizing revolutionary music from the Philippines, that I had the opportunity to get to know him. He had been out many years before me and was very flamboyant and open about his gayness. We were at the house of some KDP members for a meeting. Since some of the members weren't there yet, Ben and I decided to make the best use of our time in one of the vacant bedrooms for an intimate get-acquainted session. Needless to say, the other members were somewhat outraged by our behavior but didn't know how to "politely intervene."

In the 1970s there were few gay organizations to join, and those that existed were dominated by white males. Minorities who were members of these gay organizations were generally seen as subordinates reflecting the dominant racist attitudes in society. The experience was very isolating, and the companionship and support from other gay political activists, either minority or white, was rare. This created a degree of schizophrenia between my political and social identities. While my primary political identity and organizing efforts was directed toward issues confronting non-white minorities, specifically the Filipino community, my gay identity took on a different character in other situations.

My main social links were through places patronized by gay white males in San Francisco where minorities could be found like the Rendezvous on Sutter, Oil Can Harry's on O'Farrell, or the White Horse on Telegraph in Oakland. Often I was the only Asian or Pacific Islander in these places and usually was tagged as the "Asian Doll." If there was another Asian in the bar, I tended to avoid him so as not to infringe on his cruising domain. I knew of no minority gay organizations where I could go for support to deal with being Filipino and gay. Isolated, I felt that there was no alternative except for me to find someone who could provide me with support and companionship as a gay man. Besides, the long hours spent bar hopping—usually leading to frantic one night stands with another "friend for the night"—left me physically satiated but emotionally empty the next morning.

The first time that I fell in love within the framework of my gay identity was with Michael. Although he was white, he was another male who was also trying to define what it meant to be gay and a political activist. As fate would have it, this gay relationship was to end in three months when he was killed in a bicycle accident.

Following his death, I felt even more alone than ever before. The majority of KDP comrades didn't know how to respond to my grief since Michael was my gay lover and not my girlfriend or spouse. I did find comfort from many of his friends, and once again, in the arms of strangers for a single night.

I wanted to go to my family for comfort but couldn't since I hadn't yet come out to them. But with Michael's death, I was resolved to talk with my family and share with them that I was gay. I promised myself that in the future I would never again be isolated from the emotional support of my family if my significant other were to die. Two years later I was to make this declaration known to my mother.

All I felt at the time of Michael's death was that my family had to know that I was gay—I had to face the reality that they might not accept my lifestyle, and if necessary I would have to go on with my life without their support or understanding. Had there been a gay Filipino organization to approach at the time of Michael's death, I could at least have gathered some support and understanding for my grief.

The last time that I saw Michael alive was when he and I marched together in 1976 at my first Gay Freedom Day Parade in San Francisco. The exhilaration of declaring my gay identity through a public parade was politically liberating. There were hundreds of thousands of gay men, women, and lesbians who proudly proclaimed their right to exist. It was also in this highly charged political environment of the parade where I met Juan.

My life changed since that first introduction to Juan; he is my lifetime companion whom I have been committed to since then. The fact that he is also a man of color has created a supportive atmosphere for both of us to experience the joys of a longterm relationship. Juan is a significant part of my life. He has become not only my lover, but he has been my closest friend and confidant. Without him by my side to help me through all the different phases of my Filipino American, political, and gay identities, it would have been extremely difficult to be a minority leftist gay man.

Couples in a mixed white and non-white relationship are susceptible to cultural prejudices and racist attitudes due to the objective differences in life experiences and power relationships in a white-dominated society. This was the experience and frustration I had constantly encountered within gay social circles. Just because a white male is gay does not preclude him from being a racist. But when two minorities struggle to forge a relationship, the obstacle of race does not become an issue. Juan and I have had numerous disagreements over the years, but those have been due to issues related to adjustments in establishing our relationship and to clashes in social values rather than to racist attitudes. The continuous challenge which we experience is how to nurture the development of a long-term relationship that incorporates cross-cultural values.

The 1990s

Today, a young Filipino in the United States who decides to come out in the 1990s will still find the process to be difficult, yet, much easier than it was in the 1970s.

There are now organizations established primarily for the gay and lesbian community. In metropolitan areas where such populations are large, specific gay organizations for Asians, Pacific Islanders, or Filipinos do exist. Filipino gay organizations are rare but exist such as Barangay in San Francisco or Pan-Asian organizations like the Gay Asian Pacific Support Network in Los Angeles, which includes Filipinos among its members. The existence of these specialized gay minority organizations is often taken for granted. Few young gay Filipinos realize that there was a massive social movement in the late 1960s and early 1970s, which laid the foundation for the more tolerant and accepting attitudes, albeit minimal and uneven in our society, towards lesbians and gays today. The Stonewall Rebellion in 1969 or the Christopher Street Riots as it is sometimes referred to became the rallying point for gay liberation efforts.

The Stonewall Inn was located at 51-53 Christopher Street in New York's Greenwich Village. The New York City Police Department often raided the Stonewall Inn and other gay bars in the area as a matter of routine harassment that had been ongoing for a number of years. But around midnight on June 27, 1969, history was to change. The patrons, mainly Black and Latino drag queens and transvestites, were ejected when the police moved in to arrest the owner for selling liquor without a proper license. As the crowd of ousted patrons and onlookers grew in size, the police began to arrest people. When buses were brought in to take those arrested to jail, the bar patrons on the sidewalk resisted those efforts.

The buildup of continuous harassment and abuse, not just from this incident but the culmination of years of discrimination against all gays, was reflected in the actions of the Stonewall patrons. Their resistance became the line of demarcation in modern gay history for lesbians and gays in our refusal to accept and endure the social discrimination and abusive treatment as second class citizens in the U.S. This is not to say that today all social barriers against gays and lesbians have been lifted and that there has been a 180 degree shift in people's attitudes. Nevertheless, the visibility of lesbians and gays in all social strata of society is more recognized today than the 1970s. Openly gay men and lesbians can be found in public office as elected or appointed officials, in the legal and medical professions, as educators, business leaders, and in all walks of life. This is also true for Asian and Pacific Islander gay men and lesbians who are among all sectors of society and are open about their sexual orientation.

Today, the search for one's gay male identity as a Filipino, in any large metropolitan area of the U.S., no longer has to be as isolating an experience as it was in the 1970s. This is not to say that coming out is an easy process. The decision to come out and be openly gay in society is always difficult. What confronts gay Filipinos today is not only learning to accept their gay identity, but accepting that identity under complex heightened social prejudicial attitudes brought about by the AIDS crisis. The struggle for a positive Filipino gay identity is particularly important today given the spectre of the HIV infection rate that is approaching pandemic proportions. The social stigma of being gay is further complicated by the fact that among Asian and Pacific Islanders in the United States, Filipinos have the highest incidence of HIV infection and diagnosis for AIDS. Filipinos who embrace the gay lifestyle need not become HIV infected, so long as safe and healthy attitudes towards sex are practiced. Safer sex practices is a reorientation facing not just Filipino gays, but is an issue that society in general must address.

For the Filipino struggling openly to identify with their gayness, the trauma of determining one's sexual identity no longer has to be experienced without social support.

As I look back to that room in the 1975 where female KDP members were discussing the male chauvinist attitudes predominant among male members, I know now that those attitudes didn't apply to me. To have succumbed to the expected self-criticism for leaving Arlene was farthest from the truth. The issue wasn't so much my abandonment of her as it was the search for my gay identity. As a politicized Filipino male in a straight world, I had to deal with the issue of my self-liberation through self-acceptance and pride in the fact that I was gay. I had to take responsibility for defining what my life was to be as a gay Filipino American man, and I have found that the process of liberation is a continuous one.

Same-Sex Sexuality in Pacific Literature

*Lisa Kahaleole Chang Hall
and J. Kehaulani Kauanui*

The extreme paucity of resources on Pacific lesbian and gay literature is the result of at least two interlocking systems of exclusion. The first is the most obvious—the realities of racism, colonialism, and homophobia that determines who receives an adequate education, who is enabled to write and finally, is found worthy of publication. The second is a more subtle and profound difficulty that questions the terms and premises of racial (Pacific) and sexual (lesbian and gay) inclusion. "Pacific" is a compromise category, fully satisfying and offending no one, that is utilized both to recognize the historic similarities between its constituent groups and to consolidate their collective power. This essay therefore attempts to draw out some important complications and ambiguities involved in discussing "Same-Sex Sexuality in Pacific Literature." The difficulties begin with our use of the label "Pacific" and continue through each component of the subject of our discussion.

Within a U.S. context, the existence of indigenous Pacific peoples is often subsumed under rubrics such as "Asian/Pacific," "API," and "Asian-Pacifica" that usually address Asian Americans as their sole or primary audiences. Pacific peoples are rarely addressed even within ethnic studies, much less "mainstream" scholarship; the extent to which the U.S. has been a colonial power in the Pacific generally remains unknown and unacknowledged by both academics and the general public. Current and former U.S. colonial territories in the Pacific include Hawaii, Eastern Samoa (American Samoa), Guam, the Republic of the Marshall Islands, the Federated States of Micronesia, the Commonwealth of the Northern Mariana Islands, and Belau (the Trust Territory of the Pacific Island/Republic of Palau). In light of this colonial history and the concomitant struggles for national self-determination of the indigenous peoples, Pacific American would not be an appropriate term for most, although there are those from non-colonized islands who are American-born and might so identify. Internationally, pan-Pacific unity and identity can be an ideal or a reality depending on the context, but in the case of Aotearoa (New Zealand), for example, the complexities of multiple migrations of other colonized islanders have created tensions between the native Maori and immigrant islanders that cannot be easily resolved with the label "Pacific Islander." With all this in mind we have slipped between "indigenous Pacific peoples," "Pacific Islanders," and "Pacific" as terms that are useful in beginning to articulate the separation from "Asian Pacific." Our sources for this introductory essay were extremely limited and skewed toward Polynesians (as opposed to Melanesian Pacific peoples), and within that toward Kanaka Maoli (Native Hawaiians) and Maori. They are also skewed toward women; the space created by lesbian-feminist publishing has provided opportunities for lesbians of color to write and publish (albeit with inadequate funding and distribution) that gay men of color do not have equivalent access to within the "gay male community."

The literature of Pacific lesbians and gay men cannot be adequately understood divorced from the specific colonial histories of Pacific peoples and the Western construction of sexuality imposed upon native worldviews. Pacific peoples from Aotearoa (New Zealand) to the Hawaiian Islands have shared a cosmology in which sexuality is an integral force of life—indeed the cause of the life of the universe—and not a separable category of behavior and existence. The discrete analytical categories of "homosexuality," and more fundamentally "sexuality" itself, are a colonial imposition which only address the realities of a small part of the spectrum of Pacific people who have sexual and love relationships with members of their own sex. It also mistakenly thrusts those who transgress strict Western gender boundaries, but not sexual boundaries into this narrow conception of sexuality.

In an essay published in *Frighten the Horses*, "Being Queer in the Peace Corps," Ellen Twiname writes of her experience as a white lesbian sent to Tuvalu and Fiji.[1] Attempting to locate her "queer Tuvalan counterparts," she is puzzled by the indigenous responses to her cautious inquiries: "How could my instructor flatly deny the existence of homosexuality when the first guy I met there seemed so obviously gay?" Later she is told "that there really is no concept of homosexuality as a separate lifestyle in Tuvalan culture." The refusal of some to be subsumed into the category of gay or lesbian has often been perceived as an attempt to remain closeted and essentially dishonest about their sexual desires. In some cases this might be true; in others it is an attempt to retain control over the meaning and interpretation of those same-sex desires and relationships and to retain a pre-colonial understanding of the world and one's place in it that is not divided by Christian and capitalist dualities of spirit and flesh, sacred and profane.

John D'Emilio's influential essay , "Capitalism and Gay Identity,"[2] argues against the conception of the "eternal homosexual" who has always existed in all times and places, albeit in different forms. Gay identity, in contrast to "homosexual behavior," is a modern phenomenon that is predicated on the ability of individuals to break from kinship ties and be able to support themselves outside of those ties autonomously. It is precisely this fundamental linkage between individualism and gay identity that leads some to resist the contemporary categorizations of "gay" and "straight," not a desire to hide same-sex sexual behavior.

Others, like Maori writer Ngahuia Te Awekotuku, attempt to reclaim traditional roots of their contemporary gay identities. Her essay, "Dykes and Queers: Facts Fairytales and Fictions," in *Mana Wahine Maori: Selected Writings on Maori Women's Art, Culture and Politics* suggests that Maori lesbianism is transhistorical: "Indeed, the loving of one's own gender is an ancient, even tribal, practice, honourable and revered."[3] The profound impact of Western sexual ideology on colonized peoples has created a complex spectrum of accommodations and resistances to externally imposed conceptions of gay identity.

Though there is a rich history of same-sex sexual relations and cross-gendered roles in the Pacific, the vast majority of literature focusing on Pacific peoples is anthropological in nature and written by outsiders to the culture described. A preoccupation with "sexual deviance" is a recurrent theme. From the moments of first contact, Western concepts of Pacific sexuality have consistently distorted, misrepresented, and degraded the experiences they attempted to describe. The forms this has taken are quite different from the ideologies of "emasculation" and "asexuality" imposed on Asian men and the exoticization of Asian women. Promiscuity and savagery (whether noble or bestial) were the earliest and most enduring labels applied to Pacific peoples. From the explorers who decided the women were whores and the men weak in their lack of control over "their" women to the missionaries who recorded with appalled horror their views of native sexuality, a legacy of control and commodification of Pacific sexuality was established and persists. Because Pacific cultures had oral rather than written historical traditions, the written history that survives is filtered through the censorship of the literate and horrified missionaries. Historian Marshall Sahlins noted about Hawaii in *Islands of History*, "What a place for puritanical missionaries! One of them complained that Hawaiians had about twenty forms of what he considered illicit intercourse, with as many different names in the language; so that if any one term were selected to translate the Seventh Commandment, it was bound to leave the impression that the other nineteen activities were still permitted."[4] Needless to say, the richness of this kind of sexual tradition was not translated and passed on in English.

The contemporary context of same-sex love for Pacific peoples grows out of the deliberate colonial destruction of indigenous languages and traditions; its potential for resistance is influenced by feminist, gay liberation, and decolonization movements and ideologies. Many Pacific women were first published by feminists dedicated to the ideal of inclusion of all women's voices. A body of work proclaiming both existence and difference developed in the 1970s and 80s. Bisexual activist Lani Kaahumanu's poem "Hapa Haole Wahine" in *Bi Any Other Name: Bisexual People Speak Out*[5] delineates her identity shifts with regard to racial/political/sexual identification in a form reminiscent of a genealogical chant. In "Answers to Questions I am Frequently Asked," the only Pacific Islander work in *A Piece of My Heart: A Lesbian of Colour Anthology*, Samoan poet Lanuola Asiasiga resists *palagi* (white) definitions of her and their desire to confine her within the colonial restraints of "authenticity." "No, I don't play the guitar, sing or dance the hula.... Oh, so now you want to dismiss me/as not being the 'real' thing."[6]

Themes of fragmentation, displacement and returning home appear in the writing of Pacific gay men in *Lavender Godzilla: Voices of Gay Asian and Pacific Islander Men*. Chamorro author Vince Crisostomo's autobiographical story "Malago: Strong Brown Arms" reflects a longing for home and wholeness as he moves between Guam, Gilroy, California, and Hawaii.[7] The difficulties for displaced peoples returning home are expressed in Samoan writer Dan McMullin's short story "The Least" when Christian sexual restrictions come into conflict with the main character Kama's childhood relationship with his male cousin.[8] Similarly, from Aotearoa, Te Awekotuku notes how "the Judeo Christian legacy of guilt and punishment, of judgement and mortification has flourished on these islands."[9]

The struggle for decolonization and the reclamation of traditional practices has enabled some indigenous Pacific scholars and writers to present a more complex view of Pacific sexuality than has previously existed. In her landmark work on land tenure in Hawaii, *Native Land and Foreign Desires*, Native Hawaiian historian Lilikala Kame'eleihiwa explains the various ways Hawaiian men could traditionally increase their *mana* (divine power/status authority).[10] She notes that "if a man were handsome and somewhat talented in dance and poetry, he could be kept as an *'aikane*, or male lover, of an *Ali'i Nui* (high chief), as they were often bisexual." This distinction between the role of the 'aikane and that of the mahu has only recently been widely recognized. The term mahu has often been used as a synonym for a male homosexual, but as defined in *He Alo A He Alo: Hawaiian Voices on Sovereignty*, the term actually refers to a "homosexual, of either sex who adopts the opposite gender role. In common slang, the term is often incorrectly used to indicate any homosexual."[11]

This reclamation and recovery of traditional roles and practices reaches across the Pacific. Te Awekotuku refuses the charge that same-sex love is a Western importation: "We are the inheritors of a Polynesian tradition, of the Mahu of Hawaii, Tahiti, the Cook Islands, the Marquesas, of the Fa'afafine of Samoa, of the Fakaleti of Tonga...in (Aotearoa) we obviously have the traditions."[12] She proclaims, "My challenge is this: we should reconstruct the tradition, reinterpret the oral history of this land, so skillfully manipulated by the crusading heterosexism of the missionary ethic." Maori poet Hinewirangi looks to her beginnings in the poem "Woman" in her collection *Screaming Moko*: "...but from the beginning/ *Te Kore*/ *Te Po*/ I learnt to love you," ending with "—no white christianity/blocks your eyes."[13]

As pan-Pacific political and cultural movements continue to expand across former colonial divisions, new alliances are being produced that provide new opportunities for unpublished voices. In the U.S. context, the rapidly expanding movement for Hawaiian sovereignty and the recent Hawaii State Supreme Court decisions in favor of gay marriage rights have created an unprecedented amount of attention to issues of nationalism and sexuality in the Pacific. The newly formed group of lesbian, gay, and bisexual Hawaiians, Na Mamo o Manoa, is struggling with the appropriation and erasure of indigenous sexuality and history both by white gay activists and some sovereignty leaders. On the continental U.S., important linkages are being made between indigenous Pacific and indigenous American writers. A forthcoming anthology from Firebrand press will be edited by Maori writer and activist Cathie Dunsford and Beth Brant, a noted Mohawk writer.

New struggles and new alliances foster the conditions for more indigenous Pacific writing to be produced and expand the potential for indigenous voices to be heard. Hopefully, these new works will be received on their own terms and not erased within another's agenda.

Notes

1. Ellen Twiname, "Being Queer in the Press Crops," *Frighten the Horses* 10 (San Francisco: Hearing Seeking Publishing, 1992), 19–23.
2. John D'Emilio, "Capitalism and Gay Identity," *Power of Desire: The Politics of Sexuality*, ed. Ann Snitow, Christine Stansell, and Sharon Thompson (New York: Monthly Review Press, 1983), 100–113.

3. Ngahuia Te Awekotuku, "Dykes and Queers: Facts, Fairytales and Fictions," *Mana Wahine Maori: Selected Writings on Maori Women's Art, Culture and Politics* (Auckland: New Women's Press, 1991), 36–41.

4. Marshall Sahlins, *Islands of History* (Chicago: University of Chicago Press, 1985), 10.

5. Lani Haahumanu, "Hapa Haole Wahine," *Bi Any Other Name: Bisexual People Speak Out*, ed. Lani Kaahumanu and Loraine Hutchins (Boston: Alyson Publications, 1991), 306–23.

6. Lanuola Asiasiga, "Answers to Questions I Am Frequently Asked," *Piece of My Heart: A Lesbian of Color Anthology*, ed. Makeda Silvera (Ontario: Sister Vision Press, 1991), 232.

7. Vince Crisotomo, "Malago: Strong Brown Arms," *Lavender Godzilla: Voices of Gay Asian and Pacific Islander Men* (1992), 12–15.

8. Dan McMullin, "The Least," *Lavender Godzilla: Voice of Gay Asian and Pacific Islander Men* (1993), 24–27.

9. Te Awekotuku, 37.

10. Lilikala Kame'eleihiwa, *Native Land and Foreign Desires* (Honolulu: Bishop Museum Press, 1992).

11. American Friends Service Committee, *He Alo A He Alo: Hawaiian Voices on Sovereignty*, 1993.

12. Te Awekotuku, 37.

13. Hinewirangi, "Woman," *Screaming Moko* (Aotearoa, New Zealand: The Taranga Moana Press, 1993), 14.

II

Funny Boys and Girls:[1]

Notes on a Queer[2] South Asian Planet

Gayatri Gopinath

What does it mean to queer the diaspora[3]? The question was at the back of my mind as I walked into a recent panel discussion entitled "Queer Festivals Go Global," organized by the 1994 New York Experimental Lesbian and Gay Film Festival, and but one of a spate of recent events[4] that seem to be positing a notion of a shared alterior sexuality that exists across national boundaries. As I listened to the discussion, it became increasingly obvious to me how complicated it is to think in terms of a queer diaspora: the notions of both "queer" and "diaspora" connote highly contested terrain, where it is difficult if not impossible to avoid falling into murky territory while trying to negotiate a path around existing and competing discourses on sexuality, class, "culture," and language. In fact, I walked away from the event more aware than ever of the ways in which a project of constructing a diasporic queerness—on the part of queer activists, scholars, and cultural producers—is fraught with both pleasures and dangers.

Rather than develop any totalizing or linear narrative around these questions, I would like here to simply begin a dialogue on just what some of these pleasures and dangers might be, by focusing on the workings of a South Asian diaspora in particular. The subjective "I" in this piece functions not so much as a marker of a representative positionality but rather militates against any such reading, insisting upon the radical contingency of queer South Asian subjectivity.[5] While I am not suggesting that transnational performances of South Asian queerness work to create some kind of purely liberatory space, free from the various violences effected by the disciplinary mechanisms of the state and nation, I do want to explore the possibilities—as well as the limits—of conceptualizing a diasporic or transnational South Asian queer sexuality. Clearly, there are no answers that can be arrived at, no conclusions that can easily be drawn; all that is possible is a more rigorous interrogation of the frameworks within which we attempt to speak of queerness transnationally.

Whose Queer State? Whose Queer Nation?

There have been a number of recent attempts by queer scholars to explicitly link together questions of the state, nation and queerness. Lisa Duggan's essay on "Queering the State,"[6] for instance, calls for the necessity of formulating new strategies "at the boundary of queer and nation"[7] to combat anti-gay right-wing campaigns. It is only through a creative contestation of the politics of the state within the public sphere, she argues, that queers can hope to counter the rhetorical and legislative violence aimed at them. Similarly, Lauren Berlant's and Elizabeth Freeman's essay on "Queer Nationality"[8] analyzes Queer Nation's project of "coordinating a new nationality" through the "[reclamation of] the nation for pleasure."[9] While Berlant and Freeman express some reservations at using nationalism as a counter-hegemonic model for transgression and resistance,[10] they nevertheless hold that Queer Nation's strategies of spectacular counterpublicity redefine the terms of citizenship and nationality.

I would argue that neither Duggan nor Berlant and Freeman fully address the particularly vexed relation of many queers of color to the disciplinary and regulatory mechanisms of the state and nation, thereby inadvertently pointing up the severe limitations of any nationalist project, however transgressive. The authors suggest that the power of queer activism lies in its ability to exploit the disjuncture between queers having access to the state and its juridical privileges, that is, to citizenship, and being simultaneously denied access to the nation, to full national subjectivity.[11] Implicit in their argument, then, is that queers, for the most part, have unproblematic access to the state and to "queer citizenship"[12]; ultimately, the queer (white) U.S. citizen remains in their framework as the singular subject for and through which the public arena can and must be reterritorialized. Clearly, this uninterrogated assumption of queer citizenship as the starting point of their argument renders it inadequate in addressing the realities faced on a daily basis by a substantial number of queers—particularly those of color. As queer South Asians in the diaspora, "citizenship," queer or otherwise, is not something that we can ever take for granted. Rather, we enact a much more complicated navigation of state regulatory practices and *multiple* national spaces—one that is often profoundly mobile, contingent, and evasive, and that demands a more nuanced theorization of the interplay of state and nation. Indeed, as I hope to make clear in what follows, it is at the interstices of these various strategic negotiations that a transnational or diasporic queerness is under construction.

Diasporic Pleasure

Before addressing this question of diasporic queerness, however, we must ask what "diaspora" means for South Asians in the first place. We need to keep in mind the limitations involved in situating ourselves as "diasporic" subjects at all, even while acknowledging that the notion of diaspora is a useful and necessary one for those of us who inhabit simultaneous and often contradictory geographic, political and psychic spaces. As one critic writes, "to be cognizant of oneself as a diasporic subject is always to be aware of oneself, no matter where one is, as from elsewhere, in the process of making a not quite legitimate appeal to be considered as if one were from here."[13] It is this liminality of diasporic experience—of being inside/outside—that is so perfectly captured and negotiated by South Asian transnational popular cultural forms such as bhangra. Originally a Punjabi folk music that has been transformed through its amalgam with house, reggae, rap, and other black diasporic musical forms, bhangra is a tremendously celebratory "affirmation of particularity"[14] that testifies to the (often forced) movements of South Asians between South and East Africa, South Asia, the Caribbean, the United States, Canada, and Great Britain. Bhangra has become a general signifier for South Asian-ness from New York to London to Toronto to Bombay, calling into existence a diasporic network of "affiliation and affect"[15] that cuts across national boundaries with remarkable fluidity. In this sense, bhangra enacts a counter-public space of "diasporic intimacy" (Paul Gilroy's phrase) that resists the exclusionary norms of a bourgeois public sphere.[16] Yet, as with many constructions of community and ethnic identity, however oppositional, current articulations of diaspora tend to replicate and indeed rely upon conventional ideologies of gender and sexuality; once again, certain bodies (queer and/or female) are rendered invisible or marked as other. Within the bhangra music industry, for instance, there remain very few women producers or DJs; similarly, many bhangra lyrics and the stage personas of the performers themselves are deeply masculinist and heterosexist, imagining women as reproducers (both literally and metaphorically) of "culture" and community.[17]

So how do those of us who fall outside a normative space of monogamous heterosexuality forge diasporic networks for our own particular purposes? Perhaps the strategic appropriation of bhangra or Hindi film music by queer South Asians in the west—where both have become staples at parties and parades as a way of signifying South Asian-ness to a mainstream (white) gay community, as well as to other queer people of color—offers a glimpse into what a queered South Asian diaspora could look (and sound) like. The recontextualization of Hindi film songs within the space of queer South Asian parties, for instance, where these songs become parodic performances of conventional gender constructions,[18] indicates but one out of the many proliferating sites and strategies upon and through which new articulations of queer pleasure and desire are emerging. Indeed, it becomes clear that the question of pleasure, of constituting ourselves as desiring subjects, is critical to this project of negotiating a space of queer diasporic intimacy.[19] As one activist observes in *Khush*, Pratibha Parmar's documentary on queer South Asian identity, the pleasures of being gay are for him summed up by "two words: sex and solidarity."[20] His comment seems to speak to what Gina Dent, in her discussion of "black pleasure, black joy,"[21] refers to as "the collective basis of our conception of joy": there is a profoundly affective quality to the experience of walking into a roomful of queer brown folks lip-synching along to *Choli Ke Piche*, a phenomenally popular Hindi film song that, as one South Asian gay man playfully commented, has done more for the South Asian queer community than any conference or parade ever has. We know what a high it can be to participate in conferences like Desh Pardesh, an annual, Toronto-based festival that draws progressive South Asians together from all over the globe. Many of us are also a part of more informal networks of friends and lovers that traverse various diasporic locations, creating a transnational politics of affect that is proving to be remarkably malleable and resistant[22] to state regulation.[23] The work of British cultural workers like Paul Gilroy and Isaac Julien have taught us to take seriously this kind of politics of affect, to acknowledge its profound influence on the ways in which we imagine ourselves and our relation to each other.

On another, more formalized level, the works of emerging writers like Canadian-based Shani Mootoo[24] and Shyam Selvadurai trace, with a distinct comic sensibility, the exquisite intricacies of simultaneous sexual, racial, and national migrations. A recent anthology, *A Lotus of Another Color*,[25] maps the lines of exchange and influence between various global South Asian queer organizations, from (among others) Trikone, Shamakami, and SALGA in the U.S., to Khush in Toronto, to Shakti in London, to Sakhi and Bombay Dost in India. Meanwhile, much of the scholarly and experimental work currently being produced by queer South Asians is critically informed by and responds to the work of (U.K. "Black") British artists and cultural theorists[26]—both Asian and Afro-Caribbean—thereby underscoring the need to theorize a queer South Asian diaspora as marked and inflected by multiple, overlapping diasporas. My brief and rather random citations here are not meant to be exhaustive but rather to sketch out the shifting contours of a South Asian diasporic queerness, and to foreground the centrality of questions of pleasure and desire to the processes—both formal and informal—by which it is taking shape.

Whose Queerness?

So what about the dangers involved in framing queer sexuality diasporically? As one critic reminds us, new constructions of sexual subjectivity "[offer] an ambiguous combination of collective power and vulnerability" in its "focusing and ossifying" of identity.[27] What, then, are the implications of privileging sexuality as a primary "identity" throughout the diaspora? What possible alternative narratives of sexuality may we be shutting down in such a move?[28] How do we allow for the fact that same-sex eroticism exists and signifies very differently in different diasporic contexts,[29] while simultaneously recognizing the common forms of violence that we face everyday because of our sexuality? I would like to return here to the film festival panel and the pitfalls that it ran into, which I think are emblematic of the difficulties inherent in recent formal attempts—like festivals and conferences—in articulating a queer diaspora.

The panelists at this particular program spoke about the problems in transporting queer festivals (that were for the most part conceived of in the west) to India, Brazil, Hong Kong, and other parts of the non-western world. There was a lot of talk among various panelists and audience members about the need to avoid yet another form of "cultural imperialism," where this time around the cultural imperialists would be gay people in the west exporting and imposing their particular brand of queer identity upon unsuspecting non-western "sexual minorities." I could certainly understand where this well-intentioned concern with imposing "alien" paradigms and strategies was coming from, given that the weapon most often wielded against any struggle for queer visibility and self-definition is that same-sex sexuality is a western import, something that is not "authentically" Indian, Brazilian, etc. The necessity we feel to work against and grapple with such notions of cultural validity also plays out in the on-going debate around what to call ourselves, the language we use to signify alterior sexualities in a way that does not excise particular histories.

Yet in struggling against certain dominant discourses, we find ourselves reconsolidating a number of other, equally problematic ones. One curator at the panel, for instance, talked about how troubled she was that a program on body-piercing she had taken from New York to Brazil prompted a body-piercing trend in the Brazilian city where it was shown. Given my lack of access to the Brazilian context that was being referenced, I can only suggest that there may exist other, more enabling readings of such an instance of translated queer style. While I do not deny the power of global structures of imperialism and neocolonialism in shaping the ways in which we as queer people relate across various diasporas, it should not be assumed that consumption, on the part of the non-western "they" that the audience and panelists were referring to, can be

Funny Boys and Girls ▪▬▬▬▬

read solely as mimicry.[30] Couching this non-western "they" in such terms negates the ways in which consumption—whether of identities or style or modes of organizing—can be a productive, imaginative act, where what is consumed is not simply and passively digested but more often than not reworked and forced to resignify.[31] The evacuation of agency of the non-western "they" engendered in the name of an anti-imperialist position also necessitates a concurrent evacuation of the possible site of pleasure that a practice like body-piercing opens up. In denying this non-western "they" the power to (re)invent and claim pleasure, "they" were effectively shut out of the potential dialogue that would construct a queer diasporic subject and sensibility. Even more problematically, such an attribution of motivation (or rather the lack it) to "other" queer subjects reinscribes the conventional anthropological logic that has been so fundamental to the colonial imagination.

Fabled Territories

Such difficulties in speaking of sexuality diasporically are not easily rectified. But perhaps recognizing the uses to which queer South Asians, as I have alluded to above, put film music or bhangra or any other popular cultural form available to us is to force us to theorize queerness and diaspora in a way that at least confounds this easy cultural imperialism argument. It is to realize that such forms of transnational popular practice mean radically different things in different contexts, that it is not about a one-way flow of commodities, identities, or models of being and organizing; rather, it is about multiple and non-hierarchical sites of exchange, where queerness and ethnicity are being contested and made anew every step of the way. And it seems to do so in a way that formal attempts at forging new sexual subjectivities (the film fests and the panels) have yet to catch up to. This is not to romanticize popular culture, or to deny the dialogic relationship between theory and practice, but I do get the sense that what is going on through informal popular cultural practices exceeds the theoretical models that we have been working with so far. Paying closer attention to these varied performances of a queer South Asian counter-public demands that we theorize queer diaspora in a particular way: not in terms of an immutable, generalized queer subject that inhabits this diasporic space, nor in terms of a notion of both queerness and diaspora that replicates existing power structures between the west and the rest. Instead, the new paradigm of queerness gestured to by queer South Asian diasporic cultural practices is one that interpellates a translated geography of pleasure, what poet and activist Ian Rashid calls a "fabled territory"[32] where new sites of deterritorialized desire are continuously being produced. Yet, even within this translated geography, it remains to be seen if we can fully avoid enacting the various forms of conceptual violences that I have sought to foreground here.

Notes

I am grateful to Sarita Echavez See, Hiram Peréz, and Shabnum Tejani for getting me started; my special thanks to Hiram Peréz for sharing with me his thoughts on queerness within a discourse of "human rights," to Chandan Reddy for reading a theory of pleasure into a later draft of this essay, and to Qadri Ismail for his careful and astute criticism.

1. The title contains a reference to Sri Lankan/Canadian writer Shyam Selvadurai's novel, *Funny Boy* (London: Jonathan Cape, 1994).

2. I use the word "queer" in this article as shorthand for indicating an oppositional space outside hetero-normativity. I recognize the term as emerging out of a long and complicated history within a U.S. context (as historian George Chauncey's most recent work attests to), and that it is not one used for self-identification by many South Asians throughout the diaspora. I nevertheless find "queer" useful in that it is (or has the potential to be) gender-neutral, and connotes an entire range of alternative sexual practices and sensibilities in a way that "lesbian," "bisexual," or "gay" do not.

3. Clearly, there is no such thing as "diaspora" as such; it is hardly a given entity or a transparent term but one with an extremely problematic genealogy inflected by class, gender, and heterosexuality. However, I continue to use the term in this essay, even while recognizing its limits, to refer to the global networks of affiliation constantly being produced and reproduced along the lines of race, ethnicity, and/or sexuality.

4. To cite just two examples, the theme of New York City's 1994 Pride Parade was one of "international human rights" for "sexual minorities"; on a much smaller scale, Trikone, a queer South Asian group in San Francisco and the International Gay and Lesbian Human Rights Committee, attempted to organize an international queer film festival and conference in India for December 1994.

5. Concurrently, when I speak of or from a collectivity, an "us" or a "we," it is with the recognition that this collectivity is continuously under construction both within and outside academic discourse, and that it is one that, as I hope this essay will make clear, simultaneously inhabits and transcends identity politics.

6. See Lisa Duggan, "Queering the State," *Social Text* 39 (Summer 1994): 1-14.

7. Ibid., 3.

8. Lauren Berlant and Elizabeth Freeman, "Queer Nationality," *Boundary* 2 (Spring 1992): 149–80.

9. Ibid., 151.

10. Ibid., 154.

11. I am grateful to Qadri Ismail for bringing this point to my attention.

12. For instance, Berlant and Freeman state that "disidentification with U.S. nationality is not, at this moment, even a theoretical option for queer citizens"(154), disregarding the fact that *identification* with either nationality *or* citizenship is not an option for many queers (particularly queers of color) in the U.S.

13. Kenneth Warren, "Appeals of (Mis)Recognition: Theorizing the Diaspora." In *The Cultures of United States Imperialism*, ed. Amy Kaplan and Donald E. Pease (Durham: Duke University Press, 1993): 400–401.

14. The phrase is Paul Gilroy's, which he uses to discuss Black diasporic cultural production. See *The Black Atlantic: Modernity and Double Consciousness*, 16.
15. Ibid.
16. I am indebted to José Muñoz's recent lecture on "Latino Bodies, Queer Spaces," given at Columbia University, for this particular formulation of the counter-public.
17. One of the more transparent instances of this includes the hit song "Arranged Marriage" by the British Asian musician Apache Indian.
18. The scope of this essay precludes an adequate discussion of the subject, but it must be noted that such performances cannot be contained within the discourse of camp that is so prevalent in queer theory, but rather demand their own specific theorization. The possibilities opened up by these performances for lesbian spectatorship and desire is also a subject that remains to be further explored.
19. It is necessary to add here that pleasure, so intrinsic to a project of queer subject formation, is always available to recuperation in the service of heternormativity; that pleasure—its policing and denial—can also function as the most powerful weapon in the effacement and foreclosure of such a project.
20. *Khush*. Dir. Pratibha Parmar. Women Make Movies, 1991. 16 mm, 24 min.
21. Gina Dent, "Black Pleasure, Black Joy: An Introduction." In *Black Popular Culture*, ed. Gina Dent (Seattle: Bay Press, 1992): 10.
22. See Lisa Duggan, 12, for a discussion of "malleability and resistance" in conceptualizing an alternative model of queerness.
23. If there is a utopian strain that runs through these various articulations of diasporic queerness, it is one that perhaps gestures to what Greg Tate calls "a certain kind of romance" that even "self-defined antiessentialists" have with inhabiting particular identities (see Greg Tate, quoted in Gina Dent, "Black Pleasure, Black Joy: An Introduction": 13).
24. See Shani Mootoo, *Out on Main Street and Other Stories* (Vancouver: Press Gang Publishers, 1993).
25. Rakesh Ratti, ed., *A Lotus of Another Color: An Unfolding of the South Asian Lesbian and Gay Experience* (Boston: Alyson Publications, 1993).
26. Some of the work I have in mind includes: Paul Gilroy, *The Black Atlantic: Modernity and Double Consciousness* (Cambridge: Harvard University Press, 1993), and *There Ain't No Black in the Union Jack: The Cultural Politics of Race and Nation* (Chicago: University of Chicago, 1987); Kobena Mercer, *Welcome to the Jungle: New Positions in Black Cultural Studies* (New York: Routledge, 1994); *Looking for Langston*, Dir. Isaac Julien. Sankofa, 1989; Hanif Kureishi, *My Beautiful Laundrette and the Rainbow Sign* (Boston: Faber and Faber, 1986), and *The Buddha of Suburbia* (New York: Viking Penguin, 1990); *I'm British, But...* Dir. Gurinder Chadha. Umbi Films, 1988; and *Bhaji on the Beach*, Dir. Gurinder Chadha, 1994.
27. Rosalind Morris, "Three Sexes and Four Sexualities: Redressing the Discourses of Gender and Sexuality in Contemporary Thailand," *Positions* 2 no. 2 (Spring 1994): 29
28. I thank Hiram Peréz for asking this question.
29. We would do well to heed Morris' warning against the "homogenization of differences that emerges when...[particular] forms of alterior sexual identity are considered in fetishism's vacuum, independent of the culturally specific sex/gender systems

from which they emerge": 16.

30. I use "mimicry" here to signify a kind of parodic repetition, in Judith Butler's terms, that fails to displace its conventions.

31. This argument, of course, is not a new one, as work like Dick Hebdige's classic, *Subculture: The Meaning of Style* (London: Methuen, 1979), attests to; yet it bears repeating within the new context of a transnational queer politics.

32. Ian Iqbal Rashid, *Black Markets, White Boyfriends and Other Acts of Elision* (Toronto: TSAR, 1991): 11.

part III

"I push my pen to bleed ink, hoping against the uncertainty of a blank page and these tumultuous times, and that you will not recede into fragments."

—Martin Manalansan IV

Figuring Desire

overleaf: "Indian Aphorisms" by Allan deSouza.
Quotation from "Plague: A Dossier," 1995.

In the Shadows of a Diva

Committing Homosexuality in David Henry Hwang's *M. Butterfly*

David L. Eng

The limits of my cell are as such: four-and-a-half meters by five. There's one window against the far wall; a door, very strong, to protect me from autograph hounds. I'm responsible for the tape recorder, the hot plate, and this charming coffee table.

When I want to eat, I'm marched off to the dining room—hot steaming slop appears on my plate. When I want to sleep, the light bulb turns itself off—the work of fairies. It's an enchanted space I occupy.

Rene Gallimard, in *M. Butterfly*[1]

Prison as Closet, Closet as Prison

The prison cell from which Rene Gallimard addresses us bears a striking resemblance to a closet. Slightly larger than the average run-of-the-mill walk in, the physical limits of Gallimard's fairy-like privacy are demarcated from the opening lines of David Henry Hwang's 1988 Tony Award-winning drama *M. Butterfly*. As the prison is meant to enclose, the closet is meant to conceal. While Gallimard praises this "enchanted space"[2] for its putative ability to keep those bodies who would seek his autograph at bay, the closet offers him, more importantly, the protection of identity.

And beyond his opening confession as "least likely to be invited to a party"[3] what alternate identity does Gallimard seek to hide from us? We could begin by pondering the epistemology of the closet. In her formidable treatise on queer subjectivity of the same name, Eve Sedgwick states that in accord with Foucault's demonstration:

that modern Western culture has placed what it calls sexuality in a more and more distinctively privileged relation to our most prized constructs of individual identity, truth, and knowledge, it becomes truer and truer that the language of sexuality not only intersects with but transforms the other languages and relations by which we know.[4]

Positing sexuality as the privileged signifier of identity in modern Western epistemologies, Sedgwick's observations provide a preliminary starting point in our investigation of Gallimard's "alternate identity." We begin by invoking questions of sexuality in *M. Butterfly*: what is the language of sexuality in the drama? How should we evaluate Gallimard and Song's sexual relationship?[5] How does this relationship constitute and transform the terms of exchange by which we ultimately judge the value of the play?

These questions persist for the current critical commentaries and theatrical reviews generated by *M. Butterfly* are notable for their collective sacrifice of issues relating to homosexuality. Focusing on the drama as a testimony to cultural misunderstanding and sexist ignorance on the part of the white man, the majority of readings are remarkably uniform in so far as they examine these issues of racism and sexism within the exclusive regime of a compulsive and compulsory heterosexuality.[6]

The concerted privileging in these critical analyses of an inveterate heterosexuality over the implicit and explicit residues of a queer sensibility motivating the play from Gallimard's opening lines restricts, then, like the prison cell, any useful implications of *M. Butterfly* for a gay antihomophobic politics. This elision is particularly damaging for the issue of race and homosexuality as they intersect in the figure of Song (and Gallimard's desire for Song) imputes additional consequences of a racist homophobia against the gay male of color—in this instance, the Asian and Asian American homosexual.[7]

In this analysis of *M. Butterfly*, I hope to offer a reading against which the homosexual can emerge unhindered, unhinged. By exposing a collusion of spaces—a collusion of interests—we will deconstruct the structure of Gallimard's closet, considering the motives behind its erection and vigilant maintenance. We will interrogate the sexual orientation of our narrating diplomat, consider his fantasmatic identifications with a queer subjectivity, and explore his racist investments in his orientalized vision of Song. We will, I hope, come to recognize that Gallimard's closet—the furtive space from which he professes his tale of "heterosexual" love gone awry—is a prison, literally and figuratively, allowing the former French consul to offer us a filtered vision of his aborted affair.

Sexual Disorientation

In *The Language of Psychoanalysis*, Jean Laplanche and Jean-Bertrand Pontalis chart the scene of desire through a mechanism of the human psyche they come to label as the "fantasmatic." The fantasmatic gives shape to our lives as a "whole"[8] for it articulates our unconscious fantasies, fantasies that not only impute coherence to our identity but also determine our libidinal object choice. We must keep in mind, however, that fantasies—as Freud reminds us—are ultimately less personal than culturally inscribed through collective group structures, most notably the Oedipus complex. Human subjectivity and desire, therefore, come more to reflect a repetition of past actions than a private and essentially unrepeatable domain of individual action and experience.[9]

The pioneering work of Judith Butler extends the arena of the fantasmatic to focus specifically upon queer subjectivity. Working with the presumption that every subject functions under collective fantasies as well as collective constraints—most strikingly the prohibition against homosexuality—Butler queries in *Bodies That Matter*:

> When the threat of punishment wielded by that prohibition [against homosexuality] is too great, it may be that we desire someone who will keep us from ever seeing the desire for which we are punishable, and in attaching ourselves to that person, it may be that we effectively punish ourselves in advance and, indeed, generate desire in and through and for that self-punishment.[10]

In a society governed by compulsory heterosexuality, it comes as little surprise that homosexual desire is often reconfigured through heterosexual constructs. Gay desire often comes to be abjected and displaced by the notion of an advanced self-punishment purchased in exchange for a promise of sexual impunity.

Keeping Butler's concept of the fantasmatic as one riven through by the interdictions of a homophobic society, I suggest that we must read Gallimard's detailed memories of the events leading up to his espionage trial not as a mere chronology of his frustrated love affair with Butterfly but rather as an extravagant example of fantasmatic constraint against homosexual desire. The fact that Song Liling is a man holds significance beyond the emphasis of Gallimard's orientalism, the perfunctory cultural arrogations that lead to his ostensible blunder concerning Song's anatomical sex. On a physical level, admittedly or not on the part of our narrating diplomat, Gallimard and Song have a homosexual affair.[11] They are two males who repeatedly engage in the act of sodomy: "I let him put it up my ass!"[12] confesses a beleaguered Song, "coming out," under the farcical interrogations of Comrade Chin.

The construction of *M. Butterfly*, however, revolves around Gallimard's avowal of putative ignorance, an avowal that becomes crucial in so far as its efficacy is sanctioned and legitimated by the voice of the law: "Did Monsieur Gallimard know you were a man?"[13] emerges as the central and obsessive question of the investigating judge, swinging the all-too-familiar juridical gavel. The answer to this inquisition is, of course, never fully established by the Chinese opera singer:

JUDGE: Just answer my question: did he know you were a man?
SONG: You know, Your Honor, I never asked.[14]

Is the Asian diva's response to the repeated query of the judge so enigmatic? While the construction of his Honor's question demands a simple "yes" or "no" answer, Song's reply, however ambiguous, does little to credit Gallimard's position of ignorance. Rather, the opera singer's retort undercuts the diplomat's avowal by refusing to give the corroboration that both Gallimard and the judge so desperately seek. The structure of Song's rhetoric—"You know… I never asked"—suggests the irrelevance of the question, its facile nature as articulated by the voice of the law: I never asked because it was unnecessary to ask. I never asked because the answer is obvious. What do you think?

Nevertheless, Gallimard's position of denial—his alignment with a compulsory system of heterosexuality—is privileged from the opening lines of the drama. The diplomat's contention that for the duration of his twenty-year affair he was "loved by 'the Perfect Woman'"[15] definitively answers the judge's final question, while establishing Gallimard's avowal of ignorance as the central premise of the drama. It is this premise that renders a "sexual disorientation" between the hetero- and homosexual into M. Butterfly, and it is this disjunction that demands a detailed interrogation of Gallimard's fantasmatic identifications with and against a queer subjectivity beyond the irrefutability of his and Song's sex and sexual practices as well as the facile inquiries of the investigating judge.

David Henry Hwang's Afterword to the drama offers a fruitful starting point for our investigation. Citing the important parallels between "Rice Queens" and "Yellow Fever," the playwright states:

Gay friends have told me of a derogatory term used in their community: "Rice Queen"—a gay Caucasian man primarily attracted to Asians. In these relationships, the Asian virtually always plays the role of the "woman"; the Rice Queen, culturally and sexually, is the "man." This pattern of relationships had become so codified that, until recently, it was considered unnatural for gay Asians to date one another. Such men would be taunted with a phrase that implied they were lesbians.

Similarly, heterosexual Asians have long been aware of "Yellow Fever"—Caucasian men with a fetish for Oriental women. I have often heard it said the "Oriental women make the best wives." (Rarely is this heard from the mouths of Asian men, incidentally.) This mythology is exploited by the Oriental mail-order bride trade that has flourished over the past decade. American men can now send away for catalogues of "obedient, domesticated" Asian women looking for husbands.[16]

As described by Hwang, the concepts of "Rice Queen" and "Yellow Fever" are constructed along congruent paradigms of submission, the intersection of racism and sexism in heterosexual and homosexual economies respectively. This overlap is crucial for it definitively expands the common reading of Gallimard's heterosexual relationship with Song into the homosexual arena. The hyperfeminization of both the obedient "Oriental lady" and the effeminate gay Asian male (lesbians!) thus renders every explicitly racist and misogynist remarks of the drama (e.g.: "It's true what they say about Oriental girls. They want to be treated bad!"[17] "Her mouth says no, but her eyes say yes. The West believes the East, deep down, wants to be dominated—because a woman can't think for herself"[18]) the implicit double-edged efficacy of a racist homophobia as well.[19]

Hence, we can view Song Liling's appearance in drag not only as the figure of an inscrutable feminine and female Butterfly, but equally as the fulfillment of the Rice Queen's ultimate fantasy in which the gay Asian male literalizes the desired qualities of the effeminized oriental sissy. The potential of Song's transvestitism to be interpreted as a homosexual submission to the gay Gallimard's white male fantasy—the symptomatic Rice Queen—is read most productively against the diplomat's repressed adolescence and subsequent tenure at the French embassy.

Like all pubescent young men, the young Gallimard has his fair share of traumatic sexual encounters. However, the development of Gallimard's heterosexual desire is qualified both by his atypical reactions in these typical sexual scenarios as well as by a litany of stereotypical homosexual innuendoes throughout the drama—its campiness, Gallimard's affinity for musical opera. Gallimard's original meeting with Butterfly, as described by the boorish Marc, is certainly "monumental"[20] when juxtaposed against the pubescent diplomat's long history of intimidation by and a general aversion to the opposite sex.

Faced with the opportunity for some healthy male-female adolescent frolics—an invitation by the indefatigable Marc to his Marseille condominium—Gallimard's response is more than non-committal, fraught with homosexual anxiety:

MARC: Rene, we're a buncha of university guys goin' up to the woods. What are we going to do—talk philosophy?
GALLIMARD: Girls? Who said anything about girls?
MARC: Who cares? The point is, they come. On trucks. Packed in like sardines. The back flips open, babes hop out, we're ready to roll.
GALLIMARD: You mean, they just—?
MARC: Before you know it, every last one of them—they're stripped and splashing around my pool. There's no moon out, they can't see what's going on, their boobs are flapping, right? You close your eyes, reach out—it's grab bag, get it?

> Doesn't matter whose ass is between whose legs, whose teeth are sinking into who. You're just in there, going at it, eyes closed, on and on for as long as you can stand. (Pause) Some fun, huh?
>
> GALLIMARD: What happens in the morning?
>
> MARC: In the morning, you're ready to talk some philosophy. (Beat) So how 'bout it?
>
> GALLIMARD: Marc, I can't… I'm afraid they'll say no—the girls. So I never ask.
>
> MARC: You don't have to ask! That's the beauty—don't you see? They don't have to say yes. It's perfect for a guy like you, really.
>
> GALLIMARD: You go ahead… I may come later. [21]

Gallimard's dismissal of Marc's invitation goes beyond the trauma of adolescent clumsiness and acne. Notice the diplomat's unequivocal terror (Girls? Who said anything about girls?) as soon as he learns that the homosocial gathering of a "buncha university guys" will be marred by the presence of flapping boobs. The Frenchman's identifications with an adolescent heterosexuality are far from developed; they are nonexistent. Presented with the perfect opportunity for unqualified sex—guaranteed acceptance, no looking, no rejection, a veritable "grab bag" by Marc's estimation—Gallimard's unorthodox panic makes sense only when read in light of a heterosexual abjection, a fear of not being able to perform, a fear of not wanting to perform: You go ahead… I may come later… I may come… I may or may not come out of the closet.

Heterosexual performance emerges as a central concern of the drama of the flaccid and uncooperative penis becoming primary. The young Gallimard's personal and private masturbatory fantasies are marked by his inability to "get it up," even temporarily, for the female sex. The image of the closet is once again presented as the adolescent, quite literally, finds himself occupying this furtive space:

> GALLIMARD: …I first discovered these magazines at my uncle's house. One day, as a boy of twelve. The first time I saw them in his closet…all lined up—my body shook. Not with lust—no, with power. Here were women—a shelfful—who would do exactly what I wanted.
>
> GIRL: I know you're watching me.
>
> GALLIMARD: My throat…it's dry.
>
> GIRL: I leave my blinds open and the lights on.
>
> GALLIMARD: I can't move.
>
> GIRL: I leave my blinds open and the lights on.
>
> GALLIMARD: I'm shaking. My skin is hot, but my penis is soft. Why?…
>
> GIRL: I can't see you. You can do whatever you want.
>
> GALLIMARD: I can't do a thing. Why?[22]

The circumstances of these two situations are equivalent in both cause and effect: unqualified acceptance by women ("You can do whatever you want") greeted by a disturbing phallic inadequacy: the soft penis. However, in Gallimard's dirty magazine daydream the guaranteed privacy of the situation, the absence of direct social pressure, and the lack of immediate demands for performance are, perhaps, even a more reliable indicator of Gallimard's sexual disposition. The anxiety over sight in both passages should not be overlooked. Gallimard is overwrought by the issue of vision: of seeing and not being seen, of being seen for what he really is. The picture of Gallimard's flaccid penis coupled with his final question, repeated twice—Why can't I do a thing?—reinforces a fantasmatic allegiance with the queer; Gallimard's object choice clearly lies in a different realm of desire.

A final example: the diplomat's "heterosexual" tryst with Renee, the assertive Danish coed. It is, of course, no accident that Renee shares the feminine version of Rene Gallimard's first name.[23] The copula of the shared name immediately marks the presence of an imaginary other, a semantic Lacanian imago, so to speak, meant to impute coherence onto Gallimard's identifications. Renee, most memorable for her aggressive interactions with the diplomat provides a liberated self-expressive image towards which Rene Gallimard can aspire, but never occupy.[24]

Renee's exchange with the diplomat in which she skillfully appropriates traditional signifier of phallic power, literally by seizing Gallimard's penis and figuratively by expounding on the conflation and slippage between anatomical "weenies" and their symbolic manifestations—wars, epic fiction, large buildings—throws normative concepts of heterosexual difference into radical question. Her explication on the pernicious penis is worth quoting at length:

RENEE: Oh. Most girls don't call it a "weenie," huh?

GALLIMARD: It sounds very—

RENEE: Small, I know.

GALLIMARD: I was going to say "young."

RENEE: Yeah. Young, small, same thing. Most guys are pretty, uh, sensitive about that. Like you know, I had a boyfriend back home in Denmark. I got mad at him once and called him a little weeniehead. He got so mad! He said at least I should call him a great big weeniehead.

GALLIMARD: I suppose I just say "penis."

RENEE: Yeah. That's pretty clinical. There's "cock," but that sounds like a chicken. And "prick" is painful, and "dick" is like you're talking about someone who's not in the room.

GALLIMARD: Yes. It's a...bigger problem than I imagined.

RENEE: I—I think maybe it's because I really don't know what to do with them—that's why I call them "weenies."

GALLIMARD: Well you did quite well with…mine.

RENEE: Thanks, but I mean, really do with them. Like, okay, have you ever looked at one? I mean, really?

GALLIMARD: No, I suppose when it's part of you, you sort of take it for granted.

RENEE: I guess. But, like, it just hangs there. This little…flap of flesh. And there's so much fuss that we make about it. Like, I think the reason we fight wars is because we wear clothes. Because no one knows—between the men, I mean—who has the bigger…weenie. So, if I'm a guy with a small one, I'm going to build a really big building or take over a really big piece of land or write a really long book so the other men don't know, right? But, see, it never really works, that's the problem. I mean, you conquer the country, or whatever, but you're still wearing clothes, so there's no way to prove absolutely whose is bigger or smaller. And that's what we call a civilized society. The whole world run by a bunch of men with pricks the size of pins. (*She exits*)

GALLIMARD (*To us*): This was simply not acceptable.[25]

Gallimard's horrified reaction to the coed's incisive sartorial critique clearly lies in her unwelcomed incursion into the realm of the paternal metaphor. Renee is completely in charge: in bed she is dominant, quite literally "on top," as Gallimard admits "you did quite well with…mine" [his penis]. Outside the bedroom, she assumes a position of discursive authority, emasculating the tongue-tied diplomat by running verbal circles around him in conversation.

Renee is everything that Gallimard is not and what Gallimard wishes he could be in his most acute masculine day dreams of phallic plenitude: assertive, dominant, straight. Relegating the Frenchman to a position of powerlessness, she undercuts Gallimard's heterosexual presumption by assuming a macho subjectivity that installs him squarely on the side of lack. The diplomat's objections towards Renee revolve around the Oedipal trauma that her actions—"too uninhibited, too willing, too…masculine"[26]—trigger in his own libidinal psyche. The "unacceptability" of her actions, of course, resides in her sex as a female, her aggressive usurpation of phallic authority. If the given name that the two characters share marks a zone of unfulfilled desire on the part of Gallimard for discursive control, Renee's status as female other confounds this desire, while raising the possibility of its location outside the monopolizing realm of the symbolically heterosexual and masculine white body. Renee introduces a fantasmatic site of gender crossing and desire, a site that Gallimard finds himself, willingly or unwillingly, occupying as well.

Beyond Passing: Parables of Power

"We were worried about you, Gallimard," reveals an envious Toulon. "We thought you were the only one here without a secret. Now you go and find a lotus blossom…and top us all."[27] In one fell swoop, Manuel Toulon, corporate tool extraordinaire of the French Embassy, assuages his "worries"—his homo-phobic panic—while assuring himself of Gallimard's reassuring heterosexu-ality through his discovery of the "secret" of his own fantasies: the affair between the white man and the inscrutable oriental lotus blossom.

Thus, like all straight white males, by the virtue of his self-same body, Gallimard accedes into not only a gender but also a race privilege. His "secret" is really no secret at all, but a shared position of power within the phallic autoc-racy, monopolized by the likes of racist and sexist white men such as Toulon and vigilantly guarded by the likes of arrogant bureaucrats such as the judge pontificating under the voice of the law.[28] While clearly deficient in the art of heterosexual negotiations, Gallimard inhabits a colonial world in which the power privileges of white males are absolute, replicated, and ensured by the workings of an ideological system through the inheritance of opportunity and rights according to race—white—and sexuality—straight male.

The diplomat's awareness and subsequent indoctrination into this old boys' network comes at an early age, perhaps, without full cognition of the sweeping extent of his vested power interests. In the earlier cited masturbatory fantasy passage, we witness not only the gradual development of Gallimard's homo-sexual orientation but additionally a concomitant induction into the Name of the Father.

Though Gallimard's reaction to the dirty magazines remains uncommon of pubescent heterosexual males—his penis remains soft—the diplomat's lack of physical arousal is accompanied by a entirely typical mental awareness of his agency as a white male. The "power" over women of which Gallimard speaks, the power to make "women...do exactly as I wanted,"[29] is indicative of an incipient consciousness regarding the sweeping extents of paternal privilege.

The replication of this privilege is ensured by social institutions such as mar-riage contracts. The elder Gallimard exhibits a greater appreciation for these systems of power in arranging his marriage to the Australian Ambassador's daughter—the dowdy Helga—a marriage self-described as "practical" and lacking of any sexual affect:

GALLIMARD: I married a woman older than myself—Helga.

HELGA: My father was ambassador to Australia. I grew up among criminals and kangaroos.

GALLIMARD: Hearing that brought me to the altar—(Helga exits) where I took a vow renouncing love. No fantasy woman would ever want me, so, yes, I would settle for a quick leap up the career ladder. Passion, I banished, and in its place—practicality![30]

The institution of marriage as the bastion of sanctioned heterosexuality is rendered a farce. Gallimard's explicit confessions of a frigid marriage are displaced by the collective demands of a larger ideological concern: the continuity of white masculine control.

The diplomat's indoctrination into the full-fledged practices of paternal privilege is, however, most strongly reinforced by the French Ambassador Manuel Toulon's (mis)recognition of his affair with Butterfly as a heterosexual relationship between the white man and oriental femme fatale. Gallimard quickly learns that a consummate adeptness in perverting his gender and race entitlements are swiftly rewarded:

> TOULON: Humility won't be part of the job. You're going to coordinate the revamped intelligence division. Want to know a secret? A year ago, you would've been out. But the past few months, I don't know how it happened, you've become this new aggressive confident…thing. And they also tell me you get along with the Chinese. So I think you're a lucky man, Gallimard. Congratulations.
> *They shake hands. Toulon exits. Party noises out. Gallimard stumbles across a darkened stage.*
> GALLIMARD: Vice-consul? Impossible! As I stumbled out of the party, I saw it written across the sky: There is no God. Or, no—say that there is a God. But that God…understands. Of course! God who creates Eve to serve Adam, who blesses Solomon with his harem but ties Jezebel to a burning bed—that God is a man. And he understands! At age thirty-nine, I was suddenly initiated into the way of the world.[31]

At age thirty-nine, Gallimard is a bit slow, albeit quite melodramatic. His full cognizance of white male privilege matures only under the tutelage of Toulon who encourages the diplomat's unconscionable abuse of Butterfly with improved material, social, and political gains. What, after all, is the all-powerful "thing" that Toulon attempts euphemistically to describe but the ever-present delegated symbol of male abuse—the white heterosexual penis as phallus?[32]

While the salacious Toulon's recognition of what seems to him to be an illicit heterosexual affair provides the necessary ingredients for Gallimard to feel "for the first time that rush of power—the absolute power of a man,"[33] this power, of course, is predicated on a compulsory heterosexuality. Power and promotion within the white man's club do not tolerate difference. In refusing to relinquish this privilege, Gallimard's "secret" is not, then, his affair with Song Liling, the access of the colonizing white male to the oriental lotus blossom through a phallocentric and racist patriarchy that exalts his position over that of all others. The "secret," of course, becomes how to hide difference in a society that demands absolute compliance—racial, social, economic, and sexual. Thus, the central contradiction between Gallimard's sexual and political position of power as a gay white male is sutured through the erection and active maintenance of the closet. Gallimard's "secret" becomes the strident demarcation of a private and public sexual space through the strident demarcation of a private and public sexuality: to pass off his homosexual affair with Song Liling as a heterosexual tryst.

Commenting on the significant system of differences that arise over skin color within a homosexual economy, Earl Jackson, Jr. observes that

> white gay males occupy a peculiar position in a heterosexist society in that, as men (if they are not "out"), they potentially have full access to the very power mechanisms that repress them and their fellow "outsiders," who cannot "pass," white women and people of color of any sexual orientation. Furthermore, gay male sexuality is not simply condemned by the phallocratic order, but it is also sublimated, thematized, and fetishized in the phallocracy's own ambivalent and constitutive mythographies of the phallus and phallic primacy. While the "real" of gay male sex is demonized, the imaginary and symbolic configurations of the unisexuality assumed in phallocentrism, and sustained by the worship of the phallus in male dominant practices, finds an unwitting (and disavowed) allay in the gay male.[34]

Jackson's comments summarize well the psychological position of gay white males such as Gallimard who, by their sexual preference, may be disabled by one set of oppressions, but, in turn, by virtue of their race, have potential access to enabling positions of power. In the dominant old boy world of Ambassador Toulons, the figure of the homosexual is one of such overwhelming abjection that the option of "passing" afforded to gay white males becomes the alluring and reflexive choice of those who are not "out" of the closet. The "unwitting" complicity in an invasive phallocentric system among gay white men, thus, becomes a highly debatable issue for the rewards of "passing" are overwhelming for the closet queen: full access to the abusive mechanisms of the old boy network.[35]

For Gallimard, the option to be positioned as the supremely inept heterosexual, consummately manipulated by the scheming oriental vixen and embarrassingly ridiculed by a homophobic public is a position preferable to that of an open acknowledgment of his Rice Queen homosexuality and the subsequent consequences of violating this homosexual prohibition: ostracism from this world of privilege. This fact is validated by a weary Gallimard who, at the conclusion of *M. Butterfly*, admits that

> in public, I have continued to deny that Song Liling is a man. This brings me headlines, and is a source of great embarrassment to my French colleagues, who can now be sent into a coughing fit by the mere mention of Chinese food. But alone, in my cell, I have long since faced the truth.[36]

The statement is Gallimard's closest admission to the homosexual relationship that he and Song Liling once shared. Living by his pledge to "turn somersaults" in order to protect his vested interests, Gallimard ensures his security by learning the parables of power well: he embraces the paternal privileges offered by "passing" to the gay white male. The zone in which Gallimard finds himself beyond passing reconciles his public "face" by allowing a continuity of condoned public sexual practices in alignment with dominant political and symbolic discourse, a position that permits Gallimard, to put it somewhat inelegantly, "have his cake and eat it, too."

When Song finally disrobes in Act Three of *M. Butterfly*, the morphological unveiling of the penis threatens to devastate the structure of Gallimard's closet, to expose at once the diplomat's heterosexual presumption and destroy his well-cultivated position of phallic control. Faced with the prohibited and abject territory of the homosexual, Gallimard viciously shifts the burden of sexual identity upon the shoulders of an unwitting Song in order to ensure the continuity of a sexual and political "face." Manhandling the obstreperous diva, Gallimard attempts physically to remove Song from the area of his closet, while denying his attraction for the now male opera singer: "I think you must have some kind of identity problem,"[37] he snips at Butterfly, demonizing the oriental position through the predictable but effective practice of Asian male effeminization.

The diplomat's tenuous maneuver, however, is neither with respite nor without sacrifice. Having no other options available to recoup Song's exposure of him, Gallimard, in a monumental move of self-delusion recedes into the compensatory world of the imaginary: "Get away from me!" he orders the disrobed Song. "Tonight I've finally learned to tell fantasy from reality. And, knowing the difference, I choose fantasy."[38]

But in order to commit and thus solidify his position with the Name of the Father, Gallimard must add an ironic twist to Puccini's orientalist dictum in Madame Butterfly requiring that "Death with honor/Is better than life/Life with dishonor."[39] Now that Song is publicly a man, Gallimard must become publicly the woman. Assuming the drag appearance of the earlier Butterfly, Gallimard "straightens" their relationship once again by returning it to an "honorable" status quo male-female heterosexual union. It is an ironic transvesting act, for the price of this fantasmatic sartorial conversion is expensive: Gallimard must commit suicide, but he dies with his prison-closet structure intact and, more important, as an honorary member of the heterosexual global village.

Necessity and Extravagance

Let us detour, for a brief moment, to *Reading Asian American Literature: From Necessity to Extravagance*. In this book, Sau-ling Wong, extrapolating from Maxine Hong Kingston's *The Woman Warrior*, troubles the alignment of "Necessity" and "Extravagance" with "work" and "play" as they apply to the

Asian American and Asian American immigrant experience. The activity of play or art, Wong maintains, is "perceived as antithetical to self-justifyingly "serious" activities, which, in the Asian American context we have come to understand as the business of survival."[40] Yet, in her discussion of works by Hisaye Yamamoto, Wakako Yamauchi, and Frank Chin, Wong troubles this unproblematic division, as we witness numerous accounts of suppressed artistic activity demanding equal voice—"a return of the repressed." In the final analysis, Wong asks, "if play's imperative is so overpoweringly urgent, may it not be that play too is a need of survival—a Necessity, no less, only differently characterized and designated, and therefore customarily separated from work as if by an unbridgeable gulf?"[41] "Necessity" and "Extravagance" are not isolatable terms; they are, indeed, concepts that circulate in a closed interdependent economy, contingent upon one another and deriving value and meaning through the tensions of their interplay.

In M. Butterfly, then, David Henry Hwang seems to bring the work-play antagonism of art to a more definitive conclusion if no more than by reinforcing the ultimately symbiotic nature of the two concepts.[42] Hwang's resolution fuses the work-play antagonism of art onto an even higher level of existence in the figure of Butterfly: can we possibly separate Song the artist from Song the spy? Here, "Extravagance" in the form of performance art—acting—combines with "Necessity" in the form of espionage—spying: Acting as performing as spying.

The unity of "Necessity" and "Extravagance," acting and spying in M. Butterfly—their circulation within a closed economy—traces itself along a historical continuum in which the material realities remain constant though the political climate often changes: the artistic skills used by Song Liling under the Communist Chinese regime to "trick" Gallimard find their roots in lessons learned from Song's prostitute mother during the Nationalist Chinese era. Addressing the judge during his espionage trial, Song states:

> See my mother was a prostitute along the Bundt before the Revolution. And, uh, I think it's fair to say she learned a few things about Western men. So I borrowed her knowledge. In service to my country.[43]

Like mother, like son. The genealogy of Song's profession crosses not only generational and governmental boundaries—from Colonialist to Nationalist to Communist—but sexual boundaries as well, boundaries between the heterosexual and homosexual. If, indeed, we cannot detach the dual concepts of work and art in M. Butterfly, is it then possible to separate actively the homosexual from the heterosexual? Comrade Chin alludes to the impossibility of this separation: "Then you go to France and be a pervert for Chairman Mao!"[44] she orders the imprisoned Chin, recognizing the confluence of Song's homosexuality with the economy of work and play that is necessary for him to spy effectively.

Are not the homosexual and the heterosexual, then, in fact, two interdependent concepts circulating within a closed sexual economy similar to that of work and play, "Necessary" and "Extravagance"? The absence of critical commentaries surrounding this aspect of *M. Butterfly* would suggest not, focusing on the drama through the exclusive lens of a compulsory heterosexuality. In "The Straight Mind," Monique Wittig proffers an explanation.

> Lesbianism, homosexuality, and the societies that we form cannot be thought of or spoken of, even though they have always existed. Thus, the straight mind continues to affirm that incest, and not homosexuality represents its major interdiction. Thus, when thought of by the straight mind, homosexuality is nothing more than heterosexuality.[45]

We must keep in mind, however, that the compulsory ignorance surrounding the homosexual elision described by Wittig is further complicated by the issue of race.

Though both Gallimard and Song may be gay, clearly, their rights and privileges as white homosexual and homosexual of color are not equal. Extrapolating from Hwang's discussion of rice queens, whose expectations of their Asian counterparts do not exceed beyond the boundaries of the feminine realm, various Asian American critics have railed at the common stereotypes imposed by a dominant white—and homophobic—society that transforms the Asian woman into a hyper-feminine sex pot and always already sees the Asian male, gay or straight, as a feminized and sexless creature—the Charlie Chan sex syndrome.[46] To return to an earlier observation in my essay, we must ask ourselves why Gallimard can shift the burden of sexual identity upon the shoulders of Song with his statement, "I think you must have some kind of identity problem."[47]

The answer, of course, lies with a racist as well as homophobic explanation. The straight white mind cannot see Song Liling, whether in drag as a woman or in an Armani suit as a man, as a complete man, whose anatomical revelation in Act Three merits the recognition of a homosexual admission. If the Asian male, gay or straight, is, after all, sexless and wordless—already homosexualized of sorts—how can Gallimard's relationship with the opera singer exist at the level of same sex desire? As Richard Fung notes in "Looking for My Penis: The Eroticized Asian in Gay Video Porn," "the Asian man is defined by a striking absence down there. And if Asian men have no sexuality, how can we have homosexuality?"[48] Homosexuality is a "privilege" that the gay Asian male can never be granted—the "Extravagance" of an alternative sexual identity. Hence, in its most quotidian incarnation, Gallimard and Song's affair can only exist, in the straight mind of Wittig's homophobic audience, as a male-female union.

The playwright, however, also remains accountable. While I have argued that homosexuality is an intransigent facet of *M. Butterfly*, Hwang, in the final analysis, equivocates on the subject of gay sexuality. For instance, through an infelicitous displacement of homosexuality onto the figure of "modern" Chinese woman—the fanatical Comrade Chin sporting her dykeish haircut and butch clothing—Hwang conflates homophobia with misogyny ("What passes for a woman in modern China."[49]) The ultimate representative of female as pure hysteria, Comrade Chin is the only consistent mouthpiece of a queer sensibility in the drama, the one character who overtly speaks the "truth" of Gallimard and Song's relationship:

> Serve the revolution? Bullshit! You wore dresses! Don't tell me—I was there. I saw you! You and your white vice-consul! Stuck up there in your flat, living off the People's Treasury! Yeah, I knew what was going on! You two…homos! Homos! Homos![50]

The alignment of Comrade Chin's politically dogmatic Communism (the Red scare) with her zealous pronouncements on homosexuality works to delegitimize the queer as a viable sexual choice. Thus, in accord with a homophobic mainstream, homosexuality comes again to be pathologically inserted into the world of the "Extravagant" and hysterical; heterosexuality—by default—comes again to rest complacently on the laurels of "Necessity" and the normatively sane.[51]

At the conclusion of the Afterword to *M. Butterfly*, Hwang's sexual politics are definitively summarized. Attempting to shift the reception of his play squarely into the arena of straight cultural politics, he states:

> From my point of view, the "impossible" story of a Frenchman duped by a Chinese man masquerading as a woman always seemed perfectly explicable; given the degree of misunderstanding between men and women and also between East and West, it seemed inevitable that a mistake of this magnitude would one day take place.[52]

Why does the playwright choose to restrain the interpretative locus of the drama within a heterosexual economy—the "misunderstanding between men and women"—while suppressing the implicit and explicit issues of homosexuality that remain pervasive throughout the drama?

The answer to this question, I would argue, circles back to Wong's observations of the Asian American artist within an emerging minority discourse. It would seem that David Henry Hwang's insistence on heterosexuality at the expense of a legitimate queer sensibility in *M. Butterfly* exhibits an urgency on the playwright's part to validate his piece of Asian American literature solidly within the parameters and pressures of the dominant discourse—to carve a respectable position for himself within the established norms of a politically liberal, that is to say—white and compulsory heterosexual audience.

Gallimard, whose sexual difference would be an intolerable thorn in the old boy network of the embassy, finds an interesting correlative in Hwang's predicament as the ethnic artist within a white bourgeois artistic tradition. Like many artists of color, Hwang finds himself in a double bind that Wong describes as the impulse to suppress or distort

> all individual experiences that do not fit into white society's image of Chinese Americans. Honesty of artistic vision and acceptability by white readers thus become mutually exclusive, which poses a difficulty over and above the dilemma between artistic integrity and commercial success so familiar to the bourgeois writer.[53]

In restricting the interpretative locus of *M. Butterfly*, Hwang mimics "straightminded" critics in his suppression of the homoerotics of the drama.[54] Showing little tolerance for sexual difference by banishing homosexuality ultimately into the realm of the unmentionable, the suppression of the sexually "Extravagant" by Hwang in his play seems to become a move of "Necessity" for mainstream heterosexist commercial success and critical acceptance.

But if homosexuality lies in the realm of "Extravagance," it is no more unnecessary than "Necessity" itself. The erasure of homosexuality from the arena of Asian American literature is finally limiting, denying both a rich artistic heteroglossia and a fecund political opportunity for Asian Americans to once again vex majority expectations of well-worn stereotypes. Indeed, as Eve Sedgwick notes, the alienation of individual authority to name one's own personal sexual desire at a time when sexual discourse "has been made expressive of the essence of both identity and knowledge...may represent the most intimate violence possible.... It is, of course, central to the modern history of homophobic oppression."[55] For the Asian American community, this is an intimate violence that carries the further imputations of disempowerment and fracturing within a community already besieged by multiple forms of racism. As Richard Fung observes, although "a motto for the lesbian and gay movements has been 'we are everywhere,' Asians are largely absent from the images produced by both the political and the commercial sectors of the mainstream gay and lesbian communities."[56]

In "The Woman Warrior versus The Chinaman Pacific: Must a Chinese American Critic Choose between Feminism and Heroism?" King-Kok Cheung argues that it is precisely because the racist treatment of Asians has taken the peculiar form of sexism—in so far as the indignities suffered by men of Chinese descent are analogous to those traditionally suffered by women—we must refrain from seeking anti-feminist solutions to racism. To do otherwise reinforces not only patriarchy but also white supremacy.[57]

Extending Cheung's analysis beyond the bounds of an unspecified sexuality to focus specifically on the indignities suffered by men of Asian descent both gay and straight—for the paradigm of feminization transfers seamlessly between one and the other—we can only conclude that the need to refrain from seeking homophobic solutions to racism is as great an imperative as the need to "refrain from seeking anti-feminist solutions to racism." To do otherwise poses great danger and denies even a compensatory subject position for the Asian American male, gay or straight, in white America.

In the final analysis, who in *M. Butterfly* is afforded the last laugh? Who is the ultimate artist and trickster figure, the queen in control? Is it the caustic Song whose provisional foray out of the paternal order is quickly suppressed by Gallimard's heterosexual conversion and homosexual abjection? Or is it Gallimard, the white Frenchman diplomat, whose flawless performance as the awkward straight lover subdues the oriental diva and assures us that all will be well in status quo sexual and racial politics?

Notes

This article was first written in 1992. The impetus for the following reading of Hwang's play originally came from my dissatisfaction with the lack of criticism considering what I see as the drama's rather obvious homosexual subtext. My "queer" reading of Gallimard and Song's relationship was intended as a critical intervention into the heterosexual matrix framing the majority of previous scholarship on the drama. While I now find problematic the notion of ever being able definitively to name Gallimard as "gay white male," I believe the historical value of this essay lies in its preliminary attempts to bridge the fields of Asian American and gay and lesbian studies by introducing a queer reading into the former and by considering issues of racial difference in the latter.

For my more current reading of the play, see my forthcoming article, "Heterosexuality in the Face of Whiteness: Dividing Belief in David Henry Hwang's *M. Butterfly*." In this essay I develop what I consider a more consistently psychoanalytic argument by exploring how Gallimard could, at once, both be and not be a self-denying homosexual through the psychic mechanism of a racial and (homo)sexual fetish. This later article—part of a larger dissertation project on the intersection of race and homosexuality in Asian American literature and psychoanalytic theory—examines both the invisibility of whiteness as a racial category and its discursive alignment with a matrix of compulsory heterosexuality.

I would like to thank Sau-ling Wong, Anne McKnight, and Ella Spray, for their helpful comments on this essay, which is the expanded result of a paper I presented at the tenth annual Association for Asian American Studies Conference at Cornell University in June 1993.

1. David Henry Hwang, *M. Butterfly* (New York: Plume Books, 1988), 1–2.
2. Ibid., 2.
3. Ibid.
4. Eve Kosofsky Sedgwick, *Epistemology of the Closet* (Berkeley: University of California Press, 1990), 3.
5. In "evaluating" Gallimard and Song's sexual relationship, I am aware that I run the risk of invoking certain essentializing notions around the categories of "gay white male" and "gay Asian (American) male." Nevertheless, I believe this strategic move is worth taking, for while I am in sympathy with much of recent queer and feminist theory insisting upon the radical unknowability and unreliability of such categories as "sex," "gender," "race," and "ethnicity," in the gap between current post-structuralist theory and the contemporary historical, material context of what we familiarly call the "real world," the subject positions of the Asian (American) gay and lesbian are still overwhelmingly untenable ones. Consequently, my assessment of Gallimard and Song's sexual relationship as a homosexual relationship as well as my subsequent reading of the power disparities resulting from this homosexual relationship is executed less as an essentializing imperative than as a means to recuperate not only a (homo)sexual but also a racial positioning for the gay Asian (American) male vis-à-vis dominant white society.

   See, for instance, Richard Fung's "Looking for My Penis: The Eroticized Asian in Gay Video Porn" in *How Do I Look? Queer Film and Video* (Seattle, Washington: Bay Press, 1991), 145–60. Also see King-Kok Cheung's *"Coda" to Articulate Silences* (Ithaca, New York: Cornell University Press, 1993).
6. The reviews are too numerous to cite in their monolithic entirety. For instance, see Moira Hodgson's review in *The Nation* (April 23, 1988): 57; Leo Sauvage's review in *New Leader* (April 18, 1988): 22; John Simon's review in *New York* (April 11, 1988): 117; Gerald Weale's review in *Commonweal* (April 22, 1988): 245.

   See Marjorie Garber's *Vested Interests: Cross-Dressing and Cultural Anxiety* (New York: Routledge, 1992) for an interesting reading of the drama through the figure of the transvestite.
7. Like Sedgwick, Judith Butler makes many significant observations around the elision of homosexuality in her well-known critique of compulsory heterosexual culture found in *Gender Trouble: Feminism and the Subversion of Identity* (New York: Routledge, 1990). However, while Sedgwick and Butler do gesture to race as a category that must be considered in its specificities along with any discussion of a gay and lesbian politics, both scholars, for the most part, situate their criticism within a canonically white philosophical and literary tradition.

   My discussion of *M. Butterfly* will use much of Sedgwick and Butler's theoretical foundations to extend the particularities and parameters of queer subjectivity as they intersect with a racialized Asian American literary and material history.

8. Jean Laplanche and Jean-Bertrand Pontalis, *The Language of Psychoanalysis*, trans. Donald -Smith (New York: Norton, 1993), 317.

9. Laplanche and Pontalis, "Fantasy and Origin of Sexuality" in *Formations of Fantasy*, ed. Victor Burgin, J. Donald, and Cora Kaplan (New York: Methuen, 1986), 5–34.

10. Judith Butler, *Bodies That Matter: On the Discursive Limits of "Sex"* (New York: Routledge, 1993), 100.

11. I must emphasize that I take the coincidence of anatomical form less as an epistemological ground for homosexual subjectivity than as a starting point for my investigation of Gallimard's fantasmatic identifications. As we are aware, object choice is merely one of many resulting markers in the unconscious processes of sexual identification. See, for instance, Kaja Silverman's last chapter "A Woman's Soul Enclosed in a Man's Body: Femininity in Male Homosexuality" in *Male Subjectivity at the Margins* (New York: Routledge, 1992), 339–88.

12. Hwang, 70.

13. Ibid., 81.

14. Ibid., 83.

15. Ibid., 4.

16. Ibid., 98.

17. Ibid., 6.

18. Ibid., 83. Emphasis in original.

19. Anyone who believes such statements to be hyperbole or mere literary fiction need only to look at the recent Bay Area media controversy chronicled by the *San Francisco Chronicle* surrounding NAMBLA (The North American Man Boy Love Association), which illustrates the contemporaneousness and contemptuousness of the situation. Using public library space for meetings, NAMBLA agendas included the planning of pederastic field trips to Thailand in order to have sex with young male orphans. These "exploitation orphanages" were established and financed by NAMBLA—composed mainly of gay white members—for the exclusive purpose of these sexual excursions.

20. Hwang, 24.

21. Ibid., 8–9.

22. Ibid., 10–12.

23. It is also no accident, I think, that both the character of Renee and of the closet pinup girl are played by the same actress. This dispersal of two roles to one body underscores the pair's common psychic stake in their relationship to Gallimard's trajectory of fantasmatic desires.

24. I gesture both to the early Lacan's discussions of the sense of self imputed to the infant in "The mirror stage" and "Aggressivity in psychoanalysis," *Écrits: A Selection*, trans. Alan Sheridan (New York: Norton, 1977), 1–7, 8–29; as well as to the later Lacan's discussions of the look and the gaze in *The Four Fundamental Concepts of Psychoanalysis*, trans. Alan Sheridan (New York: Norton, 1981), 67–119 . Renee not only provides an image for Gallimard to emulate but also thwarts his ability to identify with this image by parading her look as the authoritarian gaze of the phallic authority, a right normally apportioned to the normative white heterosexual male.

See Kaja Silverman's arguments around the look and the gaze in chapter 3, "Fassbinder and Lacan: A Reconsideration of Gaze, Look and Image," of *Male*

Subjectivity at the Margins, 125–56. Silverman delineates the various methods by which the male look has traditionally been conflated with the transcendental gaze of phallic authority as well as the ways in which this conflation continually fails to sustain itself.

25. Hwang, 54–56. Emphasis in original.
26. Ibid., 54. Emphasis in original.
27. Ibid., 46.
28. Like Renee and the closet pinup girl, the roles of Toulon and the judge are also played by a single actor, I would contend, for similar psychic emphasis.
29. Hwang, 10.
30. Ibid., 4.
31. Ibid., 37–38.
32. Psychoanalytic feminist criticism has, for many years, focused much of its attention on the slippage of anatomical penis and symbolic phallus. The disentangling of this conflation is imperative for it promises additional benefits for a gay and lesbian anti-homophobic as well as an Asian American antiracist project.

    See "The Phallus Issue" 4: 1 (Spring 1992) and "Gay and Lesbian Sexualities" 3: 2 (Summer 1991) issues of *Differences: A Journal of Feminist Cultural Studies*, which approaches the penis/phallus debate from several theoretical and political perspectives.
33. Hwang, 32.
34. Earl Jackson, Jr., "Scandalous Subjects: Robert Gluck's Embodied Narratives," *Differences: A Journal of Feminist Cultural Studies* 3: 2 (Summer 1991), 121–22.
35. Jackie Goldsby has much to say about the topic of white gay male privilege as it impacts upon the realm of African American gay and lesbian politics. In her discussion of Robert Mapplethorpe's white racist photography, she summarizes: "Don't lay your hopes for freedom with a white boy—they've got too much to gain from the way things are to change anything for real." See Goldsby's article "What it Means To Be Colored Me" in *Out/Look* (Summer 1990), 9–17.

    Kobena Mercer raises a similar point in his work on Mapplethorpe's oeuvre found in the *How Do I Look* anthology. See his "Skin Head Sex Thing: Racial Difference and the Homoerotic Imaginary," in *How Do I Look? Queer Film and Video*, eds. Bad Object Choices (Seattle: Bay Press, 1991), 169–210.
36. Hwang, 92.
37. Ibid., 88. Emphasis mine.
38. Ibid., 90.
39. Ibid., 15.
40. Sau-ling Cynthia Wong, *Reading Asian American Literature: From Necessity to Extravagance* (Princeton, New Jersey: Princeton University Press, 1993), 166.
41. Ibid., 189.
42. See Wong's discussion in *Reading Asian American Literature* of "Necessity" and "Extravagance" in an earlier Hwang drama, *The Dance and the Railroad* (1981), 186–91.
43. Hwang, 82.
44. Ibid., 73. Emphasis in original.

45. Monique Wittig, "The Straight Mind" in *Out There: Marginalization and Contemporary Culture*, ed. Russell Ferguson, Martha Gever, Trinh T. Minh-ha, and Cornel West (Cambridge, MA: The New Museum of Contemporary Art and MIT Press, 1990), 54–55.

46. See Frank Chin's "Come All Ye Asian American Writers of the Real and the Fake" and the editors' "Introduction" (1989) in *The Big Aiiieeeee! An Anthology of Chinese American and Japanese American Literature*, ed. Jeffery Paul Chan, Frank Chin, Lawson Fusao Inada, and Shawn Wong, (New York: Meridian,1991), 1–92, xi–xvi; for a more detailed history and explanation of the sexual and racial politics that have been and are currently being debated within the Asian American community. The preface (1973) and introduction to the original *Aiiieeeee! An Anthology of Asian American Writers*, ed. Frank Chin, Jeffery Paul Chan, Lawson Fusao Inada, and Shawn Wong, (New York: Anchor Books, 1975), ix–xx, 3–36, also provides a background history to the sexual anxieties and racial concerns of the same four editors sixteen years earlier.

47. Hwang, 88.

48. Richard Fung, "Looking for My Penis: The Exoticized Asian in Gay Video Porn," in *How Do I Look? Queer Film and Video*, 148.

49. Hwang, 49. Emphasis mine.

50. Ibid., 71–72.

51. It is interesting to note that at the beginning of *M. Butterfly*, David Henry Hwang inserts a preface that seems rather incongruous with the device of suspense so often found in drama. Quoting from a *New York Times* article dated May 11, 1986, Hwang cites a real-life espionage trial as the inspiration for *M. Butterfly*: "A former French diplomat and a Chinese opera singer have been sentenced to six years in jail for spying for China after a two-day trial that traced a story of clandestine love and mistaken sexual identity.... Mr. Bouriscot was accused of passing information to China after he fell in love with Mr. Shi, whom he believed for twenty years to be a woman" (Playwright's Notes). By placing the truth of the former French diplomat and Chinese opera singer's relationship in the foreground, Hwang seems to shift the analysis of the viewer-reader-critic from the homosexual relationship that his two characters share to focus on the issues of the compulsory heterosexual mind: why didn't Gallimard know? How did Song pull it off? Prompted by Hwang, the straight mind justifies its own analysis over the aspects of the why and how of the issue, never entertaining the possibility of the did—that Gallimard did know, from the very beginning, Butterfly's anatomical sex.

52. Hwang, 98.

53. Wong, 177.

54. Here, it might be interesting to relate Homi Bhabha's concept of colonial mimicry to a domestic situation in which artists of color are coerced into imitative relationships with dominant aesthetic and political modes of production. See Bhabha's "Of Mimicry and Man: The Ambivalence of Colonial Discourse" in *October* 28 (Spring 1984): 125–33.

55. Sedgwick, 26.

56. Fung, 148.
    While I believe this statement is still true to a very large extent, the presence of queer

Asian Americans within the gay and lesbian arts community is beginning to be felt more decisively within large metropolitan areas such as San Francisco, New York, and Los Angeles. For instance, the 1993 Gay and Lesbian Film Festivals in both San Francisco and New York featured video works by several Asian American queer artists such as Quentin Lee, Pablo Bautista, and Ming Ma. In addition, the playwright Han Ong has written and produced several recent dramas in the San Francisco Bay Area.

The Asian/Pacific American Journal (The APA Journal), 2: 1 (Spring/Summer 1993) published out of New York City, has devoted a recent issue to lesbian, gay, and bisexual writings by Asian American and Asian Pacific writers and poets. In addition, Jessica Hagedorn's new collection *Charlie Chan is Dead: An Anthology of Contemporary Asian American Fiction* (New York: Penguin, 1993) hosts a significant gay and lesbian presence.

57. King-kok Cheung, "The Woman Warrior versus The Chinaman Pacific: Must a Chinese American Critic Choose between Feminism and Heroism?" in *Conflicts in Feminism*, ed. Marriane Hirsch and Evelyn Fox Keller (New York: Routledge, 1990), 244.

Notes on Queer 'N' Asian Virtual Sex

Daniel C. Tsang

The relationship between technology and sexuality is a symbiotic one. As humankind creates new inventions, people find ways of eroticizing new technology. Today, sex shops sell sex toys for all sorts of sex acts, but in fact, virtually anything can be a turn-on to someone. Once, lacking a real dildo, my partner and I dug out a frozen carrot from the refrigerator, thawed it under running water, and tried, rather unsuccessfuly to use it as an organic replacement. The role sex plays in human endeavor is an area always worth exploring, and despite the contemporary focus on matters sexual, one could argue that society has paid attention to sex throughout recorded history. Tierney even argues that the erotic technological impulse dates back at least to some of the earliest works of art, the so-called Venus figurines of women with exaggerated breasts and buttocks, which were made by firing clay 27,000 years ago—15 millenniums before ceramics technology was used for anything utilitarian like pots.[1]

So it is not surprising that with the advent of the information super-highway, more and more folks are discovering the sexual underground within the virtual community in cyberspace.

Like the stereotypical computer nerd, I have sat in front of my computer, pressed some keys, and connected to a remote computer, perhaps twice daily, if not more often. But unlike the desexualized computer nerd, I have used the computer to connect to a Bulletin Board System (BBS) with a significant number of gay Asian members and used it to meet others for affection, romance, love, and sex for several years. In fact, as I write, I have logged on to this board over 1,680 times, out of over 600,000 calls made by everyone to the board since its creation in September 1991. How many sexual partners I have met will remain a state secret. Of the 1,088 BBSers registered, some eighty-eight (8 percent) identify as Asian gay or bisexual males.

Initially this just seemed like the computerized, electronic version of placing or responding to a personal ad, as I had several times before. But as time went on, it dawned on me that this was something entirely different, with the potential for creativity (and mischief) largely untapped by myself and most of the others (I presumed) on the BBS.

One need not belabor the differences between pen and paper and the computer to recognize that with instantaneous communication now available, dating—and fulfilling our sexual desires—are much more immediately realizable.

Friends may bemoan months of BBSing without meeting anyone in the flesh, but they, alas, miss the point. The online experiences are ones that I cherish, not just the real live ones.

On the board, fantasy substitutes for hard reality. For a couple of years I had been chatting electronically with this college student; recently I called his college (he had given me his name and address) and found he did not exist, nor did his dormitory. Yet this was someone with whom I had even chatted "voice," i.e., on the phone. Could he have been a figment of my imagination? Or did he give me false identification? Or worse still, was an undercover government agent infiltrating the board to investigate my sex life? After all, the CIA has admitted collecting information about me and giving it away to a foreign government.[2]

It does pay to have a sense of "healthy paranoia" online. For despite the illusion of privacy, nothing one types is really truly private. The sysop [system operator] can "tap" your electronic conversations; who knows if the recipient is not "downloading" your love notes? Sometimes, in "open chat," the forum is deliberately not private, and several people can chat at once or almost at once. All participants get to read your the messages flying back and forth. Without even the National Security Agency having its Clipper chip access, BBSing is arguably more open than chatting in public. Berlet (1985), for example, argues that today's BBS sysops "are merely the modern incarnation of the pesky and audacious colonial period pamphleteeers like John Peter Zenger and Thomas Paine" and that today, "Zenger might well be a political dissident running a controversial BBS while listening to audio tapes of the 'Police' singing about surveillance," and should thus protected by privacy laws from government intrusion.[3]

But despite the best efforts of these civil libertarians to protect the privacy of BBSers, those who chat online need a wake-up call: the notion of privacy is, in the end, an illusion. Like the HIV status of your electronic mate, don't be deluded. Play safe: treat every message as public, and every sexual partner as HIV positive. The BBS challenges traditional notions of privacy and obscures the lines between private and public.

One reason BBSing is so fascinating is that the online environment truly allows one to continually reinvent one's identity, including the sexual. For once, you are in total control of your sexual identity, or identities, or at least what you decide to show the outside world.

Indeed, it is our sexualities that are on display. In real life, but more so in virtual reality, our sexualities are not fixed, but constantly in flux. In the Foucauldian sense, we re-invent our sexualities. Over time we can have more than one. And there are more than just gay or straight. And despite the protestations of the latest adherents to gay ideology that they were born gay, the online environment reminds us that our sexualities are ephemeral, to be changed with a stroke of a key. These are social constructs, not biological essentialisms.

In virtual reality, we can take on other identities than our current one, often with no one else the wiser. In time, these online identities may become more real than the physical one.

One student I know even signs on under a friend's I.D. so that he can maximize his time on the board; and he is on the board for hours daily even during exam week. Personally, I can't tell you how long it has been since I have been to a gay bar, except to pick up gay magazines; like numerous others, electronic cruising has replaced bar hopping.

The BBS I am most often on allows its members (those who pay or like me, were grandfathered in) to post not only a written biography of ourselves, answers to numerous questionnaires, but also digital portraits of ourselves. In turn, members can peruse (or "browse") these bios and questionnaire responses, as well as retrieve and download your digital image, and see you in the flesh, even nude.

Thus, with a keystroke, one can change one's biographical particulars, e.g., ethnicity, age, domestic partnership status, class, or even sexual orientation. This means, of course, that all the posted information should be taken with a grain of salt.

Age is one good example. This board, like many others, restricts membership to adults (eighteen and over). Hence, any minor who seeks access must lie about his age. In fact two had been kicked off the board because they were minors, according to the sysop. (The board is predominantly male, with only a handful of the almost 1,100 members being female.) On the other end of the age scale, because of the disdain against them, some older men do not give their true age. When I went on I put my age as thirty-six; after several years, it has been changed only by one year, to thirty-seven.

Ethnicity or race is another characteristic that can be changed, almost at will. If being Vietnamese today is not what you want to be, you could pick some other category. One BBSer from Taiwan even picked "Caucasian," and found out lots more people wanted to chat with him than when he was "Chinese," a recognition that the electronic environment does not screen out racist sentiments.

Caucasians inhabit most of this virtual space, although there is significant Asian presence (on this board, as reported above, some 8 percent). Although Caucasians will describe themselves as being of various European backgrounds, depending on the person, the distinctions may not be revealing. If Caucasians see us as the "other," we admittedly often see the white race as just monolithic. Once, when I wrote about the "rice queen" phenomenon in a gay magazine, *Frontiers*, several white readers wrote in to argue that I was racist, because I lumped all whites together. It seems to be an empirical question as to whether or not white Americans really do identify as "Italian" or "German." The dominant role race plays in American society tends to obscure the diversities that exist in all cultures.

When I was growing up in Hong Kong, I definitely could tell the British colonials apart from the other gwailos. Ethnically Chinese, my Hong Kong I.D. card was stamped "American," because my mom was born in the U.S., but I never felt American, until years after I had lived in the States. As Dana Takagi argues elsewhere in this issue, the study of gay Asians also awakens us to the dangers of essentializing the Asian American. In fact, like sexualities, Asian American identities are not static, but in constant flux. The contemporary influx of Southeast Asians and other Asian subgroups to this country makes us realize that one can no longer limit our discourse to Chinese or Japanese subcultures.

The diversity of Asian identities in the U.S. is reflected in the Asian gay or bisexual male membership of the BBS. The figures for female Asians or straight Asians on the board are too few for meaningful analysis. Although anyone can access this board by modem, given this particular BBS's location in Orange County, California, which has seen a 271 percent increase in its Vietnamese population in the decade since the 1980 census, it is surprising that only a few (thirteen) of the Asian gays or bisexuals on the board identify themselves as Vietnamese. That figure is identical to the number identifying as Japanese. In fact, the majority of the gay or bisexual Asians say they are Chinese (thirty-three in all). The 1990 census shows an increase of 191 percent in the Chinese population in the county. Pilipino gay or bisexuals are also a significant number on this board, adding up to seventeen. The 1990 census shows that Pilipinos have also increased in size in the county since the last census, by 178 percent. There are nine Amerasian or Eurasian gay or bisexuals and four Pacific Islander gays or bisexuals. There is only one Thai, and two East Indians. Although I have chatted with at least one Korean American on the board, he and any other apparently did not publicly identify their ethnicity.

Because this board was set up to serve gay males (in fact the sysop is a gay Vietnamese immigrant), there are few females on the board. Since some on the board specify they would only chat with other males, a female BBSer is at a disadvantage. She can continue to stay on the board as a female, or she can change her gender on her electronic biography. Whether anyone has done that remains an open question. Despite the preference of many to chat only with other males, the few hardy souls who are female have stuck it out, although one friend I know dropped out soon after, but also because she had relocated north.

One could argue that by signing up for the board, one is, in fact, taking the first step toward "coming out." Even though one can remain largely anonymous on the board with "handles" that are pseudonyms and not real names, the fact that a BBSer needs to identify his sexual orientation on the board makes it an important act of coming out. Many of the BBSers, for example, note in their biographies that they are just "coming out." Surprisingly, there are very few BBSers who identify as straight on the board. One might have thought that it would be easier, and less threatening to initially label oneself as straight. Undoubtedly a few do that, since they stay on the board quite a while and do engage in deep chats with those identifying as gay or bisexual. They are often asked why they are on a gay board. Yet the query is posed not to exclude but out of curiosity, I suspect, and out of a hope, perhaps, that the straight identity is indeed in flux, and moving toward a gay identity.

More of the Asians (like the non-Asians) identify themselves on the board as gay rather than bisexual. One might have thought that it would be less threatening to come out as bisexual. (If queried, many of the bisexuals would insist, however, that they are true bisexuals, and not just going through a phase). There are, however, differences within the various Asian groups as to the prevalence of bisexuals.

With the caveat that this is by no means a random sample, Japanese and Pilipinos appear to be the two groups of Asian gays with the highest percentage identifying as bisexual, if we discount the one case of a bisexual Thai man, or the two cases of East Indian men, one of whom calls himself bisexual. Thirty percent (or four out of thirteen) of the Japanese males call themselves bisexual, the rest label themselves as gay. Twenty-nine percent or five of all seventeen Pilipino males on the board identify as bisexual, with the rest calling themselves gay. One out of the four Pacific Islander males on the board identifies as bisexual. The rest identify as gay. Among Vietnamese males, only two out of thirteen (15 percent) identify as bisexual; the rest call themselves gay. Similar low percentages exist for Chinese males (almost 10 percent or three out of thirty-three). The others say they are gay. Only 11 percent or one out of the nine Amerasians or Eurasian males identifies as bisexual. The others identify as gay.

Age-wise, the Asian gay or bisexual males range from eighteen to fifty-five. Chinese gay males are generally younger (average age 24.8); with Chinese bisexual males a bit older (25.6). Among Pilipinos, gay men average almost twenty-seven years old; bisexual men average over thirty-one years old. Japanese gay males are older (average thirty-two years old), although bisexual Japanese males are younger (twenty-seven years old). Vietnamese bisexual men show the reverse trend; they are older on average (thirty-two years old) than the gay Vietnamese men (twenty-eight). The one bisexual Amerasian is aged thirty-four; the average for the eight gay Amerasians is almost twenty-nine years old. Among Pacific Islanders, the age is 25.6 on average for gay men, and nineteen for the one bisexual man. Of the two East Indians, one is a bisexual eighteen-year old man, another a twenty-four year old gay man.

It should be noted, however, that identifying as gay or bisexual on a BBS is not the same as coming out to someone directly. Because of the presumed anonymity of the board, such a disclosure is made much more easily. Often, I have had prolonged chats with someone who pours out his love life online, something he would probably only do because I am a stranger. Hotline volunteers are familiar with this phenomenon. .

As I write, Gay Asians have become more visible, the 1994 Lunar New Year celebrations marking the first time a gay and lesbian Asian contingent has marched in San Francisco's Chinatown. No one has done such a comparative study, yet, but one could postulate that it is harder for Asians (than Caucasians) to come out, given cultural and family traditions, and that the rate at which Asians come out varies by national origin.

Anthropologist Joseph Carrier and his colleagues have in fact studied the sexual habits of Vietnamese immigrants in Orange County, California. They have found that assimilated Vietnamese Americans are more ready to identify as "gay," whereas those who are more recent immigrants or less assimilated do not, even if they engage in homosexual behavior.[4] This supports Tomas Almaguer's observation that some Chicanos "come out" genitally but not cerebrally. In other words, they engage in gay sex, but without the self-identification as gay or bisexual. Loc Minh Truong, who was almost bashed to death by two Caucasian youths later convicted of gay bashing, insists he is not gay, even though he was once convicted of lewd conduct on the same beach where the hate crime later occurred.[5]

In light of the above, it is surprising that so few on the BBS actually refuse to identify as gay or bisexual. Only a handful on the board who are Asian say they are straight.

I have also argued elsewhere that just as many homosexuals attempt to pass as straight, some Asians in North America attempt to pass as white.[6] I mentioned above the case of a college student from Taiwan who, in an apparent experiment, changed his ethnic identity from Chinese to Caucasian on the

BBS, and almost immediately, received many more queries and inivitations to "chat."

That there are others who are in fact uncomfortable with their ethnic identity is suggested by the several dozen, presumably of varying ethnicities, who identify as "others" in the category for ethnicity. To be sure, many may have found the categories listed inappropriate (especially those with a multiethnic heritage). But I suspect a certain percentage decline to state their ethnicity in the hopes that their chances on the board will be improved. Ethnic identity and age are the two identifying characteristics that flash on the screen whenever a BBSer tries to contact another BBSer to chat.

Online, it is of course possible to reconstruct not only one's sexual orientation, but also one's racial and ethnic identity—and indeed one's entire biography. In a racist society, it is perhaps surprising that not more do that. Fung has argued:

> Gay society in North America, organized and commercial, is framed around the young middle-class white male. He is its customer and its product. Blacks, Asians and Latin Americans are the oysters in this meat market. At best we're a quaint specialty for exotic tastes. Native people aren't even on the shelves.[7]

Exoticized and eroticized, Gay Asian males are nonetheless considered a "quaint specialty." This became quite clear with a recent mail message from a self-described "rice queen" on the board who wrote me:

> Hi, they say opposites attract, so I am looking for an unabashed snow queen with nice patties! To rest upon my snowey [sic] slopes.... I have written to over fifteen Asians on this BBS but none of them has replied. Can you give me some helpful hints? Don't worry, I can take critisisms [sic].

Why are Asian males the subject of desire of so-called rice queens? A Japanese American I met on the board wrote in his short-lived print newsletter, Daisuki-Men, that there are three reasons: China Doll syndrome (i.e., Asian males are seen as feminine); perception that Asians are submissive; and the rice queens' obsession with things Asian (as indicated by decorating their residences with Asian knick knacks).[8]

One could go on, but the point is made. "Our (presumed) racial characteristics are fetishized by the non-API gay communities as a frozen form of desirablility—one that is derived from an Orientalist perspective. In this economy of desire, the trade is almost always unidirectional, where APIs are encouraged to use our 'exotic appeal,' our 'Oriental sensuousness,' to maximize our attractiveness..." according to Hom and Ma (1993).[9]

As Asians, we resent being treated as objects, or as the "Other," but given the mainstream definition of beauty in this society, Asians, gay or straight, are constantly reminded that we cannot hope to meet such standards. Fung writes that in commercial gay male representation, it is the image of white men that is set up as the ideal: "Although other people's rejection (or fetishization) of us according to the established racial hierarchies may be experienced as oppressive, we are not necessarily moved to scrutinize our own desire and its relationship to the hegemonic image of the white man."[10] With such lack of self-scrutiny, is it any wonder that some gravitate to the Great White Hope as their savior?[11]

For it is not just Caucasians who see Asians as a specialized taste. Asians are so specialized that for some Asians, fellow Asians are not even on the shelf.

A twenty-five-year old Japanese American sparked a recent debate on this very issue when he posted the following on a public bulletin board: "Like the stereotypical Asian, I prefer to date Caucasian men."

Now, as some subsequent BBSers pointed out, a stereotype has some basis in fact. To be sure there are Asians who feel attracted only to Caucasians. Hom and Ma have observed that since "many of us 'came out' in the Euro/American gay context, our ideals of male beauty are necessarily influenced by the dominant cultural standards of beauty and desirability."[12]

But it is probably safe to say that most Asians do not have exclusive attractions to one race. Even on this board, very few indicated publicly their attraction to their own race or to strictly another race. One suspects such a stereotype (that Asians prefer Caucasians) is based not only on self-hate and dominant beauty standards, but also because interracial couples stand out and thus are much more visible. In contrast, groups like Gay Asian Pacific Alliance (in the San Francisco Bay area) and Gay Asian Pacific Support Network (in Southern California), which provide safe spaces for Asian gays to meet each other, are largely invisible to the gay mainstream, in part because Caucasians are not in control and are in fact absent.[13] One could argue that the gay press will report the news of white gays much more than it will of nonwhite gays. It largely ignores the activities of people of color, except as they relate to HIV.

Furthermore, the online debate suffered from an implicit acceptance of a way of viewing sexuality and racial identity in dualistic terms: gay or straight, white or Asian (complementing mainstream media's black/white dichotomy). Not all Asians feel the same way, of course, nor do all Caucasians. Lumping each group together tends to obscure more than it unveils. Furthermore, there's more diversity (even on the BBS) than this white/Asian dichotomy allows. How about all the Latino Americans on the board? Or the African Americans? One can postulate, as I have argued, that our identification with the struggles of the U.S. civil rights movement draws some of us in solidarity with other people of color, so that this focus on white/Asian relationships is misleading.[14]

As I explore BBSing further, I see more transgressing of these traditional dichotomies, Asians cohabiting with Blacks or Latinos. But not just racial barriers are transgressed. Monogamy is another. On the board, romance, marriage, love, and lust are redefined. One bisexual Southeast Asian (who has a steady girlfriend he plans to marry) is an occasional fuckbuddy, visiting every so often in person, or more often, engaging in cybersex or phone sex.

The sexual practices that Asians on board find desirable run the gamut, from oral to anal sex, sadomasochism, and frottage. Some BBSers specifically ask other Asians to check out their electronic bios; others ask non-Asians to browse their sexual histories. Some readily admit their penis size, others say they are too shy. They report sizes ranging from five to eight inches. Many admit they have been tested for HIV, although some say it's too personal a question to answer. Some admit to smoking pot. Detailed analysis awaits further coding of the data.

BBSers provide more evidence that campaigns against sex in the schools have failed and that the Reagan/Bush years of sexual repression are over. The proliferation of sex boards suggests that a vibrant sexual underground has spawned right under the unsuspecting eyes of parents.

Given the prevalence of Asians in computer-related careers, one would not be surprised to find BBSers to be the places where gay or bisexual Asians gain entrance into the sexual communities that now span the globe. Given restrictive drinking ages that bar anyone under twenty-one from gay bars, BBSers have become an easy way for young gays of whatever ethnicities to enter the sexual underground. And this is not just a U.S. phenomenon. France is in many ways ahead of us; authorities there banished the telephone book (thereby saving many trees). Instead, every household received a computer terminal, thus in one stroke, bringing the French into the electronic age. Inevitably, the sex boards on the Minitel became the hottest venues for a newly electronically enfranchised constituency.[15] A comparative study of Vietnamese in Orange County and in Paris cruising on their respective sex boards would be an exciting contribution to the study of Asian sexualities.

The prevailing, if contradictory images of the Asian male as Kung Fu expert or computer nerd are ones that also renders him desexualized. In other words, the penis is missing in the dominant representation of the Asian male. In his "lifelong" quest for his lost penis, Fung found it in a Vietnamese American, going by various names including Sum Yung Mahn, who acted in gay porn videos.[16] In fact a BBSer claimed to be the same actor, but has since left the board so it has been impossible to confirm his identity.

BBSers, then challenge prevailing notions of Asian males as asexual. They provide Asians and Pacific Islanders an anonymous forum for sexually explicit dialog and for exploring their sexualities. On these boards, APIs are truly "breaking the silence" about taboo sexualities. In the process, APIs are empowered to voice our own forbidden desires and to reconstruct our own sexual identities.

Notes

1. John Tierney, "Porn, the Low-Slung Engine of Progress," *The New York Times*, 9 January 1994, Section II: 9.
2. For an early account of the case, Tsang v. CIA, see G.M. Bush, "Librarian Takes on CIA: UCI Employee Wants to Know About His File," *Los Angeles Daily Journal*, 6 February 1992, section II, 1, 18. The admission about releasing information about me to a foreign government appears in court documents. The student later explained online that because he lived in a homophobic dorm, he had given me fake identification information.
3. Chip Berlet, "Privacy and the PC: Mutually Exclusive Realities?" Paper prepared for the 1985 National Conference on Issues in Technology and Privacy," Center for Information Technology and Privacy Law, John Marshall Law School, Chicago, Illinois, June 21–23, 1985. Electronic version stored in publiceye database on PeaceNet.
4. Joseph Carrier, Bang Nguyen, and Sammy Su, "Vietnamese American Sexual Behaviors and HIV Infection," *The Journal of Sex Research* 29: 4 (November 1992): 547–60.
5. Daniel C. Tsang, "The Attack on Loc Minh Truong: The Intersection of Sexual Orientation, Race and Violence," *RicePaper* 2: 7 (Winter 1993): 10–11.
6. Daniel C. Tsang, "Gay Awareness," *Bridge* 3: 4 (February 1975): 44–45.
7. Cited in Daniel C. Tsang, "Struggling against Racism," in Tsang, *The Age Taboo* (Boston: Alyson, 1981), 163.
8. Sumo, "From the Editor…." *Daisuki-Men* 1 (1992): 4.
9. Alice Y. Hom and Ming-Yuen S. Ma, "Premature Gestures: A Speculative Dialogue on Asian Pacific Islander Lesbian and Gay Writing," *Journal of Homosexuality* 26: 2/3 (1993): 38.
10. Richard Fung, "Looking for My Penis: The Eroticized Asian in Gay Video Porn," in *Bad-Object Choices*, ed., *How Do I Look? Queer Film and Video* (Seattle: Bay Press, 1991): 149.
11. See Daniel C. Tsang, "M. Butterfly Meets the Great White Hope," *Informasian* 6: 3 (March 1992): 3–4.
12. Hom and Ma, "Premature Gestures," 37–38.
13. A rare exception to usual mainstream non-coverage is when a major newspaper published my essay, "Laguna Beach Beating Opens Closed Asian Door," *Los Angeles Times*, 18 January 1993, B5, which focused on gay Vietnamese in Southern California. Cf. Daniel C. Tsang, "Asian-Americans Come Out Actively in Orange County," *Orange County Blade* (February 1993): 39.
14. Daniel C. Tsang, "Lesbian and Gay Asian Americans: Breaking the Silence," *A/PLG Newsletter* (October 1990): 14–17.
15. See chapter 8, "Télématique and Messageries Roses" in Howard Rheingold's *The Virtual Community* (Reading, MA: Addison-Wesley, 1993): 220–40.
16. Fung, "Looking for My Penis," 149–50.

Toward a Struggle against Invisibility

Love between Women in Thailand

Took Took Thongthiraj

Lesbian-like relationships and lifestyles exist in Thailand, yet many Western (often male) analysts of Thai sexuality and homosexuality have focused solely on the gay male subculture in Thailand.[1] Unwillingness to uncover information on same-sex relationships between Thai women on the part of such analysts reinforces the multiple invisibility of these women—as women, "Third World"/Asian women, and lesbians. I hope to break such invisibilities by constructing a general discussion of lesbian-like relationships and lifestyles in Thailand as culturally, regionally, and class specific to and within Thailand. I want to stress how many Thai women in same-sex relationships are creating more terms and concepts to define their identities, thus revealing that lesbianism is not a Western import, but very Thai. Furthermore, an important argument underlining the overall discussion is that although Thailand lacks the extreme homophobia ingrained in many Western societies, discrimination against lesbian-like lifestyles and behavior persists in Thailand. Such discrimination takes on varied, subtle forms and is particularly addressed in family pressures on women to marry, have children, and take care of elders; reluctance to discuss sexuality in general; and reluctance to see lesbian-like relationships as a legitimate choice and issue. Thai women who love other women face incredible invisibility (again ramified by class and region)—an invisibility that shapes how they conceptualize their identity and struggle to change their position(s).

In a letter to the International Lesbian Information Service, Anchana Suwannanond (Tang), a thirty-three-year old Thai lesbian who organized the Asian Lesbian Network in Bangkok wrote, "It's not easy to build a network where there is a myth that lesbianism is not indigenous to Asia, but has been imported from the West."[2] In fact, according to Siriwan, a thirty-six-year old Thai lesbian now living in Los Angeles, Thai women who love other women "don't usually say they are lesbians because the word lesbian is Westernized. They don't like the word so they create their own words like 'tom' and 'dy.'"[3] Perhaps these women are disgusted with the gross distortions of lesbian-like behavior and lifestyles created and perpetuated by Euro-American sexologists and French decadent writers of the nineteenth and twentieth centuries. That is, European sexologists such as Krafft-Ebing and Havelock Ellis insisted that women who loved other women were "congenital inverts," abnormal, and suffering from familial neurosis. In addition, nineteenth-century French writers popularized lesbian eroticism by exoticizing lesbian sex and reinforcing that lesbians were evil, sinful manipulators of young, innocent women.[4] Such literary images gradually figured into non-Western literature, as revealed in Kenyan Rebecca Njau's book *Ripples in a Pool* and Indian Ismat Chugtai's tale *Lihah* (The Quilt). Thus, as Tang shares, "The word 'lesbian' is considered very bad usage amongst Thai women who love other women. To us, the word 'lesbian' only refers to sexual activity. We found it very pornographic. Sex is a start, but there are other things."[5]

In reaction to any distorted Western labels, Thai women in same-sex relationships—like their Japanese sisters of Regumi—have developed innovative terms and concepts to define their culture-specific identity. For example, several years ago the Thai lesbian organization Anjaree created the word "Anjaree," which means "someone who follows non-conformist ways."[6] Such a word attests to these women's resistance to heterosexism and compulsory heterosexuality and plays a significant role in reconstructing the Thai language, which offers no word for "lesbian"—except for a phrase translated as " 'playing with friends' (connoting) women being sexual with each other."[7]

However, the majority of Thai women involved in lesbian-like relationships have not adopted the word "Anjaree," but prefer to define themselves as either "tomboys" or "ladies." The tom and dy scene as it is called, is analogous to the butch-femme subculture found in many Western societies. The tom and dy scene is currently the lesbian-like community in Thailand, in that it is the most publicly visible. The tom and dy scene emerged into popularity some twenty years ago and has become the most widespread (at least in the cities) in the last five to ten years. According to Tang, unlike Thai gay men, "we don't have enough money to create a gathering of entertainment places which would cater only to lesbians. There is not enough paying clientele that can pay to keep the businesses going."[8] Thus, given the context where there are no lesbian bars, bookstores, or nominal support groups (Anjaree is still rather small) in Thailand, the tom and dy circle is particularly important in shaping and maintaining lesbian-like lifestyles and identities. That is, a Thai woman cannot just venture into a restaurant, cafe, department store, or discotheque (four of the major gathering spots of toms and dys) and assuredly know that every women there would be lesbian. Tang notes that:

> the only crowd where you can identify and be noticed is the tomboys and ladies crowd. There are a lot of groups of girls who go out together as "girls," but you cannot tell if they're lesbians or not. But you can tell when you see a group of girls who are dressed up as toms and ladies, and assume that they are lesbians in the sense that there can be relationships between these girls.[9]

Being a tom or dy thus facilitates social interaction among Thai women in same-sex relationships who are searching for potential partners, and as toms are noticeably not heterosexual by their appearance, it is the ladies who almost always take the initiative. As Tang observes:

> As a tom or dy you can just sit at a table next to each other and start to flirt. Dressing up as a tom is an expression that you are available to and have an interest in women, so if women are interested in you they have the courage to approach you. But, I can't see a way that a lady can start flirting with another feminine-looking woman out of the blue, with no contacts at all. I know many feminine-looking women who are lovers, but that takes time. Usually, they first become close friends, get to know each other, and then slowly start to express their attraction.[10]

Considering the social environment in Thailand, which lacks a visible, exclusive lesbian-like subculture, interchangeability between toms and dys is rare. That is, as Tang and Siriwan agree, "everyone usually sticks to their identities."[11] In fact, although Tang knew one tomboy who used to be a lady and one lady who used to be a tomboy, she clarifies that these two women are "rare cases" and that "most people don't change overnight or every other week in any way they like."[12] Unfortunately, the reasons for the lack of interchangeability amongst toms and ladies remain unclear. However, it is possible that the aforementioned lack of lesbian-designated gathering places fosters sticking to the identity of either a tom or dy. That is, contacts by word of mouth that a particular woman is a tom or dy have already been established within the circle, and thus it would be advantageous for these women to remain toms or ladies. Furthermore, in relation to the tom and dy social setting, the ladies gain a sense of empowerment and control in their relationships because they solely initiate the social interaction with toms. According to Tang,

> Ladies can recognize the tomboys, but tomboys cannot recognize the ladies. That is, any woman is a potential lover for the tomboy. So, if you don't think you are a tom and you like women, you can sort them out by recognizing if the woman is a tom or not. You know you can then approach and flirt with her. It's the ladies who are thus giving the first hint to the tomboys.[13]

In addition, not many Thai women can become toms easily, due to the strict dress code in most work settings where, according to Thitiya Glassman, a Thai social worker who has many Thai lesbian friends in Thailand, "if you don't wear a skirt, you cannot get a job."[14] Thus, for those few wealthy women who are either self-employed or work in a family business where relatives tolerate a flexible dress code, taking the identity of a tomboy is more flexible than having to change into tomboy attire after work or quitting one's job if required to wear skirts.

Still, many toms may insist that if they behave differently (i.e., like a traditionally-feminine woman), their behavior would not be natural to them. Both Siriwan and Tang agree that often toms see themselves as more like men than women—"but better than men because they are not men, and thus know how to please and (understand) women better."[15] Other tomboys "don't want to be the way they should be anymore. Tomboys say they are not girls and not men."[16] Perhaps by insisting that they are neither men nor girls in the traditional sense within a compulsory heterosexual and patriarchal society, tomboys are revealing another way to be women—one way that is more emancipatory and fulfilling.

With respect to whether or not tom and dy relationships involve oppressive gender role-playing prevalent in many heterosexual relationships, there seems to be as much diversity as in the reasons tomboys give for manifesting their particular behavior. On one level, tom and dy relationships seem to follow heterosexual guidelines of the male family breadwinner and the female housewife. As Siriwan notes (and she stressed that the women she refers to are of the upper-middle class), "The toms will usually be the ones who go out to work and come home with the money, while ladies stay home and cook. I've talked with some couples back home and they do that."[17] In Hong Kong's upper-middle class butch-femme subculture, "the one who acts in the female role has to do all the domestic work, and the other will go out and earn a living."[18] However, unlike the upper-middle class butch-femme subculture in Hong Kong, such rigid roleplaying is not the norm. According to Tang,

In many relationships the ladies are earning more than the toms. There are many couples in which older ladies are providing everything for the young toms. Thus, these relationships are not similar to heterosexual ones in the conventional economic sense.[19]

However, at the 1990 Asian Lesbian Network (ALN) conference in Bangkok, several Thai lesbians asked, "Is there a power hierarchy among them (toms and ladies)?"[20] (Whether or not the women who raised the question were lesbian-feminists is unclear; however, from my conversations with Tang and Siriwan and the conference's agenda, there is a consensus that lesbian issues should be connected to women's issues.) Unfortunately, because none of the two hundred toms and ladies who attended the conference's opening reception came to the workshops, the Thai lesbians who did conclude that "we cannot speak for them."[21] However, it is clear that toms (ladies) do not become sexually involved with other toms (ladies), but limit their interaction to friendship. According to Siriwan, a common quip among toms and ladies is, "How can two ladies love one another? You can't! It has to be one tom and one dy."[22] Nevertheless, one must stress that a rigid segregation does not exist between toms and ladies for "toms and ladies can become friends if dy doesn't like the tom as a lover."[23]

For those women in lesbian-like relationships who are neither toms nor ladies (i.e., either they change roles often or refuse to label themselves as such), interaction within the circle is limited to friendship as well. Such women who choose to be neither tomboys nor ladies are often jokingly called the Thai word for "amphibian," as their U.S. counterparts were called "kiki" by butches and femmes in the 1950s.[24] Thus, while these women can form friendships with toms and ladies, they are still treated differently—often with ambiguity. Tang shared, "I think I have a mixed identity (i.e., she may sometimes dress like a tomboy, but is reluctant to restrict herself to the identity of a tom or lady), so sometimes I'm treated differently amongst toms and ladies. They don't know how to relate with me."[25] Thus, women like Tang—"amphibians"—can face extreme invisibility, in that the only visible lesbian-like community in Thailand—the tom and dy circle—treats them with confusion, and thus the only community they can identify with is their lovers. As a result, their environment is informal, small, and thus relatively invisible, compared to the upper-middle class tom and dy scene, which is the largest, most visible aspect to lesbian-like expression in Thailand.

Yet invisibility is not only limited to those women who do not adhere to the roles of tomboys and ladies. Popular Thai newspapers and magazines focus primarily on a tom and dy community composed largely of upper-middle class women (most of whom are university and high school students). A common assumption (which is partially true) is that there are few working-class and/or poor toms and ladies because as mentioned earlier, a rather strict dress code exists in the workplace stipulating that women must wear dresses and skirts to be considered women (and thus not be harrassed). As a result, many working-class and poor women cannot afford to quit their jobs or open up their own businesses where they can dress as they please. However, despite such a barrier, there are many working-class toms and ladies, for as Tang states,

> There are a lot of toms who are of the working-class. They work in factories or do more manual work. These women in the factories can afford to dress like toms because there's no set uniform.[26]

Yet for the tomboys in the clerical sector or in workplaces bound by the traditonal dress code, life entails the survival tactic of maintaining a double identity: wearing skirts when they go to work and changing into trousers after leaving work. The tomboy-lady lifestyle is further class-specific, in that due to their economic situation, many working-class toms and ladies socially interact within an informal, and thus less visible, setting than the upper-middle class. Tang describes their situation:

> All the entertainment places in Thailand are for people who have money. Also, most of the people who don't have much education have to work longer hours and six days a week. So, it's not only working-class tomboys and ladies who haven't got a scene (to go out), but the working class in general. Working-class and poor toms and ladies usually go to cheaper department stores to walk around or to corner parks. Occasionally there are (Buddhist) temple fairs or carnivals which charge cheap admission, then a lot of working-class people, including the toms and ladies, would go.[27]

Considering the unstable economic conditions of the working class, it is highly unlikely that even if lesbian bars, night clubs, or bookstores emerge in Thailand—and are arranged merely according to who can pay—that working-class and poor tomboys, ladies, and other women who love women will gain the opportunity to further shape, affirm, and maintain their class, gender, and lesbian-like identities.

Although lesbian-like relationships and lifestyles are as much regional as class specific in Thailand, discussions on same-sex love between Thai women by the media and analysts of sexuality have virtually ignored the lives of rural Thai women who love other women. Because 43 percent of the female population in Thailand live in rural areas, affirming those lesbian-like relationships in the Thai countryside can significantly expand our knowledge about love between women in Thailand.[28] Unfortunately, due to the inadequate communication and transportation facilities in rural areas, information on these women's lives are scarce. In any case, the available information attests that village attitudes towards lesbian-like relationships are diverse, ranging from intolerance to easy-going acceptance. One Thai woman in a lesbian-like relationship found it so hard to live in her village that she migrated to Bangkok and is now working as a domestic servant in the home of one of Tang's friends. Although Tang was unsure about this woman's full predicament, she suspects that the woman's family rejected her because she desired to live in a lesbian-like lifestyle, rather than fulfill the heterosexual institutions of marriage and procreation.[29] Indeed, traditional values of heterosexuality prevail in rural villages. However, often family pressures on women to marry, have children, and stay with and care for one's natal family (youngest daughters are traditionally expected to remain at home and care for the elderly) are due to economic conditions in the countryside. Since the rural family depends on women to fulfill much of the family's and village's agricultural activities for both subsistence and exchange, rural lesbians lack the economic independence and stability needed to create a life without depending on a husband or family.[30] Futhermore, many Thai rural women in general lack spatial independence within village society, since rural families are composed of at least six members and normally one does not have a "room of one's own."[31] Rural households are situated so close to one another that every aspect of a person's life is known by others in the village. Thus, Thai rural women in same-sex relationships would find it difficult to keep their lifestyles and identities secret from village members intolerant of such relationships.

However, the possibility that not all rural societies in Thailand profess unacceptance of lesbian-like relationships reinforces regional specificity concerning societal attitudes toward a woman's right to self sex-orientation. According to Tang's personal experience, some rural village members may actually willingly participate in facilitating social interaction amongst Thai women holding lesbian-like identities.

One time when I was driving in a small van with some other women to a village and got off the van, many of the people there thought I was masculine just because I was driving the van. I don't think I was dressed in a tomboyish way because I was just dressed in trousers and a T-shirt. The clothing didn't really cover up my breasts, so they should've seen clearly that I was a woman. One of the women asked me if I wanted to see my friend. I said, "What's that?" Apparently, they were telling me that there was another tomboy-looking woman living in the next village, and that maybe they should take me there and introduce me to her.[32]

Is such tolerance merely a rare case in Thailand? Or, is it possible that because Thai rural societies are often characterized by a flexible sexual division of labor compared to urban societies—women often assume traditionally "men's work" of harvesting, threshing, and caring for water buffalo, while men often fulfill women's domestic labor and child care—women loving other women in the Thai countryside are allowed more flexibility in their sexual relationships and identity-formation than their sisters in the big cities?[33] Furthermore, how does this instance of social acceptance of lesbian-like identity complicate the subtle forms of discrimination against such an identity in the general Thai society?

Like several of their rural Thai sisters, many Thai women in same-sex relationships confront family and societal expectations that women fulfill the roles of wife, mother, and caretaker of the elderly. Except for the women with more broadminded parents, women who refuse to adhere to these daughterly duties and desire to form a lesbian-like lifestyle often face virtual disownment and the attached guilt. Siriwan describes her experience of ten years ago:

When I told my family, they were so angry that they didn't talk to me for years. One of my brothers told me, "You are a daughter. You have to get married or you will be an old maid. You have to take care of mom the rest of your life." I said to him, "There's no such thing written down that I have to take care of mom for the rest of my life. Enough is enough! I took care of her for over ten years—Now it's your turn!" Fortunately my mom doesn't pressure me to marry because she knows I can take good care of myself and that I will go back to visit the family and do as a good daughter. She knew about my first lover and that I had others, but she doesn't bother me anymore about it. But, some women have to get married, otherwise they will not please their parents. If something goes wrong—like if the parents get sick worrying about you—they blame it on you. That guilt will stay with you for the rest of your life.[34]

The notion that heterosexual marriage, motherhood, and kin-keeping are a woman's "natural" roles are so ingrained in Thai traditions, that women who do not fulfill these responsibilites are treated with pity, as if they were wretched or downtrodden. During the1990 ALN conference, Thai lesbians voiced that "single women are thought pathetic—'Too bad she couldn't find a man.'"[35] Some Thai people may even consider these women's lesbian-like relationships and lifestyles as non-enduring and appetite-whetters due to the lack of an heterosexual outlet. According to Siriwan, many heterosexual Thai men and women joke, "Oh, it's not going to last long. She'll eventually get married and have children!"[36] Despite such discriminatory attitudes subtly hidden under the cloaks of sarcasm and pity, several Thai lesbians recognized at the 1990 ALN conference, "But there is a space for us—we live with a family."[37] Indeed, since Thailand has a strong kinship system, the family may serve as a safe space for Thai women in same-sex relationships, in that Thai women can look to their natal family for financial support and residence, and thus can avoid marriage. Yet at the same time, "most women, especially tomboys and ladies, don't tell their families," for fear of disownment or publicly shaming the family.[38]

Thai women in lesbian-like relationships also must face the contradictions underlying traditional Thai attitudes towards same-sex intimacy between women. On one level few Thai people are willing to discuss sexuality in general, particularly heterosexuality. In fact, "sexuality is very undercover. There is little touching between the sexes. Only very westernized men and women would touch, and only in private."[39] More specifically, the heterosexual and patriarchal society in Thailand may not view heterosexual intimacy as for pleasure (at least for the women's fulfillment), but for procreation. However, in contrast to taboos against heterosexual intimacy in public, Thai society appears very permissive of publicly expressed same-sex intimacy between women. Unlike the inclination in Western societies for people to label a person "homosexual" if he/she is holding hands with someone of the same sex, Thai society is relatively tolerant of those "natural gestures" of women to hold hands, hug, or even sleep together in the same bed. Sunny, a forty-year old Thai lesbian living in Los Angeles for seven years comments:

> When women hug each other, Thai people don't say anything—they just think the women are close friends. Back home, I used to bring many of my girlfriends to my family's house to have dinner, and even introduced them to my mother and aunt. Even when we went out on dates, they didn't think of anything, except that we were good friends. Basically, if you do not have sex in front of them, they will not suspect anything.[40]

While many Thai women who love other women are "happy being quiet" about their relationships, many of these women expressed the need for a more visible lesbian-like community in Thailand, where they can meet to socialize and discuss the ways women like themselves have survived the invisibility.[41] The question is, how will mainstream Thai society react if lesbian-like relationships gain visibility as a legitimate issue?

It is within the context of openly discussing lesbian-like lifestyles that the contradiction in Thai society's tolerance of same-sex intimacy between women emerges. True, there are no laws prohibiting homosexuality in Thailand, and "same sex marriages are not uncommon and may have a Buddhist monk's blessing."[42] However, when I asked several Thai people how they perceived women who love other women, they argued that homosexuality is abnormal, and since Buddhism shuns abnormality, homosexuals would never reach enlightenment. I must stress, however, that such a response may be dangerously biased, in that the Thais who expressed the sentiment were born in Thailand, but have been living in the United States for over twenty-five years. Thus, their ideologies about female homosexuality may be "Westernized" and more discriminatory than the general society in Thailand. On another note, particularly revealing is the growing conservative backlash in Thailand against the tom and dy scene—which emerged into popularity some twenty years ago, but which has become the most visible aspect of lesbian-like expression and youth culture in Thailand. Several years ago, the Ministry of Education criticized the tom and dy scene for corrupting Thai youth culture. According to Tang, the Ministry's complaint was that "apart from not paying attention to school, the tomboys and ladies were not 'normal' women to them."[43] In addition, when the song, "Not Wrong," by Unchalee Jongkadeekit—a popular Thai singer and rumored tomboy—was released in the middle of 1985, "it drew a lot of attention from the public and was criticized by the conservative sector of the press for being bold and giving young people misleading and bad examples."[44] Undoubtedly, the lyrics disturbed much of the conservative public, for they explicitly challenge the notions that same-sex love between women is "strange" and "wrong":

> I've met a young woman of impressive smiles. I have the right to think, the right to love, don't I, when my heart thinks? If she gives me the right, I think I'm not wrong.... Not at all, not at all. Anyone may think it's wrong, but that's not important. Love is from the heart, so how can one forbid it. How can you say I'm wrong.... I don't understand. Who set the rules? I give my honesty...and what's wrong about that? I've realized I'm not wrong. Why should I worry? Like I've said, love is from the heart so it's not wrong to love. Everybody has the right...so don't you worry too much. It's not strange if we fall in love. It's not wrong if we fall in love.[45]

It must be noted that much of the recent public concern over lesbian-like relationships (especially tom and dy relationships) in Thailand has been accentuated or perhaps even ignited, by the growing Western influence in Thailand that is most directly expressed by pressures to modernize. During the last ten years, the Thai school system has undergone drastic changes. While the majority of the schools previously were sex-segregated until the university level, the government is quickly converting the schools to coed institutions, hoping to model the system after American schools. Thus, many young Thai women will not be able to benefit from the lesbian-like paradise of female support, solidarity, and intimacy found in all-girl's schools, convent schools, and the like.

With their sources of interaction and identity under potential threat, many Thai women in lesbian-like relationships are slowly struggling to maintain national and international support networks through such groups as Anjaree, ALN, and ALOA (Asian Lesbians Outside Asia). That is not to say that Thai women who love other women should look to the West for strategies of resistance, as if the West holds the standards of survival and community-building, while non-Western women are merely suffering a "false consciousness." To the contrary, Thai women in same-sex relationships will undoubtedly emancipate themselves from their oppression(s) in the same ways they have conceptualized their lesbian-like identities with cultural, regional, and class specificity, in the hopes of ensuring that love between women remains indigenous to Thailand.

Notes

1. Studies on male homosexuality in Thailand have been made by the following writers: Eric Allyn and John P. Collins, *The Men of Thailand* (San Francisco and Bangkok: Bua Luang, 1987); Peter A. Jackson, *Male Homosexuality in Thailand*, (New York: Global Academic Publishers, 1989); Geoff Puterbaugh, *Encyclopedia of Homosexuality*, ed. Wayne R. Dynes (New York: Garland Publishing, Inc., 1990).
2. Anchana Suwannanond (Tang), letter to *ILIS Newsletter* 10: 1 (1990): 10.
3. Personal interview, Siriwan, Santa Monica, California, May 16, 1991.
4. Lillian Faderman, *Surpassing the Love of Men* (New York: William Morris & Company, Inc., 1981), 229–94.
5. Personal interview, Anchana Suwannanond, telephone interview to Bangkok, Thailand, May 1991.
6. Ibid.
7. Shelley Anderson, "Asian gay/lesbian life has a long history," *Equal Time*, (23 November 1989): 2–3.
8. Personal interview, Anchana Suwannanond.
9. Ibid.
10. Ibid.
11. Personal interview, Anchana Suwannanond; Siriwan.
12. Personal interview, Anchana Suwannanond.
13. Ibid.
14. Personal interview, Thitiya Glassman, telephone interview to Minneapolis, Minnesota, April 1991.
15. Personal interview, Anchana Suwannanond.
16. Alice Henry, Tsehai Berhane-Selassie, and Ruth Wallsgrove, "Feminism in Thailand," *Off Our Backs* (March 1985): 3.
17. Personal interview, Siriwan.
18. Lenore Norrgard, "Opening the Hong Kong Closet," *Out/Look* (Winter 1988): 60.
19. Personal interview, Anchana Suwannanond.
20. Workshop papers from Asian Lesbian Network conference, Bangkok, Thailand, December 7–10, 1990.
21. Ibid.
22. Personal interview, Siriwan.
23. Ibid.
24. Shelley Anderson, "Asian gay/lesbian life has a long history," *Equal Time* (23 November 1989): 2.
25. Personal interview, Anchana Suwannanond.
26. Ibid.
27. Ibid.
28. Ann Olson and Joni Seager, *Women in the World: an International Atlas* (New York:

Simon & Schuster, 1986), country tables.

29. Personal interview, Anchana Suwannanond.

30. However, since the Thai government's implementation of an economic development strategy that has decreased agricultural investmest and increased support for an export-oriented economy, many Thai women from rural villages have been forced by landlessness and poverty to seek employment in the big cities. Most of them find work in Thailand's sex industry as prostitutes, bar girls, masseures, and go-go dancers. For many women, this unfortunate separation from the family often gives them the opportunity to form lesbian-like relationships in the cities, often with women in similar predicaments. A particularly moving testimony is that of Sai (nineteen years old) in *Vindication of the Rights of Whores*, ed. Gail Pheterson (Seattle: Seal Press, 1989), 64, 152, 155–56.

31. Chamrieng Bhavichitra, "Thai Marriage and Family," graduate paper (Indiana University Press, 1962): 35.

32. Personal interview, Anchana Suwannanond.

33. Chamrieng Bhavichitra.

34. Personal interview, Siriwan.

35. Workshop papers from ALN conference, Bangkok, Thailand, 1990.

36. Personal interview, Siriwan.

37. Workshop papers from ALN conference, Bangkok, Thailand, 1990.

38. Ibid.

39. Alice Henry, Tsehai Berhane-Selassie, & Ruth Wallsgrove, "Feminism in Thailand," *Off Our Backs* (March 1985): 4.

40. Personal interview, Sunny, Santa Monica, California, May 16, 1991.

41. Workshop papers from ALN conference, Bangkok, Thailand, 1990.

42. Robin Morgan, ed., *Sisterhood is Global* (Garden City, New York: Anchor Press/Doubleday, 1984), 669.

43. The information on the conservative sector's attitudes towards the tom and dy scene derives from the personal interview with Anchana.

44. Derived from Anchana Suwannanond's English translation of Unchalee Jongkadeekit's song "Not Wrong."

45. Ibid.

15

Gregg Araki and the Queer New Wave

Kimberly Yutani

Los Angeles filmmaker Gregg Araki has been getting attention in what has been conveniently dubbed the "Queer New Wave." Film festivals in 1992 have been dominated by a group of gay films including Araki's *The Living End*. These films are some of the "hippest" of independent films, providing fresh, distinctive, and challenging points of view and aesthetics distinguished by unconventionality. They've proven to be marketable—to the point of being screened in mall cineplexes. However, the films receiving the press and funds are for the most part by and represent white males, excluding lesbians and gays of color, and lesbians in general.

Gregg Araki's films came to my attention at the American Film Institute (AFI) film festival with the description of his second film, *the long weekend (o' despair)* (1989): "a minimalistic gay/bisexual postpunk antithesis to the smug complacency of regressive Hollywood tripe like *The Big Chill*." Then PBS aired his first feature, *three bewildered people in the night* (1987), which I found equally self-absorbed, dark, humorous, and entertaining. Both films were made on $5,000 budgets with Araki doing everything: financing, directing, shooting, editing. These raw, grainy, black-and-white films set an example for what

Director Gregg Araki. Photograph
courtesy of Eric Nakamura/Eyebox.

independent cinema strives for (or at least should)—and represent the unrep-
resented in the mainstream Hollywood movies. Araki is first to admit that his
films "come from a dark, personal place" and makes no qualms about representing a subculture of a generation of twenty-ish characters defined more by
what music they listen to than anything else. His characters are predominantly
artists, gay/lesbian/bisexual, alienated, and filled with "post-modern angst" to
the hilt, who wander through an eerily glamorous and uninhabited nighttime
Los Angeles (Araki eschews location permits) of mini-malls, parking structures, and darkened apartments.

More recently, Araki's film *The Living End*, incorporates all of the rawness,
anger, quirkiness, and despair of his previous films to create a color, bigger-
budgeted movie that challenges the "couple on-the-run road movie" genre by
having two gay HIV-positive lovers as its protagonists, and bashes back at some
of the more "evil and oppressive" members of society (gay bashers; gay bashers
in sex, lies, and videotape T-shirts; police; Bush) and has a lot of cathartic fun
along the way. *The Living End* also has received both independent and mainstream attention during the past year amidst the Queer New Wave.

Indeed, calling the group of exceedingly popular and successful films made
by and representing gays and lesbians a "Queer New Wave" is controversial.
Although positive feedback (critically and financially) proves queer films have
an audience, such labels are simply convenient and pigeonhole and limit the
works and filmmakers, overlooking the fact that lesbians and gays have always
made movies. Most concisely, B. Ruby Rich explains:

Of course, the new queer films and videos aren't all the same, and don't share a single aesthetic vocabulary or strategy or concern. Yet they are nonetheless united by a common style. Call it Homo Pomo: there are traces in all of them of appropriation and pastiche, irony, as well as a reworking of history with social constructionism very much in mind. Definitively breaking with older humanist approaches and the films and tapes that accompanied identity politics, these works are irreverent, energetic, alternately minimalist and excessive. Above all, they're full of pleasure.[1]

With this, films by Christopher Munch, Tom Kalin, and Derek Jarman come to mind. These films "out" the past and reevaluate history: Kalin's *Swoon* (1992) is another depiction, along with Hitchcock's *Rope* (1948) and Fleischer's *Compulsion* (1959), of the murderers Leopold and Loeb—yet this time they are eplicitly lovers. Munch's *The Hours and Times* (1991) also takes on famous subjects, John Lennon and Beatles' manager Brian Epstein, their weekend trip to Barcelona and explores the extent of the relationship between the men. While Kalin and Munch are relatively new names to the "queer film scene," Derek Jarman is a pioneer of sorts with his films: *Sebastiane* (1975), *Jubilee* (1977), *Angelic Conversation* (1984), and *The Last of England* (1987). His most recent, *Edward II* (1991), goes back in history to out Christopher Marlowe, Marlowe's play, and a king—and examines homophobia and misogyny—within a narrative that combines the period piece with the contemporary radical political action of Britain's OutRage.

When discussing the Queer New Wave of the 90s, the big winners of the 1991 Sundance Film Festival cannot be overlooked. Todd Haynes' *Poison* (1991) and Jennie Livingston's documentary *Paris Is Burning* (1990) are groundbreaking works. Not only did they reveal a definite audience for gay films, Haynes' Genet-inspired *Poison* took risks in creating a non-linear narrative to interweave three tales (Hero, Horror, Homo) into one film, to make an idiosyncratic but coherent work. It also created a controversial (and ticket selling) stir with the NEA. At the same time, Livingston's winning documentary of New York City drag balls featuring black and Latino gay men exposes a marginalized group within a marginalized group. Meanwhile Gus Van Sant—whose *My Own Private Idaho* (1991) used two "teen idol" actors (Keanu Reeves and River Phoenix) to explore the world of Portland street hustlers, experimenting with narrative by slipping Shakespeare's *Henry IV* into his gritty, funny, and sensitive work.

For the most part, the Queer New Wave has been dominated by white males as both artists and subjects, and Gregg Araki's *The Living End* is commonly included in mass media. Araki defines himself as "a gay Asian American" and "a card-carrying (albeit controversial) member of two, count 'em, two, 'oppressed' subcultural groups."[2] During the summer of 1992, when Araki emblazoned an *LA Weekly* cover (August 21–27, 1992) as the "guerrilla godard," a friend of mine remarked, "He's beautiful.... Why doesn't he have Asian characters in his films?" Indeed, his "lacking of color" in his films is a point that deems him controversial, particularly in the Asian American community. So far all of his films have only featured white characters. The absence of characters of color in his three films make it difficult to discuss his films in any context of ethnicity. Yet looking at his films and judging from what he says, for Araki, ethnicity isn't necessarily an issue. I spoke to him about this point to which he responded, "I've always wanted to have an Asian character in my films but it just comes down to who the best actor is. I mean, I think I should choose the best actor before I judge ethnicity."[3] While in the past he was working under extremely limited budgets, his more substantially funded upcoming film, *Totally F***ed Up*, his "gay John Hughes movie directed by Godard," features a multiethnic (Latino, half African-American, Persian, and half, yes, Asian) cast of teens. Such a film might appease some of his critics—with this addition of color—yet is his philosophy "acceptable"? Araki says of *Totally F***ed Up*, "The parts are not written in any sort of ethnic way. Their ethnicity was completely interchangeable. The ethnicity of the characters was like wardrobe, essentially."[4] Again, as in all of his films, the relationships are bound not by ethnicity, but by the interests and sexuality of Americanized, "integrated," characters. Filmmaker Roddy Bogawa takes a similar stance and questions expectations from him as an Asian American and filmmaker: "Why should the work be discussed in terms of my racial identity?"[5]

Few Asian American filmmakers (gay or straight) are discussing gay or lesbian issues in an Asian context with perhaps, the exception of Richard Fung and a few others (incidentally, Fung's piece in *Moving the Image* is recommended reading regarding the mutual exclusiveness of "gay" and "Asian" work). In addition, the issues at hand are complicated. Fung remarks, "Many Asian or gay and lesbian tapes and films are still guided by notions of 'positive images'."[6] Within a marginalized group, there is a concern as to how one is being portrayed in respect to "the bigger picture." What distinguishes the new queer films from say, the TV movie of the week, is the idea of "political correctness" or "positive images." *My Own Private Idaho* was criticized for its narcoleptic hustler character, *Swoon* boldly tackles the gay murderers Leopold and Loeb, while *The Living End* is ironically billed as "an irresponsible movie by gregg araki." Araki's HIV-positive lovers aren't distracted by preachy morality, but are guided by a *carpe diem* philosophy in their nihilistic situation where they wield guns, extinguish their enemies, hit the road, and have unsafe sex. In short, what is occurring is an unselfconscious group of filmmakers taking narrative and formal risks and creating complex characters.

While most of the criticism of the Queer New Wave concerns the absence of women, a good deal of criticism of *The Living End* comes from the representation of women. In *The Living End* the women are inconsequential. The protagonists are on the run from the law, in an opposites attract, l'amour fou genre film made gay. Jon (Craig Gilmore) is a cute, uptight film critic while Luke looks and acts like a queer frat boy but is a likeable, complete romantic. The hitchhiking Luke (Mike Dytri) has a run-in with two "killer" lesbians (a sensitive subject since the *Basic Instinct* uproar). The women are minor, innocuous, campy characters, and simply add to the over-the-top tone of the hostile city life that the protagonists escape. The lesbian characters (Fern and Daisy, played by performance artist Johann Went and ex-Warhol actress Mary Woronov) are amusing, inefficient killers who function more as targets to ridicule lesbians who stereotypically listen to folk music—"Don't these wenches listen to anything besides k. d. lang and Michelle Shocked?" Luke wonders. However, what does deserve criticism is the character of Darcy, played by Darcy Marta who starred in Araki's three bewildered people. Darcy serves as the ultimate fag hag—she's an artist herself (frustrated), has an inert boyfriend, is Jon's confidant who listens to his problems, worries about him to the point that her own life is disrupted, waits for his calls (collect), cleans up matters for him while he's being irresponsible. Perhaps it's an attempt to echo the relationship in three bewildered people between the straight woman (Alicia) and David, the gay male, but where it's handled less skillfully. In the love triangle between Alicia, David, and Craig—Alicia is essential to the narrative (and even has equal share in complainer and complainee status)—whereas in *The Living End*, Darcy's presence is disruptive and intrusive to the main, "real" story of the boys on the road.

Not only is the representation of lesbians and women in general lacking, but lesbian filmmakers are conspicuously absent from the queer cinema movement. Lesbian filmmakers have been subject to limited funding, hence confining their work to video—although in fact, eighteen year-old Sadie Benning has been a film fest favorite with her twenty-dollar budgeted self-as-subject videos shot with a Fisher-Price Pixelvision camera. However, according to Cherry Smyth: "It is hardly surprising, in terms of economics alone, that more queer women are working in photography than in film or video. In the New Queer Wave, lesbians are drowning."[7] Apparently there are lesbian filmmakers in the film festival circuit (working in video, creating short films, documentaries), but they are vastly overshadowed by the men who are making the feature-length, narrative films that attract the attention of both funding and press. British filmmaker Pratibha Parmar's documentaries *A Place of Rage* (not necessarily queer but "queer positive" feminist, featuring Angela Davis, Alice Walker, and Trinh T. Minh-ha) and *Khush* are impressive works but are seldom mentioned alongside the works of Araki, Kalin, Haynes, etc.

Parmar echoes Smyth's sentiments and adds: "these festivals are programmed predominantly by white gay men and women, who prioritize their own constituencies, further marginalizing queers of color."[8] Parmar has a point, but that is not to say filmmakers of color (although mostly male) are not getting attention in the Queer New Wave. Marlon Riggs's *Tongues Untied,* featuring the sensual poetry of Essex Hemphill and looking unabashedly at "black men loving black men" caused a stir when PBS aired the film in its P.O.V. series. Isaac Julien from Britain, whose *Passion of Remembrance* (1986) and *Looking for Langston* (1989) now seem like gay "classics," made *Young Soul Rebels* (1991), which takes on an interracial relationship between a punk and a soul boy, and racial and homophobic violence in London during the Queen's Silver Jubilee in 1977. At the same time and locale is Hanif Kureishi's *London Kills Me* (1992), which in Kureishi's directing debut, chose to explore street life and drugs rather than his "expertise" of sexual politics and racial issues of his previous screenwritings, *My Beautiful Laundrette* (1984) and *Sammy and Rosie Get Laid* (1987).

The absence of lesbian filmmakers and representation within queer cinema, and lesbians and gays of color is problematic, and disturbingly replicates the mainstream in a sense. Although gender and racial inequality exists in what is an exciting movement of progress, optimistically, the queer films being made are creating the space for lesbians and lesbians and gays of color. The queer films are unconventional, risk-taking, and thought-provoking—all of the characteristics that I have consistently seen in Gregg Araki's work—and deserve a permanent space in an independent film forum. Araki's upcoming *Totally F***ed Up* is definitely something to look forward to, featuring half-Vietnamese actor Jimmy Duval, whom he boasts is his new superstar ("my Joe Dallesandro"). And perhaps the superficial "Queer Cinema" label will be shed with the aforementioned Chris Munch, Jennie Livingston, Todd Haynes making films sans "gay themes." Araki adds that his fifth, his "straight" film promises to be his most offensive and shocking, reassuring that his edge is a permanent fixture in independent cinema.

Notes

1. B. Ruby Rich, "A Queer Sensation," *The Village Voice,* 24 March 1992, 42.
2. Gregg Araki, *Moving the Image: Independent Asian Pacific American Media Arts* (Los Angeles: Asian American Studies Center, UCLA and Visual Communications, 1991), 69.
3. Author interview with Araki, March 5, 1992.
4. Lawrence Chua, "Profiles and Positions," *BOMB* (Fall 1992): 27.
5. Roddy Bogawa, "An(other) Refection on Race?" *Moving the Image,* 209.
6. Richard Fung, "Center the Margins," *Moving the Image,* 67.
7. Cherry Smyth, "Trash Femme Cocktail," *Sight and Sound* (September 1992): 39.
8. Pratibha Parmar, "Queer Questions," *Sight and Sound* (September 1992): 35.

Looking for My Penis
The Eroticized Asian in Gay Video Porn

Richard Fung

> Several scientists have begun to examine the relation between personality and human reproductive behavior from a gene-based evolutionary perspective.... In this vein we reported a study of racial difference in sexual restraint such that Orientals > whites > blacks. Restraint was indexed in numerous ways, having in common a lowered allocation of bodily energy to sexual functioning. We found the same racial pattern occurred on gamete production (dizygotic birthing frequency per 100: Mongoloids, 4; Caucasoids, 8; Negroids, 16), intercourse frequencies (premarital, marital, extramarital), developmental precocity (age at first intercourse, age at first pregnancy, number of pregnancies), primary sexual characteristics (size of penis, vagina, testis, ovaries), secondary sexual characteristics (salient voice, muscularity, buttocks, breasts), and biologic control of behavior (periodicity of sexual response predictability of life history from onset of puberty), as well as in androgen levels and sexual attitudes.[1]

This passage from the *Journal of Research in Personality* was written by University of Western Ontario psychologist Philippe Rushton, who enjoys considerable controversy in Canadian academic circles and in the popular media. His thesis, articulated throughout his work, appropriates biological studies of the continuum of reproductive strategies of oysters through chimpanzees and posits that degree of "sexuality"—interpreted as penis and vagina size, frequency of intercourse, buttock and lip size—correlates positively with criminality and sociopathic behavior and inversely with intelligence, health, and longevity. Rushton sees race as the determining factor and places East Asians (Rushton uses the word *Orientals*) on one end of the spectrum and blacks on the other. Since whites fall squarely in the middle, the position of perfect balance, there is no need for analysis, and they remain free of scrutiny.

Notwithstanding its profound scientific shortcomings, Rushton's work serves as an excellent articulation of a dominant discourse on race and sexuality in Western society—a system of ideas and reciprocal practices that originated in Europe simultaneously with (some argue as a conscious justification for[2]) colonial expansion and slavery. In the nineteenth century these ideas took on a scientific gloss with social Darwinism and eugenics. Now they reappear, somewhat altered, in psychology journals from the likes of Rushton. It is important to add that these ideas have also permeated the global popular consciousness. Anyone who has been exposed to Western television or advertising images, which is much of the world, will have absorbed this particular constellation of stereotyping and racial hierarchy. In Trinidad in the 1960s, on the outer reaches of the empire, everyone in my schoolyard was thoroughly versed in these "truths" about the races.

Historically, most organizing against racism has concentrated on fighting discrimination that stems from the intelligence-social behavior variable assumed by Rushton's scale. Discrimination based on perceived intellectual ability does, after all, have direct ramifications in terms of education and employment, and therefore for survival. Until recently, issues of gender and sexuality remained a low priority for those who claimed to speak for the communities.[3] But antiracist strategies that fail to subvert the race-gender status quo are of seriously limited value. Racism cannot be narrowly defined in terms of race hatred. Race is a factor in even our most intimate relationships.

The contemporary construction of race and sex as exemplified by Rushton has endowed black people, both men and women, with a threatening hypersexuality. Asians, on the other hand, are collectively seen as undersexed.[4] But here I want to make some crucial distinctions. First, in North America, stereotyping has focused almost exclusively on what recent colonial language designates as "Orientals"—that is East and southeast Asian peoples—as opposed to the "Orientalism" discussed by Edward Said, which concerns the Middle East. This current, popular usage is based more on a perception of similar physical features—black hair, "slanted" eyes, high cheek bones, and so on—than through a reference to common cultural traits. South Asians, people whose backgrounds are in the Indian subcontinent and Sri Lanka, hardly figure at all in North American popular representations, and those few images are ostensibly devoid of sexual connotation.[5]

Second, within the totalizing stereotype of the "Oriental," there are competing and sometimes contradictory sexual associations based on nationality. So, for example, a person could be seen as Japanese and somewhat kinky, or Filipino and "available." The very same person could also be seen as "Oriental" and therefore sexless. In addition, the racial hierarchy revamped by Rushton is itself in tension with an earlier and only partially eclipsed depiction of *all* Asians as having an undisciplined and dangerous libido. I am referring to the writings of the early European explorers and missionaries, but also to antimiscegenation laws and such specific legislation as the 1912 Saskatchewan law that barred white women from employment in Chinese-owned business.

Finally, East Asian women figure differently from men both in reality and in representation. In "Lotus Blossoms Don't Bleed," Renee Tajima points out that in Hollywood films:

> There are two basic types: the Lotus Blossom Baby (a.k.a. China Doll, Geisha Girl, shy Polynesian beauty, et al.) and the Dragon Lady (Fu Manchu's various female relations, prostitutes, devious madames).... Asian women in film are, for the most part, passive figures who exist to serve men—as love interests for white men (re: Lotus Blossoms) or as partners in crime for men of their own kind (re: Dragon Ladies).[6]

Further:

> Dutiful creatures that they are, Asian women are often assigned the task of expendability in a situation of illicit love.... Noticeably lacking is the portrayal of love relationships between Asian women and Asian men, particularly as lead characters.[7]

Because of their supposed passivity and sexual compliance, Asian women have been fetishized in dominant representation, and there is a large and growing body of literature by Asian women on the oppressiveness of these images. Asian men, however—at least since Sessue Hayakawa, who made a Hollywood career in the 1920s of representing the Asian man as sexual threat[8]—have been consigned to one of two categories: the egghead/wimp, or—in what may be analogous to the lotus blossom-dragon lady dichotomy—the kung fu master/ninja/samurai. He is sometimes dangerous, sometimes friendly, but almost always characterized by a desexualized Zen asceticism. So whereas, as Fanon tells us, "the Negro is eclipsed. He is turned into a penis. He *is* a penis,"[9] the Asian man is defined by a striking absence down there. And if Asian men have no sexuality, how can we have homosexuality?

Even as recently as the early 1980s, I remember having to prove my queer credentials before being admitted with other Asian men into a Toronto gay club. I do not believe it was a question of a color barrier. Rather, my friends and I felt that the doorman was genuinely unsure about our sexual orientation. We also felt that had we been white and dressed similarly, our entrance would have been automatic.[10]

Although a motto for the lesbian and gay movements has been "we are everywhere," Asians are largely absent from the images produced by both the political and the commercial sectors of the mainstream gay and lesbian communities. From the earliest articulation of the Asian gay and lesbian movements, a principal concern has therefore been visibility. In political organizing, the demand for a voice, or rather the demand to be heard, has largely been responded to by the problematic practice of "minority" representation on panels and boards.[11] But since racism is a question of power and not of numbers, this strategy has often led to a dead-end tokenistic integration, failing to address the real imbalances.

Creating a space for Asian gay and lesbian representation has meant, among other things, deepening an understanding of what is at stake for Asians in coming out publicly.[12] As is the case for many other people of color and especially immigrants, our families and our ethnic communities are a rare source of affirmation in a racist society. In coming out, we risk (or feel that we risk) losing this support, though the ever-growing organizations of lesbian and gay Asians have worked against this process of cultural exile. In my own experience, the existence of a gay Asian community broke down the cultural schizophrenia in which I related on the one hand to a heterosexual family that affirmed my ethnic culture and, on the other, to a gay community that was predominantly white. Knowing that there was support also helped me come out to my family and further bridge the gap.

If we look at commercial gay sexual representation, it appears that the antiracist movements have had little impact: the images of men and male beauty are still of *white* men and *white* male beauty. These are the standards against which we compare both ourselves and often our brothers —Asian, black, native, and Latino.[13] Although other people's rejection (or fetishization) of us according to the established racial hierarchies may be experienced as oppressive, we are not necessarily moved to scrutinize our own desire and its relationship to the hegemonic image of the white man.[14]

In my lifelong vocation of looking for my penis, trying to fill in the visual void, I have come across only a handful of primary and secondary references to Asian male sexuality in North American representation. Even in my own video work, the stress has been on deconstructing sexual representation and only marginally on creating erotica. So I was very excited at the discovery of a Vietnamese American working in gay porn.

Having acted in six videotapes, Sum Yung Mahn is perhaps the only Asian to qualify as a gay porn "star." Variously known as Brad Troung or Sam or Sum Yung Mahn, he has worked for a number of different production studios. All of the tapes in which he appears are distributed through International Wavelength, a San Francisco-based mail order company whose catalog entries feature Asians in American, Thai, and Japanese productions. According to the owner of International Wavelength, about 90 percent of the Asian tapes are bought by white men, and the remaining 10 percent are purchased by Asians. But the number of Asian buyers is growing.

In examining Sum Yung Mahn's work, it is important to recognize the different strategies used for fitting an Asian actor into the traditionally white world of gay porn and how the terms of entry are determined by the perceived demands of an intended audience. Three tapes, each geared toward a specific erotic interest, illustrate these strategies.

Below the Belt (1985, directed by Philip St. John, California Dream Machine Productions), like most porn tapes, has an episodic structure. All the sequences involve the students and *sense* of an all-male karate *dojo*. The authenticity of the setting is proclaimed with the opening shots of a gym full of *gi*-clad, serious-faced young men going through their weapons exercises. Each of the main actors is introduced in turn; with the exception of the teacher, who has dark hair, all fit into the current porn conventions of Aryan, blond, shaved, good looks.[15] Moreover, since Sum Yung Mahn is not even listed in the opening credits, we can surmise that this tape is not targeted to an audience with any particular erotic interest in Asian men. Most gay video porn exclusively uses white actors; those tapes having the least bit of racial integration are pitched to the specialty market throughout outlets such as International Wave-lengths.[16] This visual apartheid stems, I assume, from an erroneous perception that the sexual appetites of gay men are exclusive and unchangeable.

A Karate dojo offers a rich opportunity to introduce Asian actors. One might image it as the gay Orientalist's dream project. But given the intended audience for this video, the erotic appeal of the dojo, except for the costumes and a few misplaced props (Taiwanese and Korean flags for a Japanese art form?) are completely appropriated into a white world.

The tape's action occurs in a gym, in the students' apartments, and in a garden. The one scene with Sum Yung Mahn is a dream sequence. Two students, Robbie and Stevie, are sitting in a locker room. Robbie confesses that he has been having strange dreams about Greg, their teacher. Cut to the dream sequence, which is coded by clouds of green smoke. Robbie is wearing a red headband with black markings suggesting script (if indeed they belong to an Asian language, they are not the Japanese or Chinese characters that one would expect). He is trapped in an elaborate snare. Enter a character in a black *ninja* mask, wielding a *nanchaku*. Robbie narrates: "I knew this evil samurai would kill me." The masked figure is menacingly running the nanchaku chain under Robbie's genitals when Greg, the teacher, appears and disposes of him. Robbie explains to Stevie in the locker room: "I knew that I owed him my life, and I knew I had to please him [long pause] in any way that he wanted." During that pause we cut back to the dream. Amid more puffs of smoke, Greg, carrying a man in his arms, approaches a low platform. Although Greg's back is toward the camera, we can see that the man is wearing the red headband that identifies him as Robbie. As Greg lays him down, we see that Robbie has "turned Japanese"! It's Sum Yung Mahn.

Greg fucks Sum Yung Mahn, who is always face down. The scene constructs anal intercourse for the Asian Robbie as an act of submission, not of pleasure: unlike other scenes of anal intercourse in the tape, for example, there is no dubbed dialogue on the order of "Oh yeah...fuck me harder!" but merely ambiguous groans. Without coming, Greg leaves. A group of (white) men wearing Japanese outfits encircle the platform, and Asian Robbie, or "the Oriental boy," as he is listed in the final credits, turns to lie on his back. He sucks a cock, licks someone's balls. The other men come all over his body; he comes. The final shot of the sequence zooms in to a close-up of Sum Yung Mahn's headband, which dissolves to a similar close-up of Robbie wearing the same headband, emphasizing that the two actors represent one character.

We now cut back to the locker room. Robbie's story has made Stevie horny. He reaches into Robbie's pants, pulls out his penis, and sex follows. In his Asian manifestation, Robbie is fucked and sucks others off (Greek passive/French active/bottom). His passivity is pronounced, and he is never shown other than prone. As a white man, his role is completely reversed: he is at first sucked off by Stevie, and then he fucks him (Greek active/French passive/top). Neither of Robbie's manifestations veers from his prescribed role.

To a greater extent than most other gay porn tapes, *Below the Belt* is directly about power. The hierarchical dojo setting is milked for its evocation of dominance and submission. With the exception of one very romantic sequence midway through the tape, most of the actors stick to their defined roles of top or bottom. Sex, especially anal sex, as punishment is a recurrent image. In this genre of gay pornography, the role-playing in the dream sequence is perfectly apt. What is significant, however, is how race figures into the equation. In a tape that appropriates emblems of Asian power (karate), the only place for a real Asian actor is as a caricature of passivity. Sum Yung Mahn does not portray an Asian, but rather the liberalization of a metaphor, so that by being passive, Robbie actually becomes "Oriental." At a more practical level, the device of the dream also allows the producers to introduce an element of the mysterious, the exotic, without disrupting the racial status quo of the rest of the tape. Even in the dream sequence, Sum Yung Mahn is at the center of the frame as spectacle, having minimal physical involvement with the men around him. Although the sequence ends with his climax, he exists for the pleasure of others.

Richard Dyer, writing about gay porn, states that:

> although the pleasure of anal sex (that is, of being anally fucked) is represented, the narrative is never organized around the desire to be fucked, but around the desire to ejaculate (whether or not following from anal intercourse). Thus, although a level of public representation gay men may be thought of as deviant and disruptive of masculine norms because we assert the pleasure of being fucked and the eroticism of the anus, in our pornography this takes a back seat.[17]

Although Tom Waugh's amendment to this argument—that anal pleasure is represented in individual sequences[18]—also holds true for *Below the Belt*, as a whole the power of the penis and the pleasure of ejaculation are clearly the narrative's organizing principles. As with the vast majority of North American tapes featuring Asians, the problem is not the representation of anal pleasure per se, but rather that the narratives privilege the penis while always assigning the Asian the role of bottom; Asian and anus are conflated. In the case of Sum Yung Mahn, being fucked may well be his personal sexual preference. But the fact remains that there are very few occasions in North American video porn in which an Asian fucks a white man, so few, in fact, that International Wavelength promotes the tape *Studio X* (1986) with the blurb "Sum Yung Mahn makes history as the first Asian who fucks a non-Asian."[19]

Although I agree with Waugh that in gay as opposed to straight porn "the spectator's positions in relation to the representations are open and in flux,"[20] this observation applies only when all the participants are white. Race introduces another dimension that may serve to close down some of this mobility. This is not to suggest that the experience of gay men of color with this kind of sexual representation is the same as that of heterosexual women with regard to the gendered gaze of straight porn. For one thing, Asian gay men are men. We can therefore physically experience the pleasures depicted on the screen, since we too have erections and ejaculations and can experience anal penetration. A shifting identification may occur despite the racially defined roles, and most gay Asian men in North America are used to obtaining pleasure form all-white pornography. This, of course, goes hand in hand with many problems of self-image and sexual identify. Still, I have been struck by the unanimity with which gay Asian men I have met, from all over this continent as well as from Asia, immediately identify and resist these representations. Whenever I mention the topic of Asian actors in American porn, the first question I am asked is whether the Asian is simply shown getting fucked.

Asian Knights (1985, directed by Ed Sung, William Richhe Productions), the second tape I want to consider, has an Asian producer-director and a predominantly Asian cast. In its first scenario, two Asian men, Brad and Rick, are seeing a white psychiatrist because they are unable to have sex with each other:

Rick: We never have sex with other Asians. We usually have sex with
    Caucasian guys.
Counselor: Have you had the opportunity to have sex together?
Rick: Yes, a coupla times, but we never get going.

Homophobia, like other forms of oppression, is seldom dealt with in gay video porn. With the exception of safe sex tapes that attempt a rare blend of the pedagogical with the pornographic, social or political issues are not generally associated with the erotic. It is therefore unusual to see one of the favored discussion topics for gay Asian consciousness-raising groups employed as a sex fantasy in *Asian Knights*. The desexualized image of Asian men that I have described has seriously affected our relationships with one another, and often gay Asian men find it difficult to see each other beyond the terms of platonic friendship or competition, to consider other Asian men as lovers.

True to the conventions of porn, minimal counseling from the psychiatrist convinces Rick and Brad to shed their clothes. Immediately sprouting erections, they proceed to have sex. But what appears to be an assertion of gay Asian desire is quickly derailed. As Brad and Rick make love on the couch, the camera cross-cuts to the psychiatrist looking on from an armchair. The rhetoric of the editing suggests that we are observing the two Asian men from his point of view. Soon the white man takes off his clothes and joins in. He immediately takes up a position at the center of the action—and at the center of the frame. What appeared to be a "conversion fantasy" for gay Asian desire was merely a ruse. Brad and Rick's temporary mutual absorption really occurs to establish the superior sexual draw of the white psychiatrist, a stand-in for the white male viewer, who is the real sexual subject of the tape. And the question of Asian-Asian desire, though presented as the main narrative force of the sequence, is deflected, or rather reframed from a white perspective.

Sex between the two Asian men in this sequence can be related somewhat to heterosexual sex in some gay porn films, such as those produced by the Gage brothers. In *Heatstroke* (1982), for example, sex with a woman is used to establish the authenticity of the straight man who is about to be seduced into gay sex. It dramatizes the significance of the conversion from the sanctioned object of desire, underscoring the power of the gay man to incite desire in his socially defined superior. It is also tied up with the fantasies of (female) virginity and conquest in Judeo-Christian and other patriarchal societies. The therapy session sequence of *Asian Knights* also suggests parallels to representations of lesbians in straight porn, representations that are not meant to eroticize women loving women, but rather to titillate and empower the sexual ego of the heterosexual male viewer.

Asian Knights is organized to sell representations of Asians to white men. Unlike Sum Yung Mahn in *Below the Belt*, the actors are therefore more expressive and sexually assertive, as often the seducers as the seduced. But though the roles shift during the predominantly oral sex, the Asians remain passive in anal intercourse, except that they are now shown to want it! How much this assertion of agency represents a step forward remains a question.

Even in the one sequence of *Asian Knights* in which the Asian actor fucks the white man, the scenario privileges the pleasure of the white man over that of the Asian. The sequence begins with the Asian reading a magazine. When the white man (played by porn star Eric Stryker) returns home from a hard day at the office, the waiting asian asks how his day went, undresses him (even taking off his socks), and proceeds to massage his back.[21] The Asian man acts the role of the mythologized geisha or "the good wife" as fantasized in the mail-order bride business. And, in fact, the "house boy" is one of the most persistent white fantasies about Asian men. The fantasy is also a reality in many Asian countries where economic imperialism gives foreigners, whatever their race, the pick of handsome men in financial need. The accompanying cultural imperialism grants status to those Asians with white lovers. White men who for various reasons, especially age, are deemed unattractive in their own countries, suddenly find themselves elevated and desired.

From the opening shot of painted lotus blossoms on a screen to the shot of a Japanese garden that separates the episodes, from the Chinese pop music to the chinoiserie in the apartment, there is a conscious attempt in *Asian Knights* to evoke a particular atmosphere.[22] Self-conscious "Oriental" signifiers are part and parcel of a colonial fantasy—and reality—that empowers one kind of gay man over another. Though I have known Asian men in dependent relations with older, wealthier white men, as an erotic fantasy the house boy scenario tends to work one way. I know of no scenarios of Asian men and white house boys. It is not the representation of the fantasy that offends, or even the fantasy itself, rather the uniformity with which these narratives reappear and the uncomfortable relationship they have to real social conditions.

International Skin (1985, directed by William Richhe, N'wayvo Richhe Productions), as its name suggests, features a Latino, a black man, Sum Yung Mahn, and a number of white actors. Unlike the other tapes I have discussed, there are no "Oriental" devices. And although Sum Yung Mahn and all the men of color are inevitable fucked (without reciprocating), there is mutual sexual engagement between the white and nonwhite characters.

In this tape Sum Yung Mahn is Brad, a film student making a movie for his class. Brad is the narrator, and the film begins with a self-reflexive "head and shoulders" shot of Sum Yung Mahn explaining the scenario. The film we are watching supposedly represents Brad's point of view. But here again the tape is not targeted to black, Asian, or Latino men; though Brad introduces all of these men as his friends, no two men of color ever meet on screen. Men of color are not invited to participate in the internationalism that is being sold, except through identification with white characters. This tape illustrates how an agenda of integration becomes problematic if it frames the issue solely in terms of black-white, Asian-white mixing: it perpetuates a system of white-centeredness.

The gay Asian viewer is not constructed as sexual subject in any of this work—not on the screen, not as a viewer. I may find Sum Yung Mahn attractive, I may desire his body, but I am always aware that he is not meant for me. I may lust after Eric Stryker and imagine myself as the Asian who is having sex with him, but the role the Asian plays in the scene with him is demeaning. It is not that there is anything wrong with the image of servitude per se, but rather that it is one of the few fantasy scenarios in which we figure, and we are always in the role of servant.

Are there then no pleasures for an Asian viewer? The answer to this question is extremely complex. There is first of all no essential Asian viewer. The race of the person viewing says nothing about how race figures in his or her own desires. Uniracial white representations in porn may not in themselves present a problem in addressing many gay Asian men's desires. But the issue is not simply that porn may deny pleasures to some gay Asian men. We also need to examine what role the pleasure of porn plays in securing a consensus about race and desirability that ultimately works to our disadvantage.

Though the sequences I have focused on in the preceding examples are those in which the discourses about Asian sexuality are most clearly articulated, they do not define the totality of depiction in these tapes. Much of the time the actors merely reproduce or attempt to reproduce the conventions of pornography. The fact that, with the exception of Sum Yung Mahn, they rarely succeed—because of their body type, because Midwestern-cowboy-porn dialect with Vietnamese intonation is just a bit incongruous, because they groan or gyrate just a bit too much—more than anything brings home the relative rigidity of the genre's codes. There is little seamlessness here. There are times, however, when the actors appear neither as simulated whites nor as symbolic others. There are several moments in *International Skin*, for example, in which the focus shifts from the genitals to hands caressing a body; these moments feel to me more "genuine." I do not mean this in the sense of an essential Asian sexuality, but rather a moment is captured in which the actor stops pretending. He does not stop acting, but he stops pretending to be a white porn star. I find myself focusing on moments like these, in which the racist ideology of the text seems to be temporarily suspended or rather eclipsed by the erotic power of the moment.

In "Pornography and the Doubleness of Sex for Women," Joanna Russ writes:

> Sex is ecstatic, autonomous and lovely for women. Sex is violent, dangerous and unpleasant for women. I don't mean a dichotomy (i.e., two kinds of women or even two kinds of sex) but rather a continuum in which no one's experience is wholly positive or negative.[35]

Gay Asian men are men and therefore not normally victims of the rape, incest, or other sexual harassment to which Russ is referring. However, there is a kind of doubleness, of ambivalence, in the way that Asian men experience contemporary North American gay communities. The "ghetto," the mainstream gay movement, can be a place of freedom and sexual identity. But it is also a site of racial, cultural, *and* sexual alienation sometimes more pronounced than that in straight society. For me sex is a source of pleasure, but also a site of humiliation and pain. Released from the social constraints against expressing overt racism in public, the intimacy of sex can provide my (non-Asian) partner an opening for letting me know my place—sometimes literally, as when after we come, he turns over and asks where I come from.[24] Most gay Asian men I know have similar experiences.

This is just one reality that differentiates the experiences and therefore the political priorities of gay Asians and, I think, other gay men of color from those of white men. For one thing we cannot afford to take a libertarian approach. Porn can be an active agent in representing *and* reproducing a sex-race status quo. We cannot attain a healthy alliance without coming to terms with these differences.

The barriers that impede pornography from providing representations of Asian men that are erotic and politically palatable (as opposed to correct) are similar to those that inhibit the Asian documentary, the Asian feature, the Asian experimental film and videotape. We are seen as too peripheral, not commercially visible—not the general audience. *Looking for Langston* (1988),[25] which is the first film I have seen that affirms rather than appropriates the sexuality of black gay men, was produced under exceptional economic circumstances that freed it from the constraints of the marketplace.[26] Should we call for an independent gay Asian pornography? Perhaps I am, in a utopian sort of way, though I feel that the problems in North America's porn conventions are manifold and go beyond the question of race. There is such a limited vision of what constitutes the erotic.

In Canada, the major debate about race and representation has shifted from an emphasis on the image to a discussion of appropriation and control of production and distribution—who gets to produce the work. But as we have seen in the case of *Asian Knights*, the race of the producer is no automatic guarantee of "consciousness" about these issues or of a different product. Much depends on who is constructed as the audience for the work. In any case, it is not surprising that under capitalism, finding my penis may ultimately be a matter of dollars and cents.

Discussion

> AUDIENCE MEMBER: You made a comment about perceived distinctions between Chinese and Japanese sexuality. I have no idea what you mean.
>
> RICHARD FUNG: In the West, there are specific sexual ambiences associated with the different Asian nationalities, sometimes based on cultural artifacts, sometimes on mere conjecture. These discourses exist simultaneously, even though in conflict with, totalizing notions of "Oriental" sexuality. Japanese male sexuality has come to be identified with strength, virility, perhaps a certain kinkiness, as signified for example by the clothing and gestures in *Below the Belt.* Japanese sexuality is seen as more "potent" than Chinese sexuality, which is generally represented as more passive and languorous. At the same time, there is the

cliché that "all Orientals look alike." So in this paradox of the invisibility of difference lies the fascination. If he can ascertain where I'm from, he feels that he knows what he can expect from me. In response to this query about "ethnic origins," a friend of mine answers, "Where would you like me to be from?" I like this response because it gently confronts the question while maintaining the erotic possibilities of the moment.

SIMON WATNEY: I wanted to point out that the first film you showed, *Below the Belt*, presents us with a classic anxiety dream image. In it there is someone whose identity is that of a top man, but that identity is established in relation to a competing identity that allows him to enjoy sexual passivity, which is represented as a racial identity. It's as if he were in racial drag. I thought this film was extraordinary. Under what other conditions are Caucasian men invited to fantasize ourselves as racially other? And it seems to me that the only condition that would allow the visibility of that fantasy to be acted out in this way is the prior anxiety about a desired role, about top and bottom positions. This film is incredibly transparent and unconscious about how it construes or confuses sexual role-playing in relation to race. And the thrust of it all seems to be the construction of the Asian body as a kind of conciliatory pseudoheterosexuality for the white "top," who has anus envy, as it were.

FUNG: I completely agree. The film says too much for its own good by making this racist agenda so clear.

RAY NAVARRO: I think your presentation was really important, and it parallels research I'm doing with regard to the image of Latino men in gay male porn. I wondered if you might comment a bit more, however, about the class relations you find within this kind of work. For example, I've found a consistent theme running throughout gay white male porn of Latino men represented as either *campesino* or criminal. That is, it focuses less on body type—masculine, slight, or whatever—than on signifiers of class. It appears to be a class fantasy collapsed with a race fantasy, and in a way it parallels the actual power relations between the Latino stars and the producers and distributors, most of whom are white.

FUNG: There are ways in which your comments can also apply to Asians. Unlike whites and blacks, most Asians featured in gay erotica are younger men. Since youth generally implies less economic power, class-race hierarchies appear in most of the work. In the tapes I've been looking at, the occupations of the white actors are usually specified, while those of the Asians are not. The white actors are assigned fantasy appeal based on profession, whereas for the asians, the sexual cachet of race is deemed sufficient. In *Asian Knights* there are also sequences in which the characters' lack of "work" carries connotations of the housewife or, more particularly, the house boy.

But there is at least one other way to look at this discrepancy. The lack of a specified occupation may be taken to suggest that the Asian actor is the subject of the fantasy, a surrogate or the Asian viewer, and therefore does not need to be coded with specific attributes.

TOM WAUGH: I think your comparison of the way the Asian male body is used in gay white porn to the way lesbianism is employed in heterosexual pornography is very interesting. You also suggested that racial markers in gay porn tend to close down its potential for openness and flux in identifications. Do you think we can take it further and say that racial markers in gay porn replicate, or function in the same way as gender markers do in heterosexual pornography?

FUNG: What, in fact, I intended to say with my comparison of the use of lesbians in heterosexual porn and that of Asian male bodies in white gay male porn was that they're similar but also very different. I think that certain comparisons of gender with race are appropriate, but there are also profound differences. The fact that Asian gay men are *men* means that, as viewers, our responses to this work are grounded in our gender and the way gender functions in this society. Lesbians are *women*, with all that that entails. I suspect that although most Asian gay men experience ambivalence with white gay porn, the issues for women in relation to heterosexual pornography are more fundamental.

WAUGH: The same rigidity of roles seems to be present in most situations.

FUNG: Yes, that's true. If you notice the way the Asian body is spoken of in Rushton's work, the terms he uses are otherwise used when speaking of women. But it is too easy to discredit these arguments. I have tried instead to show how Rushton's conclusions are commensurate with the assumptions everywhere present in education and popular thought.

AUDIENCE MEMBER: I'm going to play devil's advocate. Don't you think gay Asian men who are interested in watching gay porn involving Asian actors will get ahold of the racially unmarked porn that is produced in Thailand or Japan? And if your answer is yes, then why should a white producer of gay porn go to the trouble of making tapes that cater to a relatively small gay Asian market? This is about dollars and cents. It seems obvious that the industry will cater to the white man's fantasy.

FUNG: On the last point I partially agree. That's why I'm calling for an independent porn in which the gay Asian man is producer, actor, and intended viewer. I say this somewhat halfheartedly, because personally I am not very interested in producing porn, though I do want to continue working with sexually explicit material. But I also feel that one cannot assume, as the porn industry apparently does, that the desire of even white men are so fixed and exclusive.

Regarding the first part of your question, however, I must insist that Asian Americans and Asian Canadians are Americans and Canadians. I myself am a fourth-generation Trinidadian and have only a tenuous link with Chinese culture and aesthetics, except for what I have consciously searched after and learned. I purposely chose not to talk about Japanese or Thai productions because they come from cultural contexts about which I am incapable of commenting. In addition, the fact that porn from those countries is sometimes unmarked racially does not mean that it speaks to my experience or desires, my own culture of sexuality.

ISAAC JULIEN: With regard to race representation or racial signifiers in the context of porn, your presentation elaborated a problem that came up in some of the safe sex tapes that were shown earlier. In them one could see a kind of trope that traces a circular pattern—a repetition that leads a black or Asian spectator to a specific realm of fantasy.

I wonder if you could talk a bit more about the role of fantasy, or the fantasy one sees in porn tapes produced predominantly by white producers. I see a fixing of different black subjects in recognizable stereotypes rather than a more dialectical representation of black identities, where a number of options or fantasy positions would be made available.

FUNG: Your last film, *Looking for Langston*, is one of the few films I know of that has placed the sexuality of the black gay subject at its center. As I said earlier, my own work, especially *Chinese Characters* (1986), is more concerned with pulling apart the tropes you refer to than in constructing an alternative erotics. At the same time I feel that this latter task is imperative, and I hope that it is taken up more. It is in this context that I think the current attack on the National Endowment for the Arts and arts funding in the United States supports the racial status quo. If it succeeds, it effectively squelches the possibility of articulating counter-hegemonic views of sexuality.

Just before I left Toronto, I attended an event called "Cum Talk," organized by two people from Gay Asians Toronto and from Khush, the group for South Asian lesbians and gay men. we looked at porn and talked about the images people had of us, the role of "bottom" that we are constantly cast in. Then we spoke of what actually happened when we had sex with white men. What became clear was that we don't play out that role and are very rarely asked to. So there is a discrepancy between the ideology of sexuality and its practice, between sexual representation and sexual reality.

GREGG BORDOWITZ: When Jean Carlomusto and I began working on the porn project at Gay Men's Health Crisis, we had big ideas of challenging many of the roles and positionings involved in the dominant industry. But as I've worked more with porn, I find that it's really not an efficient arena in which to make such challenges. There is some room to question assumptions, but there are not many ways to challenge the codes of porn, except to question the conditions of production, which was an important point raised at the end of your talk. It seems to me that the only real way to picture more possibilities is, again, to create self-determining groups, make resources available for people of color and lesbians and other groups so that they can produce porn for themselves.

FUNG: I only partly agree with you, because I think, so far as is possible, we have to take responsibility for the kinds of images we create, or re-create. *Asian Knights* had a Chinese producer, after all. But, yes, of course, the crucial thing is to activate more voices, which would establish the conditions for something else to happen. The liberal response to racism is that we need to integrate everyone —people should all become coffee-colored, or everyone should have sex with everyone else. But such an agenda doesn't often account for the specificity of desires. I have seen very little porn produced from such an integrationist mentality that actually affirms my desire. It's so easy to find my fantasies appropriated for the pleasures of a white viewer. In that sense, porn is most useful for revealing relationships of power.

JOSÉ ARROYO: You've been talking critically about a certain kind of colo-nial imagery. Isaac's film *Looking for Langston* contains not only a decon-struction of this imagery in its critique of the Mapplethorpe pho-tographs, but also a new construction of black desire. What kind of strategies do you see for a similar reconstructing of erotic Asian imagery?

FUNG: One of the first thing that needs to be done is to construct Asians as viewing subjects. My first videotape, *Orientations* [1984], had that as a primary goal. I thought of Asians as sexual subjects, but also as viewing subjects to whom the work should be geared. Many of us, whether we're watching news or pornography or looking at advertising, see that the image or message is not really being directed at us. For example, the sex-ism and heterosexism of a disk jockey's attitudes become obvious when we or she says, "When you and your girlfriend go out tonight...." Even though that's meant to address a general audience, it's clear that this audi-ence is presumed not to have any women (not to mention lesbians!) in it. The general audience, as I analyze *him*, is white, male, heterosexual, mid-dle-class, and center-right politically. So we have to understand this pre-sumption first, to see that only very specific people are being addressed.

When I make my videotapes, I know that I am addressing Asians. That means that I can take certain things for granted and introduce other things in a completely different context. But there are still other ques-tions of audience. When we make outreach films directed at the straight community—the "general public"—in an effort to make lesbian and gay issues visible, we often sacrifice many of the themes that are important to how we express our sexualities: drag, issues of promiscuity, and so on. But when I made a tape for a gay audience, I talked about those same issues very differently. For one thing, I *talked* about those issues. And I tried to image them in ways that were very different from the way the dominant media image them. In *Orientations* I had one guy talk about park and washroom sex—about being a slut, basically—in a park at midday with front lighting. He talked very straightforwardly about it, which is only to say that there are many possibilities for doing this.

I think, however, that to talk about gay Asian desire is very difficult, because we need to swim through so much muck to get to it. It is very difficult (if even desirable) to do in purely positive terms, and I think it's necessary to do a lot of deconstruction along the way. I have no ready-made strategies; I feel it's a hit-and-miss sort of project.

LEI CHOU: I want to bring back the issue of class. One of the gay Asian stereotypes that you mentioned was the Asian house boy. The reality is that many of these people are immigrants: English is a second language for them, and they are thus economically disenfranchised by being socially and culturally displaced. So when you talk about finding the Asian penis in pornography, how will this project work for such people? Since pornography is basically white and middle-class, what kind of tool is it? Who really is your target audience?

FUNG: If I understand your question correctly, you are asking about the prognosis for new and different representations within commercial porn. And I don't think the prognosis is very good: changes will probably happen very slowly. At the same time, I think that pornography is an especially important site of struggle precisely for those Asians who are, as you say, economically and socially at a disadvantage, or those who are most isolated, whether in families or rural areas; print pornography is often the first introduction to gay sexuality—before, for example, the gay and lesbian press or gay Asian support groups. But this porn provides mixed messages: it affirms gay identity articulated almost exclusively as white. Whether we like it or not, mainstream gay porn is more available to most gay Asian men than any independent work you or I might produce. That is why pornography is a subject of such concern for me.

Notes

I would like to thank Tim McCaskell and Helen Lee for their ongoing criticism and comments, as well as Jeff Nunokawa and Douglas Crimp for their invaluable suggestions in converting the original spoken presentation into a written text. Finally, I would like to extend my gratitude to Bad Object-Choices for inviting me to participate in "How Do I Look?"

1. Phillipe Rushton and Anthony F. Bogaert, University of Western Ontario, "Race versus Social Class Difference in Sexual Behavior: A Follow-up Test of the r/K Dimension," *Journal of Research in Personality* 22 (1988): 259.

2. Feminists of color have long pointed out that racism is phrased differently for men and women. Nevertheless, since it is usually heterosexual (and often middle-class) makes whose voices are validated by the power structure, it is their interests that are taken up as "representing" the communities. See Barbara Smith, "Toward a Black Feminist Criticism," in *All the Women Are White, All the Blacks Are Men, But Some of Us Are Brave: Black Women's Studies* (Old Westbury, N.Y.: The Feminist Press, 1982), 182.

4. The mainstream "leadership" within Asian communities often colludes with the myth of the model minority and the reassuring desexualization of Asian people.

5. In Britain, however, more race-sex stereotypes of South Asians exist. Led by artists such as Pratibha Parmar, Sunil Gupta, and Hanif Kureishi, there is also a growing and already significant body of work by South Asians themselves, which takes up questions of sexuality.

6. Renee Tajima, "Lotus Blossoms Don't Bleed: Images of Asian Women," *Anthologies of Asian American Film and Video* (New York: A distribution project of Third World Newsreel, 1984), 28.

7. Ibid, 29.

8. See Stephen Gong, "Zen Warrior of the Celluloid (Silent) Years: The Art of Sessue Hayakawa," *Bridge* 8, no. 2 (Winter 1982–83): 37–41.

9. Frantz Fanon, *Black Skin, White Masks* (London: Paladin, 1970), 120. For a reconsideration of this statement in the light of contemporary black gay issues, see Kobena Mercer, "Imaging the Black Man's Sex," in *Photography / Politics: Two*, ed. Pat Holland, Jo Spence, and Simon Watney (London: Comedia/Methuen, 1987); reprinted in *Male Order: Unwrapping Masculinity*, ed. Rowena Chapman and Jonathan Rutherford (London: Lawrence and Wishart, 1988), 141.

10. I do not think that this could happen in today's Toronto, which now has the second largest Chinese community on the continent. Perhaps it would not have happened in San Francisco. But I still believe that there is an onus on gay asians and other gay people of color to prove our homosexuality.

11. The term *minority* is misleading. Racism is not a matter of numbers but of power. This is especially clear in situations where people of color constitute actual majorities, as in most former European colonies. At the same time, I feel that none of the current terms are really satisfactory and that too much time spent on the politics of "naming" can in the end be diversionary.

12. To organize effectively with lesbian and gay Asians, we must reject self-righteous condemnation of "closetedness" and see coming out more as a process or a goal, rather than as a prerequisite for participation in the movement.

13. Racism is available to be used by anyone. The conclusion that—because racism = power + prejudice—only white people can be racist is Eurocentric and simply wrong. Individuals have varying degrees and different sources of power, depending on the given moment in a shifting context. This does not contradict the fact that, in contemporary North American society, racism is generally organized around white supremacy.

14. From simple observation, I feel safe in saying that most gay Asian men in North America hold white men as their idealized sexual partners. However, I am not trying to construct an argument for determinism, and there are a number of outstanding problems that are not easily answered by current analyses of power. What of the experience of Asians who are attracted to men of color, including other Asians? What about white men who prefer Asians sexually? How and to what extent is desire articulated in terms of race as opposed to body type or other attributes? To what extent is sexual attraction exclusive and/or changeable, and can it be consciously programmed? These questions are all politically loaded, as they parallel and impact the debates between essentialists and social constructionists on the nature of homosexuality itself. They are also emotionally charged, in that sexual choice involving race has been a basis for moral judgment.

15. See Richard Dyer, *Heavenly Bodies: Film Stars and Society* (New York: St. Martin's Press, 1986). In his chapter on Marilyn Monroe, Dyer writes extensively on the relationship between blondness, whiteness, and desirability.

16. Print porn is somewhat more racially integrated, as are the new safe sex tapes—by the Gay Men's Health Crisis, for example—produced in a political and pedagogical rather than a commercial context.

17. Richard Dyer, "Coming to Terms," *Jump Cut*, no. 30 (March 1985): 28.

18. Tom Waugh, "Men's Pornography, Gay vs. Straight," *Jump Cut*, no. 30 (March 1985): 31.

19. *International Wavelength News* 2, No. 1 (January 1991).

20. Tom Waugh, "Men's Pornography, Gay vs. Straight," 33.

21. It seems to me that the undressing here is organized around the pleasure of the white man in being served. This is in contrast to the undressing scenes, in, say, James Bond films, in which the narrative is organized around undressing as an act of revealing the woman's body, an indicator of sexual conquest.

22. Interestingly, the gay video porn from Japan and Thailand that I have seen has none of this Oriental coding. Asianness is not taken up as a sign but is taken for granted as a setting for the narrative.

23. Joanna Russ, "Pornography and the Doubleness of Sex for Women," *Jump Cut*, no. 32 (April 1986): 39.

24. Though this is a common enough question in our postcolonial, urban environments, when asked of Asians it often reveals two agendas: first, the assumption that all Asians are newly arrived immigrants and, second, a fascination with difference and sameness. Although we (Asians) all supposedly look alike, there are specific characteristics and stereotypes associated with each particular ethnic group. The inability to tell us apart underlies the inscrutability attributed to Asians. This "inscrutability" took on sadly ridiculous proportions when during World War II the Chinese were issued badges so that white Canadians could distinguish them from "the enemy."

25. Isaac Julien (director), *Looking for Langston* (United Kingdom: Sankofa Film and Video, 1988).

26. For more on the origins of the black film and ideo workshops in Britain, see Jim Pines, "The Cultural Context of Black British Cinema," in *Blackframes: Critical Perspectives on Black Independent Cinema*, ed. Mybe B. Cham and Clair Andrade-Watkins (Cambridge, Mass.: MIT Press, 1988), 26.

part IV

"Love Your Asian Body, Get Tested for HIV"
> —Asian Pacific AIDS Intervention Team

Bloodlines

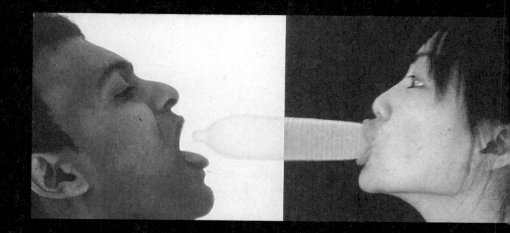

·

overleaf: "Nexus" by Allan deSouza and Yong Soon Min.
Quotation from HIV Testing slogan, Asian Pacific AIDS
Intervention Team, Los Angeles, 1992.

Communion

A Collaboration on AIDS

Ric Parish, James Sakakura, Brian Green,
Joël B. Tan, and Robert Vázquez Pacheco

Introduction —*Joël B. Tan*

The AIDS crisis in Asian America is riddled with complexities. Because sexuality, death, substance (mis)use, and homosexuality are taboo subjects among many Asian cultures, AIDS has yet to be discussed honestly and openly among Asian Americans. An organized mobilization against AIDS has been extremely difficult for Asian Americans because "Asians" do not share a common culture, history, or language.

While epidemiological AIDS reports and journalistic articles have been published, there have been few accounts written by Asian and Pacific Americans themselves who live with the retrovirus, HIV, and with AIDS. Thus I offered to organize this collaborative work from the perspective of insiders living with HIV and AIDS, for selfish reasons. Perhaps having worked in the AIDS movement for the last six years, I've saved up a lot of experiences. Having lost too many to AIDS, my heart and memories contain the spirits of friends, brothers, and sisters who are clamoring to be heard. I promised that I would never forget them. I also know many people who are living with HIV or AIDS.

Sharing time and space with them to produce these essays is an effective means to tell our stories and histories, to publicly account for our losses, and to celebrate our strengths.

Three years ago, I was one of the many individuals who helped to establish the Asian Pacific AIDS Intervention Team in Los Angeles. This work gave me a clearer understanding about the challenges that face us today. Providing adequate and effective education/service to Asians and other people of color communities is difficult. On the one hand, we are dealing with a political and medical health care system that is insensitive to our particular social, cultural, and language needs. On the other hand, Asian Americans find it difficult to discuss issues of sexuality, illness, death, drug (mis)use, and other subjects that are linked with AIDS. But as a result of doing AIDS work, I have also met dedicated and brave activists/artists who continually challenge the system as well as their home communities.

The topic of AIDS in any community of color involves a thorough discourse on AIDSphobia, racism, homophobia, sex(uality), sexism, classism, and other social diseases that compose the total realities of the pandemic. Given the restrictions of limited space and resources, the authors of this "communion" were only able to touch upon a few of these issues.

We authors are not all of Asian descent. The Asian experience in the United States cannot be discussed without an exploration of our shared histories with other communities of color. You will hear from Ric Parish, activist, artist of Pilipino and African American descent living with HIV. His essay entitled, "'Round Midnight" discusses the social and political complexities of AIDS in Asian America. You will hear from James Sakakura, a Japanese American (Yonsei, fourth generation) activist and artist living with AIDS. His essay entitled " 'til death do us part" uncovers the raw, emotional and erotic truth about his life with his partner, Brian Green. You will also hear Brian's truth in his essay "Vigil." Green is an African American artist living with HIV. I've contributed a slice of life in my essay entitled, "Faith" that intertwines my reality as a Pilipino HIV-negative activist/artist with confessions of love to my lover, Robert Vázquez Pacheco. Robert is a long-time Puerto Rican AIDS activist and artist living with AIDS. His essay "La Fe que Consuela" (Faith that Consoles) testifies to his personal history and experience with AIDS and the joys and complexities of our relationship. In a way, these essays are like family letters, corresponding one to the next, bridging our perspectives and constructing our collective truths.

These men are my family. Traditionally, families are defined as persons who are bound by blood and a common history. My family of gay men of color and other "queer families" is also bound by blood and history. AIDS has brought us together and kept us together. Mortality is our worse enemy and our greatest gift. Our losses and our fears have motivated us to live and love fiercely. We have founded, continued to work for, and sustain efforts movements and institutions to battle this pandemic. Our courage, strength, and genuine affection for each other keeps us joyful and hopeful in our darkest times. *Yup, you could say we had to learn how to make slammin' lemonade.*

Sex is, and must be, discussed explicitly in this essay. Lovemaking, fucking, and sucking are juxtaposed against our romances, unions, fears, and hopes. We simply cannot discuss AIDS without discussing sex. We cannot discuss sex without describing our bodies, motions, and emotions. Sexually speaking, this essay takes risks because 1) it talks about sex explicitly, 2) boldly declares that HIV positive men continue to be sexual despite AIDSphobia, and 3) speaks about unions among gay men of color.

Sex with/among HIV positive men is still a subject that has not been fully explored (if at all), and especially in Asian (American) literature. These essays are perhaps the first to approach the issue of sexuality among men who are both infected and affected. Yes, HIV positive men are still having sex, great sex, not so good sex, romantic sex, sex with HIV-negative men, sex with each other. HIV infection is a constant in the lives of gay men of color. Statistics tell us that the face of AIDS is changing. Gay men of color are among those who are highest at risk for HIV infection and transmission. We are being systematically destroyed. If racism, classism, or homophobia can't kill us, AIDS sure will.

Finally, we thought it was important to assemble gay men of color from different races and ethnicities. In popular culture, interracial relationships are usually discussed as white and "the other." This has become an important element in our definition of "interracial." Whiteness is the constant whenever interracial relations is discussed. Why is that? Well, the truth is, gay people are not automatically immune from internalizing white racism or other forms of oppressive, self-destructive attitudes and behavior. The cycle of hate is that deep and powerful. The reality is that the gay community and the gay movement are white-led and white-run (therefore all forms of cultural production reflect this obsession with whiteness). This is evident in the images that are produced in gay media. The blond, the buffed, and the blue-eyed remain the crowning rulers in the sexual hierarchy, while the other exotics wade below waiting to be defined and recognized as somebody. Well, yes girl, I *am* somebody, and I don't need a white supremist gay community to tell me who I am.

Gay Afrocentric culture has brought the beauty of "black on black love" to fruition. Similarly, gay Latino and Asian and Pacific Islander cultures are also mirroring the practice of loving one's own (unfortunately, I know very little about Native American culture to comment). This is an important step in the empowerment of gay men of color.

Loving thyself is beautiful, but I don't think we should stop there. People of color have shared histories in the United States, and we are not taught to recognize our shared oppression or victories. Similarly, gay men of color in cosmopolitan settings also drink from common philosophical waters. This collaborative work is one of the first to discuss gay male relationships from a "color on color" perspective. "Color on Color" love is vital in interracial discourse. I believe that celebrating the unions among gay men of color is a revolutionary step in challenging and affecting multitudinous levels of the hegemony. People of color loving one another is a political act.

"Communion" is a public yet personal statement. AIDS is a personal issue as well as a political one. We wanted to introduce you to the role that HIV/AIDS has played through our lives and the lives of those who are infected and affected by this disease. We invite you to read these narratives with an open heart and an open mind.

We believe in the power of the written word. We hope that in some way this work will communicate our thinking and change yours. If you feel strongly, we encourage you to respond and to continue this dialogue.

Peace, love, and adobo grease... Joël B. Tan
January 1995

Acknowledgments: Again, special shout outs and faithful love to my "big" daddy Russell Leong and my sistahs Ric "Rita" Parish, James "Yoko" Sakakura, Brian "Mimi" Green, and un beso con lengua for my boo-boo, Robert "Papo" Vázquez-Pacheco. We did it ! Pa-daw...big babies!

'Round Midnight   —*Ric Parish*
August 1991

Friday night, like most Friday nights, I find myself standing in line, ready to pay eight bucks for a few hours of escape. As I am buzzed in, the door, like a vault, slams shut behind me. I feel an immediate sense of relief. It takes a few minutes for my eyes to adjust to the darkness as I feel my way to the bathroom. "Shit, another line" I think.

The place is packed, there are a lot of gym bunnies here tonight. Lots of young guys, lots of crystal meth and ecstasy too. I don't know what they're cutting this stuff with these days, but the guys seem a lot hornier or something. They seem a lot more willing to do almost anything sexually.

I notice quite a few Asian boys here tonight. Most of them are fawning over the white boys. They seem to travel in packs. Some Thai, some Vietnamese, but mostly Pilipino.

I find my way into what looks like a prisoner of war camp, complete with metal bars and camouflage overlays. Jesus, they spent some money on this

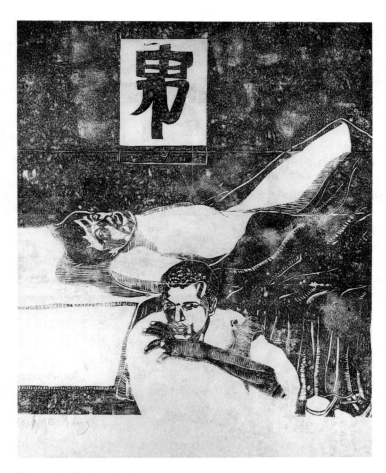

"Afro-Asian" by Stanley Roy, 1978.

place. A crowd has gathered around five or six hot bods. They look like poster boys for Gold's Gym. They are lined up in front of the metal bars, some holding, others just leaning, but all getting blow jobs. In a way they look like synchronized swimmers, reminding me of the double mint twins, and I can't help but laugh out loud. That kind of breaks the spell for a moment. but they all resume quickly. After a lengthy suck fest they begin cumming one by one. But the boys on their knees are not withdrawing. Only one pulls back, and the little stud muffin shoots his wad onto the leg of the guy standing next to him. That was just the incentive the other guy needed, and he begins to erupt himself. The kid at the bottom doesn't pull away, he goes with it, and he swallows with a sense of urgency that seemed to outweigh any danger or possible risk that now looms over his head. He looks up. It's one of the Pilipino kids I saw earlier. One by one the other boys followed suit. There is another Asian boy down there but I can't tell what his ethnicity is. Some of the on lookers watched in horror, while others eagerly waited their turns.

Suddenly a song is blasting over the sound system. The lyrics are screaming over and over "I wanna fuck you in the ass.... I wanna fuck you in the ass...." Needless to say it doesn't take much to get these guys going. Before long the sweet and pungent smell of freshly showered ass is in the air, but wait! Where are the condoms I think. Not a single condom.

I go to the lounge near the entrance. Next to the coffee pot is a huge fish-bowl full of condoms with a sign above that reads: "Anyone caught engaging in unprotected sex will be asked to leave this establishment." "Bullshit" I think, and I sit on the black leather couch and have a cup of coffee.

November 1991

There are about eight of us from the Asian Pacific AIDS Intervention Team standing in front of Faces Disco, a popular hang out and only dance club in L.A. that caters to Gay Asian Men (and the men who hunt for them). We figure there are few safe "queer spaces" for gay Asian men to congregate in Los Angeles, so we use this sad reality to our advantage in an attempt to outreach to them with information on safer sex practices.

With much lobbying to the owner of Faces, he agrees to allow us to set up outside in the parking lot. We are handing out condoms and safer sex infor-mation in English and about ten of the Asian languages. We get a lot of stares and polite rejections. Some of the guys are willing to talk to us.

I find myself talking to a young Vietnamese guy who seemed really excited to see something about AIDS written in his language. I'm handing him a con-dom when a tall blond haired blue eyed Aryan type steps up. He snatches the condom pack and literature from the kid's hand and throws them back onto the outreach table. "He Doesn't Need That!!" he says as he pulls the kid away by the arm.

I want to lose all sense of professionalism and cut the blond guy's throat. At the very least kick his ass. But of course that would jeopardize the entire oper-ation so all I can do is document the incident and keep going. We hand out over one hundred condoms and conduct sixty one-on-one interviews. It was a good night.

December 1991

It's a Sunday afternoon and I, along with some other API friends are sitting at our favorite coffee house in "Boys' town." Everyone else is talking about how fucked up the system is or something, and I'm just daydreaming about how nice it would be to tie up and spank the hot little blond number sitting next to us. Love/hate attraction is a bitch.

I overhear one of the younger Pilipino kids sitting at the table say "I wish my nose wasn't so flat… maybe if I got a nosejob I could score better in West Hollywood."

I then hear "Sista..LOVE YO' ASIAN BODY!" I look up and of course it is my best "girlfriend" Joël Tan giving the naive youth a retort and commentary on the importance of developing self esteem and self nurturing. "Besides, little sista, why do you want to spend so much time and money trying to impress white boys, when their dicks look like raw turkey necks anyway? You need to find you a good brown husband who will love you for the beautiful island girl you are, Missy!"

I loved Joël's humorous command of American dialects. He had a point—not about the "raw turkey necks" but about the self esteem issues. If we were going to reach anybody, we were going to have to speak to that. If not, we would be just communicating the same tired message as everyone else in the AIDS industry. And an "industry" it was.

Joel's comment was something every gay (API) Asian Pacific Islander youth should hear, I thought. It gave me an Idea.

March 1992

It's been two months since our "Love Your Asian Body, Get Tested for HIV" ad campaign has been running. It is the first time in Los Angeles we will see an API face on anything pertaining to AIDS on any significant scale.

I'm not sure if this is the most effective route to go, but we have to begin somewhere. Will gay API men and youth get tested just because of a quarter page advertisement buried in the back of *Frontiers*, a predominantly gay white newspaper? Probably not, but we got the funding. There was no way of avoiding getting consumed by funding cycles and scopes of work in this new business we endeavored to invade. Yet, we carried the responsibility to create a message that would reach our gay API youth and make a difference.

I am flipping through the rag looking for our new ad. Page after page is filled with smiling white boys, fabulously clothed or half-naked with perfect bodies and airbrushed skin. The images merge into images of my past. I can remember walking through the aisles of the grocery stores in Manila and seeing the pictures of smiling white babies on milk bottles and boxes of pampers. Smiling white people on cereal boxes and cosmetic display cases. Even the most famous celebrities in Manila were the ones that looked white. It was amazing how much the Philippines seemed to be a mere extension of American pop culture. I was struck by how much we so wanted to be white Americans.

My eyes focused back onto the pages of the magazine and find the quarter-page ad. I'm thinking that perhaps one of the API kids we are trying to reach will stumble across an image of himself amongst all of this propaganda on the fabulous gay white life, then maybe it will spark something in him. At least get him to think.

"Love Your Asian Body." What a radical concept. Even more radical, was the fact that we portrayed two API gay men who were very much into each other. White was not a factor in the ad, which made some people uncomfortable. It actually infuriated a few. No matter where people were on the opinion scale, it really didn't matter. They were reading the ad, and they were talking about it. That was the point wasn't it? Or was it?

June 1992

Well, the reports are in from the L.A. County AIDS Programs Office. The numbers of APIs getting tested are at about the same as they were the previous year. The rate of increase of infected, however, continues at an alarming rate. My director quietly reviews the numbers and with a look of disappointment, goes into his office and closes the door behind him. Despite my AIDS intervention work, why do I suddenly feel personally responsible for the increased numbers?

Must be that API "Shame" shit.

'til death do us part   —*James Sakakura*

I came home from work around midnight to find Brian huddled on the far corner of our king-sized bed, shaking, his eyes dilated as a deer's frozen by on-coming headlights. He was sweaty, smelly, paranoid, and afraid of the imaginary police staked outside our doors and windows.

It was Spring 1990 and he was tweaking once again from a night of sucking on the glass dick. I felt betrayed, frustrated, helpless, and angry, once again. The same thing several nights a week for most of the past year.

Something snapped in me that night. I couldn't take it anymore. My heart was breaking, watching my best friend and life partner dying a little bit more each night before my very eyes. I had him on a lifeline, pulling him to shore. But each night the tide became a little stronger, pushing him further and further away, overwhelming my efforts to pull him back to me.

Nothing was working. I'd cuddle and caress him to let him know I loved him. We'd break the pipe night after night. He'd promise to call me at work when the demons started calling his name. He usually didn't. I only wanted to save him, to help him return to the confident, ambitious, and principled young man I fell in love with. I knew how ashamed he was, how guilty he felt about his inability to stop. I was desperate. Maybe if I made him watch me get high, he would be so concerned about me, so ashamed of himself, that he would stop.

I grabbed the pipe and the last remaining rock, dropped it into the bowl, and lit up. My heart started pounding: I was rocketing through the roof, my head was expanding into a cloud of vapor. A few minutes later I caught my breath; my racing heart slowed, and I returned to earth.

Now I'd done it, crossed over the River Styx into Hades. I was hooked. He called the dealer, who delivered a new batch. We smoked ourselves into oblivion. When it was gone, we sat on the bed, trembling, feeling empty and dead. The only thing left to do was to turn to each other, reeking of cocaine sweat, and unsteadily tear off each other's clothes. Desperate, we were trying to reconnect with life by pressing the flesh. Repulsed, but so needy, we fumbled and sucked and fucked, barely able to even get hard.

Spring 1991. Clean and sober, both of us had just completed drug rehab. After our one hour weekly group therapy sessions, Brian drove me to the sober living house in San Pedro. I moved in with six other recovering men who were also getting clean. There were strict rules about visitors and conjugal visits were forbidden.

That night no one was home, so I invited Brian into my room and locked the door. Uncertain that we could heal our fragile relationship, we were only able to see each other once a week. Still, we loved each other deeply and passionately. We began to kiss. Fumbling at each others shirt and pants without even bothering to take our shoes off, we fell onto the bed. We jostled into a "sixty-nine" position, rolling off the bed onto the floor.

I heard the front door shut. We scooted, still on the floor, into the bathroom and locked the door behind us. I rolled Brian over, positioning him on all fours. Then I buried my face in his ass, feasting on his beautiful, round cheeks, reveling in the taste and smell of a day's funk. Sweet, damp, musky, his puckered hole beckoned me. I pushed my tongue into his hole until it relaxed, opening and closing like a winking eye. He lowered his upper body so his butt was in the air, giving me a better angle to eat. I drooled saliva into his gaping hole. Slowly, I placed the head of my penis into him, sliding in little by little. Eventually I was all the way in, my pelvis pressed up against the back of his ass. Slowly, I began to rock back and forth inside him, pulling out and pressing back in a little more each time. With my pants still around my ankles I straddled him, doggy-style, while I reached around him and fondled his oozing hard-on. Warm, wet, and hungry, his asshole swallowed my dick again until I couldn't hold it any longer. Pulling out at the last second, I exploded over Brian's back. I laid down on the cold floor and pulled him on top of me. We kissed as I spit on my hand and yanked on his dick until he shot all over my stomach. Then we quickly wiped up. Not wanting to get caught breaking house rules, Brian sneaked out the bathroom window.

A year passed—Spring 1992. Brian had gone to the dentist that morning. He had his teeth scraped clean, leaving microsopic cuts in his gums. Invisible to our eyes, these cuts were big enough for viruses and other unwanted organisms to enter.

Later that evening, I lied to Brian, telling him that I was going to an AA meeting. I had actually invited over a new trick I had met the other day.

As the trick and I settled onto my bed still fully dressed, I heard a key opening the door. It was Brian. He had his own key and had stopped by to surprise me when I got home from the meeting. This wasn't the first time I cheated that he knew of but it was the first time that he actually caught me.

Indignant, Brian proclaimed he was my lover and told the trick to leave as soon as possible. He did just that, slamming the door behind him.

Next, Brian turned to me. "How could you do this to me? I meet people all the time, but I can control myself."

I said nothing, angering him even more. He grabbed me by the shirt collar and swung me against the closet door. Then he pushed me onto the coffee table where the T.V. and stereo sat. He raised his fist as if to hit me. As he started to take a swing he stopped himself. I dared him, begging him to hit me. I deserved it. Still holding onto my shirt collar, he spun me around again and pinned me down on the bed, still screaming at me.

Finally, he stood up and stormed out the door. After a few seconds, he came back in. Tears were welling in his eyes: "How can you just let me walk out and say nothing, don't you know how much I love you?"

He grabbed me and threw me down on the bed again. Kissing me hard, he pushed my pants down to the ankle and flipped me over so that my butt was facing him. He buried his face in my ass, entering my hole repeatedly with his tongue. I became aroused. He pulled my dick under and between my legs and swallowed it to the base of my balls. He ran his tongue around my balls, working the ridge between my balls and my hole and then back again. As he undid his pants he returned to eating my ass, then quickly entered me with one swift lunge. With passion fueled by hurt and anger, he had finally stopped screaming. I was grateful that my punishment was so pleasurable, grateful that he still desired me.

Brian was the third person I told about my HIV status, on our second date back in 1986. Quiet and composed, he had stood up from the bed where we were sitting next to each other. He paced back and forth a few times, then sat down, turned and hugged me. He said it didn't make any difference to him, that life was full of risks and that he was willing to become infected with HIV to be with me. We never discussed what sexual practices would be acceptably safe for us. We seldom spoke about HIV if at all. When we did, it was usually in the context of my current health status. In August of 1993, Brain tested postive for HIV antibodies.

Vigil   —*Brian Green*

I had properly accessorized when I dressed that morning. I was aware of my gold bracelet dangling on my right wrist and my leather watchband snugly gripping my left. What I did not know was that if I remained perfectly still I would feel the rhythm of my watch's secondhand as it swept across its face.

I steadied myself as I slowly turned the doorknob. Sunlight filled the room and spilled over my body which had already broken into a cold sweat.

Dr. Young walked into the room wearing his signature smile. His smile could only mean "You're safe, girl." You are not positive, I told myself. His lips began to open, and I could anticipate his soft assuring voice. The soothing tones carried me back to the time when I had first laid eyes upon James.

It was never about sex. I simply knew that he was destined to be my husband. Never mind the fact that I met him in the love nest he had built with his lover of several years. I had waited for Mr. Right for twenty-one years, and on my first day in California the gods had shown him to me—James Sakakura. He was all that I had wanted. I knew this because in his presence I was not only excited but felt comfortable and whole. I decided then and there I would wait. My vigil began. We became friends, double-dated, planned outings together. All the while I kept my feelings in check and out of sight. Hell, when he and his boyfriend, Morrell would break up, I would put them back together.... This was unconditional love, honey.

I knew my day was coming and then I would rock his whole foundation. The waiting game continued for two years. Then finally a wedge had formed between James and his lover... there was no putting their humpty dumpty love back together again. I politely extended my hand and friendship to James. Yet, our time had still not arrived. Allowing him two years for grieving, separation anxiety, sex with others and spiritual growth, I distanced myself from day-to-day contact with him. But I never lost track of him.

1986, and the living was easy. Things had come together for me in every way, except I was with the wrong man at the wrong time. Again, the gods intervened. Just two months before I planned to move to San Francisco, I found myself single in a crowded bar called Rage, gazing from a distance upon the man whom I had decided would be my future husband. Oiled with alcohol, I felt no reservations. I whispered to my girlfriend, "Engage his date in a conversation, and I will do the rest." I crossed the room. In a moment, I would allow my tongue its natural sway....

With great haste I expressed my attraction and my desire to nurture him. I told him that the fact was I would soon be gone from L.A. and from his life forever. Then, at 3:00 A.M. my phone rang and we were on!

It was never about sex. In the beginning, there was no flash of lightning, thunder or heated sweaty passion, though I had experienced this with others as I am sure James had too. Five years of making love went by before my tight-lipped kisses gave way to wet deep smootches. But baby, let me tell you I have never given myself so completely, fallen victim to the joy of him laying beneath me or on top of me, or gazing into eyes that love me....

The sound of my secondhand ticking, escalating in volume brings me back to the present. Dr. Young's words reach my ears. "You are positive and nothing is different today than yesterday. With proper care and maintainance you will live a long fruitful life, and I am here to see to that."

Faith —*Joël B. Tan*
For Robert, again.

Lately, I've been renting a lot of seventies porn. It really turns me on. You know, the really, really dirty stuff. In the seventies, *everybody* got to do what they wanted. Sweat dripped, bodily fluids were swapped. Now, that's unacceptable. I don't really get off on the guys in the porno. Bad haircuts and cheesy disco are not my idea of fun. What turns me on is what they do. I can always bring myself off imagining that Robert and I can do what these guys are doing. I'm twenty-six now. That means that the seventies passed me by before I even reached puberty. The weird part is that most of these guys that I jack off to are probably dead now. In the seventies, everybody got to do what they wanted. Now, everything is covered in latex.

James and Brian have an eternal bond. They've been going out for almost a decade—that's *two* lifetimes for gay men and *four* eternities for gay men of color. They love each other very much—no doubt. They've broken up, gotten together, moved in, moved out, did drugs together, recovered together, dated again and cheated on each other more times than they can remember. They are both HIV-positive. Well, Brian is HIV-positive. James has AIDS.

Many Pilipinos believe that prayer can conquer anything. I hope so because we have a lot to pray for. Among the Asians and Pacific Islanders living in the United States, Pilipinos have the highest cases of AIDS. The large majority of the Pilipino American AIDS cases are comprised of men who have sex with men. Why Pilipinos? I don't really know. Do we fuck more (unsafely) than the Chinese, the Japanese, or the Samoans? When my grandmother found out that I was working in the AIDS movement she advised me to pray. She said God protected those who believed. Every morning, I pray for God's forgiveness and protection. I sure hope that my grandmother was right.

There are conflicting messages about the risk factors involving oral sex and HIV. My dentist cautioned me that the lining under the tongue is extremely fragile. He said that lining is only one cell layer thin. Also, microscopic cuts occur in the insides of the mouth, that are difficult, if not impossible to detect. There have been recorded testimonies of gay men who claimed that they sero-converted as a result of engaging in oral sex without a condom. Furthermore, some of these gay men also claimed to have stopped sucking just short of ejaculation. However, it is a known fact that saliva contains acids that are strong enough to destroy HTLV-III. On the other hand, there are anecdotal testimonies of gay men who claim that they have been engaging in unprotected oral sex for as long as AIDS has been around, and they have remained negative. There are those who believe that contracting HIV through oral sex is almost impossible. As of yet, there aren't any clear findings to determine the risks involved in sucking dick. Everybody I know still sucks dick—without a condom. I guess, you live or die acccording to what you believe or want to believe.

Pilipinos believe that anything can be conquered by faith. The faith healers of the Philippines are legendary. God has endowed these Pilipinos with the ability to conduct surgery without the use of knives or scalpels. In fact, these Pilipinos are so blessed they don't even need to cut into you to remove a cyst or a gall stone or *anything*. They simply push their hand into your body and take out whatever ails you. I've seen footage of it. It is amazing. There are no traces of surgery, save the dripy gooey mess these healers have in their hands. Although, these milagros happen quite often, they don't happen all the time. They only happen for those who believe. Western medicine and modern science can't explain this phenomenon. Faith cannot be measured by science. The Pilipinos are a people who believe. I am really proud to be Pilipino.

I asked James what they could have possibly been thinking. He said, he didn't know. Didn't Brian know that James was infected? He did. In fact, Brian was one of the first people who knew but they fucked and sucked without protection anyway. The only thing I can gather was that Brian believed that love would protect him. Well, love alone didn't protect Brian from James' sexual addiction, but I guess you believe what you want to believe when you're in love. I asked James again what they could have possibly been thinking. Averting my eyes, he said, he didn't know. They're trying to maintain a friendship.

In the first week of our courtship, Robert kiddingly confessed that he wished for a negative with a deathwish. Officially, Robert has AIDS. As of my last test, I have remained HIV-negative. I laughed. Kiddingly, I told him to be careful of what he wished for, it just might come true.

James was driving me to LAX. I was leaving for D.C. to spend Thanksgiving with Robert. James is the older brother I never had. He was thrilled that I was finally in love. I told him that I couldn't wait for him to meet Robert. They had a lot in common. That day, I was excited, delirious with joy. I believed that nothing could go wrong. The future was nothing but promise ahead. After we said our goodbyes and be safes, he looked at me soberly and said, " Honey, you need to start making more friends who are HIV-negative. You just have to." Averting his eyes, I waved goodbye again....

I was really shy the first time I saw it. The first thing I noticed was that it leaked a lot. I put my hand around it and kissed him some more. I worked my way down to his nipples and stuck my tongue in his navel. I shoved my nose in his pubic hair. He smelled like pencils— newly sharpened. I love him. I've never felt this way before. God, is he the one? I closed my eyes and closed my mouth around it and gripped it with my lips. I took it in one swallow. Faith will carry me through—it always has.

La Fe que Consuela   —*Robert Vázquez Pacheco*

Faith is the force of life.
—Leo Tolstoy

I believe that I have been infected probably since the early 80s. How do I know, you ask? Well, I've had this swollen lymph node since 1983. At least, that's as far back as I remember. HIV infected for maybe eleven years. Maybe longer. Who can tell. I've spent more than a decade living with this killer in my blood. I am still healthy and still asymptomatic through no conscious effort of my own. Unlike some people I know, my life does not focus around my HIV infection. Both my own treatment and my practice of "safer" sex have been fairly hit or miss. Actually my practice of "safer" sex has been more conscious and consistent than my application of treatments, alternative or otherwise. I've kinda practiced "safer" sex for years. I qualify that statement because naturally I've had difficulty in sticking to the "Ten Commandments." Yeah, I did say naturally. There exists an assumption in the wonderful and wacky world of HIV prevention that the practice of "safer" sex is something easy or painless. Most "safer" sex campaigns have traditionally adopted the Nike philosophy, "Just Do It." I'd like to think that the assumption is changing. Even today, in year thirteen of the epidemic, condoms are not something that gay men or even straight men automatically go for. The reasons for this are various. We all know how complex human sexual behavior can be normally. Add the cosmic monkey wrench of HIV, and you now have a situation even more involved. I believe that one of the barriers to the practice of safer sex is just basic human need. Maybe I'm a romantic, but I believe there is something fundamentally important in the sharing of bodily fluids. I believe it is something we need to do naturally as animals and human beings. So the interruption of that process (i.e. "safer" sex) can cause major behavioral stress. That's why the Nike philosophy doesn't work. Another barrier is the fact that we carry our individual histories (i.e. emotional baggage) into that bedroom as well. Yet another is the fact that men have never really been sexually responsible. Look at the history of birth control.

The practice of "safer" sex has never been easy for me. The rules change based on my knowledge or even lack of knowledge of my sexual partner's serostatus. What I do with another HIV-positive man or another man living with AIDS might be different from what I do with my HIV-negative lover. As horrible as that might sound to some, I know I am not alone in this practice. That's a reality that HIV prevention programs have yet to face up to. And I am not "relapsing." Relapsing (a term from the substance abuse industry) means that you are returning to previously destructive or at least potentially harmful behavior. Sucking and fucking without condoms is not previously destructive behavior. It isn't merely "unsafe" sex. It's just "normal" human sexual behavior. (Note: I include homosexuality and bisexuality under the rubric of normal sexuality.) Hey, I remember the seventies. I've survived expulsion from the sexual Garden of Eden. I remember sex before AIDS. I miss it. No amount of current unsafe sex can recapture that experience, although the smell of semen can elicit a Proustian response from me. Those memories of boys, baths, and disco music have become more than what they actually are. Memories have the tendency to do that, and those memories, to quote Gladys Knight, get in my way. But my inconsistent practice of safer sex is not merely nostalgia for lost times. No condom can stretch enough to accommodate the host of issues arising for gay men about "safer" sex.

Faith is to believe what we do not see; and the reward of this faith is to see what we believe.
—St. Augustine

Teenagers aren't the only ones who believe they'll live forever. I have buried enough people to begin to kinda sorta believe that I'll make it at least to the millennium. This is not based on any logical scientific information but after all, AIDS is not a logical disease. I seem to keep going, even with my fifty-nine T-cells, no AZT, and occasional unsafe sex. My grandmother's explanation is that my work here on earth isn't finished. She and my mom pray for me regularly. And as AIDS is not a logical disease, my grandma's theory is about as accurate as anything else, and the prayers certainly can't hurt. Does my faith in my own survival contribute to my "relapses"? I certainly am not arrogant about being asymptomatic for so long. I am humbled by the deaths of so many of my friends and lovers, and I am grateful for the ability to keep living and contributing . But whatever questioning faith I may maintain in my ability to reach the ripe old age of forty-four, I most certainly have an unquestioning faith in the transmissibility of HIV. Hence my uncomfortableness with my HIV-negative lover's giving me head without a condom. As we know the jury is still out on that one. I believe that given the amount of queens I know who suck dick without a condom, if oral transmission was a common transmission route, there would be a lot more HIV-positive queens. But my slightly flippant and essentialist theorizing doesn't preclude the reality of actual risk, no matter how miniscule. For the first time, I understand my own responsibility in transmitting the virus to another, and it terrifies me. Is it love or at least this particular romance with this particular man that brings this terrifying realization? Although the answer to this specific question is obviously a topic for therapy, the horror, guilt, and remorse I feel at the fact that I may have infected other men is a distant personal hell my Catholic upbringing is positively drooling over.

In retrospect, I realize that since I learned about my infection, my most "unsafe" sex has been with other HIV positive men or men with AIDS. At least, I really want to believe that. More immediate is my fear of possibly hurting the man I love. I look at him, young, intelligent, so vibrant, and so excited about everything. He is a gay man of color, like me. We speak of historical similarities between Puerto Ricans and Pilipinos, both peoples on islands conquered by Spain and the United States, both groups looked down upon by the larger Asian Pacific Islander and Latino communities. We are both island niggers, proud and powerful. I adore him.

Faith is the substance of things hoped for, the evidence of things unseen.
—Hebrews XI.I

I now understand how my lover Jeff felt when he learned he had Kaposi's sarcoma in 1982. He immediately wanted to stop having sex with me and was depressed for the longest time because he thought he had infected me. I now remember watching him sicken and eventually die. I understand his not wanting me to experience that physical and emotional pain. Despite all the warm, fuzzy, and empowering messages put out there about HIV/AIDS, having AIDS is a bitch. A barely functioning immune system is no picnic. As I sit here, rubbing a topical ointment on the rash I'm getting from the medication that is supposed to keep me from getting a life threatening opportunistic infection, I realize I really wouldn't wish HIV or AIDS on my worst enemy. I certainly wouldn't wish it on my HIV-negative lover. This is no simple situation and no easy answer presents itself. Nike philosophy doesn't help. Abstinence is out of the question, despite my non-existent sex drive. The strict application of outmoded moral codes, like the Judeo-Christian system, to sexual behavior can be problematic. There are situations where right and wrong are difficult to clearly sort out. For me, resolution may come through self-understanding and an increased sense of responsibility. That's certainly what I'll tell my therapist. An intimate exploration of personal motivations opens up a lifetime of pain, fear, and insecurity. I don't think I'm unique in this. Can we do this though as individual members of a community that continues to be decimated? It needs to be done while we take care of the sick and dying and fight to protect the next generation from a rabid right-wing government. What strategies do we develop that can engender "responsible" sexual behavior? Can we even define "responsible" behavior for an individual as well as a community, given the diversity of race/ethnicity, class, sexual identity, sexual practices, and histories of homophobia and abuse. The framing of AIDS as a public health crisis as opposed to an individual one is a double-edged sword but given the current political climate, this strategy can have only limited success. The burdens of HIV infection and the prevention of its transmission are both individual and collective but understanding where the rights and freedoms of individuals end and the rights of the community begin is difficult to ascertain. At least it is for me. Yeah, sure, I want to reenact the seventies with my lover, complete with patchouli incense and water beds, but to what end and at what cost. I understand that the transmission of HIV involves two people and both the infected and the uninfected are equally responsible for HIV prevention. He is as responsible as I am, but where does that leave us? The more I examine the paradox of life in the age of AIDS, the more questions I have, and they are questions many people don't even want to hear. Despite the romantic fantasies of my people, neither faith in a higher power nor the love of a good man is the answer, but I believe this tells me that they might just be one of the means to the end of this pandemic. These are strategies, strategies of survival for those of us living in the new holocaust.

Our social and individual lives are woven with uncertainty. Chance forms a substantial part of our very nature, in that space of existential anguish of that as yet inexplicable and uncertain, where faith claims its right to help go on living. Doubtless, the path to follow is the hard one of conquering objective knowledge, real control over our environment and ourselves. But while we still cry, hundreds of thousands of years of drum magic will be in our blood.
—Natalia Bolívar, *Las Orishas en Cuba*, 1990

climbs out between my fingers… It takes him

—Janice Mirikitani

A Tongue in Your Ear

overleaf: Gaye Chan, "Angel on a Folding Chair."
quotation from Janice Mirikitani, *Shedding Silence:
Poetry and Prose* (Berkeley: Celestial Arts, 1987).

My Grandmother's Third Eye

Thelma Seto

In my grandmother's Japan
there was no word for lesbian.
That came with the Westerners,
their black suits and white skin,
the Caucasian dichotomy—
Light and dark,
Male and female,
religion and sex.

A shadow in a nether region,
I disappear in your language,
mine now I've been dispossessed.
I flounder in a trough
off the Galapagos Islands
in the doldrums of August.
Untranslatable,
I am a squid riding the waves.
My tentacles ejaculate black ink
into this estuary
of self-exile.

Your vocabulary translates me
from a pictograph
into a nonsense verse
that makes sense
only in English.
The erotic has its own
etymologies.
Like me,
it defines itself.

Each morning while she prayed at her altar
to our ancestors, my grandmother
had multiple orgasms.
She understood death.
Eros ran through her
like sweat,
honoring her
with hallucinations
of the third,
most marvelous
eye.

Bak Sze, White Snake

Kitty Tsui

Author's Note: *Bak Sze, White Snake* is an historical novel that begins in China in 1900 and ends in San Francisco forty years later. It is the story of a woman who escaped death by drowning as an infant. Rescued by a man who ran an all-girl opera troupe, she becomes a Chinese opera singer. In 1922, she travels to Gold Mountain to star at the Liberty Theater on Broadway.

In this excerpt, White Snake, who has been manipulated into marriage by a fellow actor, Handsome Au, is confronted by her female lover, Red, who has followed her to San Francisco as the dresser of Peony, White Snake's childhood rival in the all-girl opera troupe. Red also cross-dresses as the actor, Dragon. White Snake and Peony are both headlining at rival theaters on Gold Mountain.

There was a cautious knocking on the door.

"He is not here. He is at the pool hall," White Snake called, expecting it to be one of Handsome Au's cronies.

"No, for you. Someone here for you." Apprentice Tan's excited face peered through the door. "There is a gentleman to see you. Shall I show him to the parlor?"

"To see me? Who is the gentleman?"

But Apprentice Tan giggled and hurried off without replying.

When White Snake approached, she could see a tall, still figure standing with his back to the door. He was wearing a Western suit and leather boots. The man turned at the sound of her footsteps. His hair was slicked down on his head, and his face was in shadow. But when he walked towards her, she saw that it was Little Red.

White Snake could not contain the scream that issued from her mouth. She was horrified and delighted all at once.

"Oh, Little Red, look at you," she said in wonder, "all grown up, and dressed like a man!"

"Liar! You are a liar! You betrayed my love for you."

The vehemence of the words struck her like a slap on the face.

"Little Red, wait, let me explain…."

"Explain? Explain what? Explain why you are married? Explain all the rubbish talk you want. I have heard the stories of the beautiful White Snake and the handsome Au," she hissed, her words tumbled out in a furious avalanche, gathering speed and fury. "You promised me your heart. You promised you would send for me. You betrayed me. I loved you. Damn you, you betrayed me with a man."

"Little Red, please, just listen to me for…."

"I am no longer your Little Red. Do not ever call me by that name again. I am the actor, Dragon. Look at me. These eyes that looked on you with adoration will never look at you again. These hands that touched you in love will never touch you again. These lips that kissed you will now kiss other women."

As Red turned to walk away, White Snake reached out to her.

"Oh, my love, you are breaking my heart. Forgive me, I had no choice but to marry. He is my husband in name only. You are the one I love."

"Rubbish words! You lie. I know you live in one room as man and wife. I know he touches you. Deny that he touches you then. Deny that he kisses you," she sobbed, heaving with emotion.

White Snake, too, began to cry.

"There, see! You cannot deny that you live together as man and wife. Right, then. I was a fool to believe you. I was a fool to think you loved me. Look at me. Look at me! Yes, I am dressed like a man. That's what you want, isn't it? I was your lover, but I was not a man, so you betrayed me and married a man. I was a fool to fall for your words. I was a fool to love you. Never again will I love you. Not in this life or any other."

She tore the jade heart from her neck, threw it onto the floor, and turned on her heel.

White Snake ran to her room and collapsed onto the bed, shaking. She felt weak, as if her bones could no longer hold her body up. A wave of emotion threatened to engulf her. Her heart knotted in anguish. How could this be happening? This was a nightmare of the worst kind, wretchedness beyond compare. Little Red had followed her to the Gold Mountain and found out that she was married. Yes, it was indeed turning out to be a nightmare of the worst kind. She was married to a man.

Peony sat staring intently at her face in the mirror. She tilted her head this way, then that, to one side, then the other. She knew she was beautiful; she saw it in men's eyes. She knew how to use her beauty to her advantage. Men pursued her with gifts and propositions. In Shanghai, a doctor had even proposed marriage. But she could not accept; their lives were too different. She was beautiful but she would never think to boast about it. Why would she have to? One look, that would be all the words that were needed.

Peony had beauty, fame, and fortune. But two things eluded her. Revenge on her old enemy, Number Four, and sexual satisfaction. Since the day Hsiao Hao, the clown, had sodomized her when she was fifteen, she had been unable to enjoy the act of clouds and rain. There were many men with whom she had tried. It was not that the men were incompetent lovers, but no matter how gentle they were, she could not find pleasure. And it was Number Four's fault.

Now Peony was in the Gold Mountain, and her rival was none other than Number Four, who now called herself White Snake. But Peony had the advantage. She knew her enemy. White Snake was in the dark.

Let her stay in the shadows, thought Peony, *until I am ready to kill.*

Her reflection in the mirror turned ugly.

"What is wrong with Dragon?" asked Peony of Prosperous Ma. "Since this afternoon she has been silent and brooding, as if someone had dishonored her mother and she is plotting revenge."

"Aiyah, I do not know what is wrong with her. She looks like she has a bitter pill in her mouth. And during the performance too. I will have a talk with her. Aiyah, shows she has no training. It does not matter what has happened, even if someone has dishonored her mother. It does not matter if her mother has died. When you are onstage, that is the world. When you are onstage, that is the only world."

Prosperous Ma paused, "Curious though, I heard talk that Dragon was seen at the lodging-house of Producer Ming's company."

"That cannot be true. What could she be doing there?"

"I heard she went to see White Snake."

It never failed. The mere mention of the name was enough to make Peony seethe. Dragon and White Snake? What was their connection?

Peony knocked lightly on the door of Red's room.

"Go away."

"It is I, Peony, and I must come in."

"Go away. I am not well. Go away, I tell you."

Peony opened the door and entered the room. Red was lying on the bed dressed in street clothes.

"Oh, where have you been? I see you were out on the street as Dragon."

"Well, what of it? Now you are my guardian as well as Prosperous Ma?" snapped Red.

"Do not get touchy with me. You are forgetting your place here."

"Am I?"

"Yes, you are," replied Peony pointedly. "You are my dresser, do not forget that. Do not for one moment think that you are of the same caliber as I. But, come, do not let us argue."

Red's jaw tightened, but she kept her silence.

Peony's voice changed. It became as sweet as orange blossom honey.

"Tell me what is wrong. Are you not well?"

She sat on the bed and reached for Red's hand.

"What is the matter? Did something happen?"

Red felt her insides knot up. The pain was unbearable. Her temples felt tight. Her heart was about to explode. She wanted to scream. She wanted to hit something. She wanted to hurt someone.

Peony was sitting beside her on the bed, stroking her arm, whispering soothing words in her ear. She was so close Red could smell her scent, feel her breath against her face. Peony unfastened the top button and loosened the collar of Red's shirt. Red began to cry, great sobs shaking her chest.

"What is it, Red? Someone hurt you, didn't they? Who broke your heart? Who did that to you?"

Red wanted to name her tormentor. She wanted to tell Peony who had betrayed her. She wanted to scream curses at the top of her voice. But she could only cry tears.

Finally she whispered: "White Snake betrayed me."

So, Peony thought, Red is lovesick and the object of her desire has spurned her. She slipped into the bed beside her and took her in her arms.

"Calm yourself. Everything will be all right."

Peony brushed her wet cheeks with her lips.

"Lie still and let me hold you. Cry if you must. Let the tears come out, then the pain will leave you."

Red's body shook violently in her arms. Peony felt a sudden sensation of arousal. Red's wet face was underneath her. On an impulse, Peony leaned down to kiss her. Red's lips opened, and she was drawn into a cavern of sweet warmth. Her mouth filled with song. Peony's hands sought out the mystery of the other woman's body. Red's body was firm, as muscular as a man's but her skin was hairless and as smooth as porcelain. Peony let her fingers travel over the warm plain of Red's stomach to her groin. They kissed again. Red opened her thighs and responded with her own need.

Peony heard a mellifluous voice lift and soar and realized it was her own. She was moaning in pleasure for the first time in her life.

20

Tita Aida

(for Jorge F. Casaclang)

R. Zamora Linmark

The Almighty

If the fever does not go away, fasten your seat belts, girlfriends, and wait for St. Jude to cross your legs. If he takes too long, sweep your thoughts together and call the Hotline. No charge, girlfriends, and the voices you hear are real. Tell 'em about the chills, night sweats, and runs you've been having. Open your palms and read to 'em the expeditions you took, how many, and where. Don't worry, girlfriends, we've all been there before, and it's all in the name of confidentiality. Don't forget to mention any shipwrecks, perished pilots, and moss growing on your skin. When those closet doors swung open and spit froze in our eyes, did we whimper and make a U-turn? No, girlfriends, we flexed our muscles and painted our nails suck-me violet. Then we took a blowtorch and burnt the damn closet to thy kingdom come. Not my kingdom, but theirs, girlfriends, the ones over there with the jasmine crucifix and fornicating beards who pounded the carpenter's table when we laughed at the flames. The first few nights are always the hardest. The spiking fever, delirious lips, and skin so dry you could peel it off and make sandwich bags. But, like catechism and singles bars, you'll get used to it and begin to take it as it is without asking why no one comes up to you anymore and hands over a calling card with a name written in magic markers. You'll even learn how to float without tire tubes or air mats. So hang in there, girlfriends, and the vines will surely get to you. Grow your hair a few inches longer and you'll feel like Rapunzel, abandoned, but still waiting pretty. Remember: Think straight and the voices you hear are real. Don't wait too long for Jude because he might be on vacation and won't be able to find your lungs by the time he asks you to breathe deep and hold.

The Father

Yikkety yak yak. Shut your mouth, asshole. You swore on your mother's grave, and we're today's headline. You make me sick. Look at yourself, you're worse than a dried prune. Such a goddamn ugly twig, even freaks are scared of you. Stop calling me Dad because I stopped being your father ever since you sashayed out of this house in your ringlets and bobbypins and corset or whatever fuck you call it. Fucking purple queer, alright. I can't even think right because everyone wants to know who put those goddamn spots between your ass. Yikkety yak yak, and I get fish eyes breathing on my skin. Don't look at me as if you never asked for it either because you had your ass all ready for anyone who tripped on your satin gown. Some satin trick. Think I didn't know what you were doing behind my back. Stop pretending that you're sorry, asshole, because you loved every goddamn minute of it. Should've been there when you had heaven groped so I could record it and play it for you over and over and over again. So stop giving me this drama crap and don't even dare think for a second that I'm gonna touch you. Won't need to. All I have to do is breathe on you, and you'll be out of here. Look at this, finally make the front page, and you had to share it with one hundred other people. Front page with colored picture and all, they mixed you up with another guy and got your name spelled wrong. You swore on your dead mother three times, asshole, and I have to answer for everything. Even yakked about the first one. Conspiring under the mango grove with a married man. You make me sick with stories. So many and he had you fished out. If only you hadn't worn so much eyeshadows and put on those plastic tits. You better shut your fucking mouth, asshole. Better yet, get up and go tell 'em how you invented everything. Put a map over your body and tell 'em self-affliction. Get up, asshole, and show 'em how you stood in the dark and never got enough.

The Son

He is a picture spoiled by the rain that enters through the wooden slats. I remember his face when Mercy comes over for siesta to write the date and my name on the wall. Only three rusty nails, but so many thorns. When I go, forget pounding nails through these palms. Got enough blood jetting out from every hole of this body. Just tell me to spit, and I'll fill up a milk bottle. Kiss the thorns goodbye because I got enough headache to last me for the afterlife. I wish I were Mercy who's pumping-iron strong and used to lead when I wanted to cha cha cha the boring afternoon away. I don't dance anymore, gave up on the beat, threw my arms and legs to the monkey bar forever. I just swallow capsules and watch Mercy put numbers and words on the wall. When I go, she promised to paint my nails, soft-shell red, and dress me up in a beaded gown, my runaway gown, and pin a tiara made from mango leaves. I love Mercy. She taught me how to peel the blue strips off the capsules and save them for souvenir. They make fantastic ribbons. Indigo for rainy nights. Turquoise for summer solstice. Electric blue for fiesta dances. She keeps them in an old biscuit tin under the broken phonograph stand. When she wipes the siesta sweat off me and takes my temperature, I remember his face, and Mercy starts to make-up the past. Me in golden curls and pink muscle-T. Patty-cake, patty-cake, sores and shakes, nobody else but me. Cha cha, cha cha cha, it's flaming hot and nobody else but me. I love Mercy and think Mercy and she keeps her promise, soft-shell red because I remember the picture, mango-leaf tiara, and indigo because it's a rainy night, a beaded gown, and I pull my tongue out, and tie tie tie the words and numbers around my tongue, indigo, and cha cha cha and tie tie tie, and pull hard and tight, again and again and again, for souvenir, baby, for souvenir.

21

River Deep
& All Those Pretty Women

Elsa E'der

like so many bridges
they are / bending over me
marking some geography

perpetual beginnings
endings / piercing needle stitches
into river sand / hands holding nothing

I must somehow flow
past / curving my back
to the impossible anchors of her sharp edges

pulling at the shores I left
long, long ago / where
romances lie rootless in abandoned flood waters

my way is liquid motion
no seeds no roots / no memory
union is nature's last aborted mission

all river want is bring back
her flesh / in exile
earth / body / river sister

union is nature's last aborted mission

all those pretty women
river deep / woman struggle too long
she fear she drown the current drags bottom to top

she wants to walk on water
I want to pray / she wants me
bless her sorrow for another

so she cry at the river
lonely / her heart is
naked as the seasons change again

river belly cut
wide open / desire for oceans for oceans
of love with no home

woman bleed in the river
angry / river deep
and lonely bridges bend while river eyes turn

now your wound is my wound
seagulls circle / ready to feed
should I fall into the sea

it is me who must leave her
Dios Solar / suck the tears away
water rising to destroy its own path

all those pretty women
drowning at the gates
love looking for home

I will leave
miles of river / in the floods
nature's last aborted mission

seeds, roots, memory.

—1993

22

Grandma's Tales

Andrew Lam

A day after Mama and Papa took off to Las Vegas Grandma died. Nancy and I, we didn't know what to do. Vietnamese traditional funeral with incense sticks and chanting Buddhist monks were not our thing.

"We have a big freezer, Nancy said, why don't we freeze Grandma. Really, why bother Mama and Papa—what's another day or two for Grandma, now anyway?

Since Nancy's older than me and since I didn't have any better idea, we iced Grandma.

Grandma was ninety-four-years eight months and six days old when she died. She had seen lots of things and lived through three wars and two famines. She lived a full hard life if you ask me. America, besides, was not all that good for her. She had been confined to the second floor of our big Victorian home as her health was failing and she did not speak English and only a little French. French like *Oui monsieur, c'est évidemment un petit monstre.* And, *Non, Madame, vous n'etes pas du tout enceinte, je vous assure.* She was a head nurse in the maternity ward of the Hanoi hospital during the French colonial time. I used to love her stories about delivering all these strange two-headed babies and Siamese triplets connected at the hip whom she named Happy, Liberation, and Day.

Grandma died a quiet death really. She was eating spring rolls with me and Nancy. Nancy was wearing this real nice black miniskirt and her lips were painted red and Grandma said, "You look like a high-class whore."

And Nancy made a face and said she was preparing to go to one of her famous San Francisco artsy-fartsy cocktail parties where waiters are better dressed than most Vietnamese men of high-class status back home and the foods are served on silver trays and there is baby corn, duck paté, salmon mousse, and ice sculptures with wings and live musicians playing Vivaldi music. "So eat, Grandma, and get off my case because I'm no whore."

"It was a compliment," Grandma said, winking at me, "but I guess it's wasted on you, child." Then Grandma laughed, her breath hoarse and thinning, her deep wrinkled face a blur. Still she managed to say this much as Nancy prepared to leave, "Child, do the cha-cha-cha for me. I didn't get to do much when I was young, with my clubbed foot and the wars and everything else."

"Sure Grandma," Nancy said, and rolled her pretty eyes toward the chandelier. Then Grandma just dropped her chopsticks on the hardwood floor—clack, clack, clatter, clack, clack—leaned back, closed her eyes, and stopped breathing. Just like that.

So we iced her. She was small enough that she fit right above the TV dinner trays and the frozen yogurt bars we were going to have for dessert. We wrapped all of grandma's five-foot-three, ninety-eight pounds lithe body in saran wrap and kept her there and hoped Mama and Papa would get the Mama-Papa-come-home-quick-grandma's-dead letter that we sent to Circus-Circus where they were staying, celebrating their thirty-third wedding anniversary. In the meanwhile Nancy's got a party to go to, and I have to meet Eric for a movie.

It was a bad movie too, if you want to know the truth. But Eric is cool. Eric has always been cool. Eric has eyes so blue you can swim in them. Eric has this laugh that makes you warm all over. And Eric is really beautiful and a year older than me, a senior. *Dragon*, the movie is called, *Dragon*, starring this Hawaiian guy who played Bruce Lee. He moaned and groaned and fought a lot in the movie but it just wasn't the same. Bruce Lee is dead. Bruce Lee could not be revived even if the guy who played him has all these muscles to crack walnuts and lay bricks with. Now Grandma was dead too.

So Eric and I got home and necked on the couch. Eric liked Grandma. Grandma liked Eric. Though they hardly ever spoke to one another because neither one knew the other's language, there was this thing between them, you know, mutual respect like, like one cool old chick to one cool young dude thing. (Sometimes I would translate but not always 'cause my English is not all that good and my Vietnamese sucks). What's so cool about Grandma is that she's the only one who knows I'm bisexual. I mean, I hate the term but I'm bisexual, I suppose, by default 'cause I don't have a preference and I respond to all stimuli. And Eric stimulated me at the moment, and Grandma who for some reason, though Confucian bound and trained, and a Buddhist and all, was really cool about it. One night, I remember, we were sitting in the living room watching a John Wayne movie together and Eric was there with me and Grandma while Mama and Papa had just gone to bed. (Nancy is again at some weird black-and-white ball or something like that). And Eric leaned over and kissed me on the lips, and Grandma said, "That's real nice." I translated and we all laughed and John Wayne shot dead five mean old guys. Just like that. But Grandma didn't mind, really. She'd seen Americans like John Wayne shooting her people before and always thought John Wayne was a bad guy in the movies, and she'd seen us more passionate than a kiss on the lips and didn't mind. She used to tell us to be careful and not make any babies—obviously a joke—'cause she's done delivering them. She also thought John Wayne was uglier than a water buffalo's ass, but never-you-mind. So, you see, we liked Grandma a lot.

Now Grandma's packed in -12 degrees Fahrenheit. And the movie sucked. On the couch in the living room, after a while I said, "Eric, I have to tell you something."

"What," asked Eric?

"Grandma's dead," I said.

"You're kidding me, Eric whispered, showing his beautiful white teeth.

"I kid you not," I said.

"She's dead, and Nancy and me, we iced her."

"Shit!" said Eric, "Why?"

"Cause she would start to smell otherwise, duh, and we have to wait for my parents to perform a traditional Vietnamese funeral." We fell silent for a while then, holding each other.

Then Eric said, "Can I take a peek at Grandma?"

"Sure," I said, "Sure you can, she was as much yours as she was mine," and we went to the freezer and looked in.

The weird thing was the freezer was on defrost and Grandma was nowhere in sight. There was a trail of water and saran wrap leading from the freezer to her bedroom though, so we followed it. On the bed, all wet and everything, there sat Grandma counting her Buddhist rosary and chanting her diamond sutra. What's weirder still is that she looked real young. I mean around fifty-four now, not ninety-four. The high cheekbones came back, the rosy lips. When she saw us she smiled and said: "What do you say we all go to one of those famous cocktail parties that Nancy's gone to, the three of us?" Now, I wasn't scared, she being my Grandma and all, but what really got me feeling all these goose bumps on my neck and arms was that she said it in English, I mean accentless, Californian English. I mean the way Mrs. Collier, our neighbor, the English teacher speaks English. Me, I have a slight accent still but Grandma's was really fine.

"Wow, Grandma," said Eric, "your English is excellent."

"I know," Grandma said, "that's just a side benefit of being reborn. But enough with compliments, we got to party."

"Cool," said Eric.

"Cool," I said, though I was a little jealous 'cause I had to go through junior high and high school and all those damn ESL classes and everything to learn the same language while Grandma just got it down cold—no pun intended—'cause, so it would seem, she was reborn. And Grandma put on this nice brocaded red blouse and black silk pants and sequined velvet shoes and fixed her hair real nice, and we drove off downtown.

Boy, you should've seen Nancy's face when we came in. I mean she nearly tripped over herself and had to put her face on the wing of this ice sculpture that looked like a big melting duck to calm herself. Then she walked straight up to us, all haughty like and said, "It's invitation only, how'd y'all get in?"

"Calm yourself, child," said Grandma, "I told them that I was a board member of the Cancer Society and flashed my jade bracelet and diamond ring and gave the man a forty-dollar tip." And Nancy had the same reaction Eric and I had: Grandma, your English is flawless! But Grandma was oblivious to compliments. She went straight to the punch bowl to scoop up some spirits. That's when I noticed that her clubbed foot was cured, and she had this elegant grace about her. She drifted, you might say, across the room, her hair floating like gray-black clouds behind her, and everyone stared, mesmerized.

Needless to say Grandma was the big hit of that artsy-fartsy party. She had so many interesting stories to tell. The feminists, it seemed, loved her the most. They crowded around her like hens around a barn yard rooster and made it hard for the rest of us to hear. But Grandma told her stories all right. She told them how she'd been married early and had eight children while being the matriarch of a middle-class family during the Viet Minh Uprising. She told them about my grandfather, a brilliant man who was well versed in Moliere and Shakespeare and who was an accomplished violinist but who drank himself to death because he was helpless against the colonial powers of the French. She told everyone how single-handedly she had raised her children after his death and they all became doctors and lawyers and pilots and famous composers. Then she started telling them how the twenty-four-year-old civil war divided her family up, and brothers fought brothers over some stupid ideological notions that proved terribly bloody but pointless afterwards. Then she told them about our journey across the Pacific Ocean in this crowded fishing boat where thirst and starvation nearly did us all in until it was her idea to eat some of the dead and drink their blood so that the rest of us could survive to catch glimpses of this beautiful America and become Americans.

She started telling them, too, about the fate of Vietnamese women who must marry and see their husbands and sons go to war and never to come back. Then she recited poems and told fairy tales with sad endings, fairy tales she herself had learned as a child, the kind she used to tell me and my cousins when we were real young. There was this princess, you see, who fell in love with a fisherman, and he didn't know about her 'cause she only heard his beautiful voice singing from a distance and so when he drifted down river one day she died, her heart turning into this ruby with the image of his boat imprinted on it. There was also this faithful wife who held her baby waiting for her war-faring husband every night on a cliff and one stormy night, out of pity, the gods turned her and her child into stone. In Grandma's stories, the husbands and fishermen always come home, but they come home always too late and there was nothing the women could do but mourn and grieve.

Grandma's voice was sad and seductive and words came pouring out of her like rain and the whole place turned quiet and Nancy sobbed because she understood. Eric, he stood close to me and put a hand on my shoulder and squeezed slightly and I, leaning against him, cried a little too.

"I lost four of my children," Grandma said, "twelve of my grandchildren and countless relatives and friends to wars and famines, and I lost everything I owned when I left my beautiful country behind. Mine is a story of suffering and sorrow, sorrow and suffering being the way of Vietnamese life. But now I have a second chance, and I am not who I was. And yet I have all the memories so wherever I go, I figure, I will keep telling my stories and songs."

There was this big applause then and afterwards a rich looking man with gray hair and a pin-stripe suit came up to Grandma, and they talked quietly for a while. When they were done Grandma came to me and Nancy and Eric and said goodbye. She said she was not going to wait for my parents to come home for a traditional funeral. She has got a lot of living still to do since Buddha had given her the gift to live twice in one life and this man, some famous novelist from Columbia, was going to take her places. He may even help her write her book. So she was going to the mediteranee to get a tan and to Venice to see the festivals and ride the gondolas, and maybe afterward she'd go by Hanoi and see what they'd done to her childhood home and visit some long forgotten ancestral graves and relatives, and then who knows where she'll go after that? She'll send post cards though and don't you wait up. Then before we knew it Grandma was already out of the door with the famous novelist and the elevator music started up again and people felt pretty good. They hugged each other, and there was this magical feeling in the air. And if those ice sculptures of ducks and fat little angels with bows and arrows started to come alive and fly away or something, I swear, nobody would have been surprised. Eric and I ran out after Grandma after we got through the hugging frenzy, but she was already gone. Outside there was only this beautiful city under a velvety night sky, its high rises shining like glass cages with little diamonds and gold coins kept locked inside of them.

Mama and Papa came home two days later. They brought incense sticks and ox hide drums and wooden fish and copper gongs and jasmine wreaths and Oolong tea and paper offerings—all the things that we were supposed to have for a traditional funeral. A monk had even sent a fax of his chanting rate and schedule and "please choose the appropriate time because he was real busy" and the relatives started pouring in.

It was hard to explain then what had happened, what we had always expected as the tragic ending of things, human frailty, the point of mourning and grief. And wasn't epic loss what made us tell our stories? It was difficult for me to mourn now, though. Difficult 'cause while the incense smoke drifted all over the mansion and the crying and wailing resounded like cicadas humming on the tamarind tree in the summer back in Vietnam, Grandma wasn't around. Grandma had done away with the easy plot for tragedy and life after her was not going to be so simple anymore.

23

Queer Pilipino Rebolusiyon
with ms. nikki giovanni to thank for

Joël B. Tan

yesterday
on live television
prime time
mr. newsman asked me
who i thought our
great white hope
was for this election year and
i said, "this
colored
queer
don't
have a hope to drop-dead on"

i called for
rebolusiyon
cause i got
real tired of asking

real nice like
for our human rights
and i figure what would it
matter anyway,
since they don't
listen to queers
or coloreds
unless they get
downright
aggressive
and mean
and use big words like
rebolusiyon

all of a sudden
they get these
malnutritioned visions of apocalypse
in their minds about
killin' people and burnin' shit up.
rebolusiyon is a big smart
benevolent
word
that involves more than violence

rebolusiyon
starts with the mind
and the self
like bright yellow
knowledge imploding in your brain
merging with your deep
deepest
soul-part
then coming out your mouth
out your hands
out your private parts
and falling dead smack in the middle of your
heart.

so you see
rebolusiyon ain't scary.
uh-uh, in fact,
rebolusiyon

is a freeing,
mango-juicy
dope
fat, fresh, fly
liberating
emancipating
ejaculating
gyrating
titillating
bootie-grooving
earth-moving
this is the dawning of the age of aquarius
love thang
wrapped up in a whole lot of
historical
common sense.

word.

funny thing is since
i look like a monkey in suits
and t.v. only gives you
five seconds to speak your peace
i thought that rebolusiyon was
like
offering the world
a one-word
poëm.

—October 1992

24

Fascination, Gravity, and a Deeply Done Kiss

Lisa Asagi

There was nothing at all significant that caused me to tell of this, except for a sudden lapse in perception. How steam holds long enough to play against any conjured change in temperature, how a reaction can be so visibly shaken out of something as mundane as a shower in the middle of an ordinary evening. Perhaps it was an inadequate amount of ventilation. Whatever the case, I had never found myself before a room so vividly filled with vagueness, instilling an inertia normally reserved for a slipping off a very steep cliff. It had nothing to do with contemplation. I simply turned off the water, parted the curtains, and found myself not being able to find my towel. So unlike me. No not nude. Naked. In a fog. It could have been a smoke-filled room and my last moment. I could have died. But instead, I am alone and worried about it.

There is a painting that hangs in a museum two miles from my apartment. It is a watercolor by Paul Klee. Smaller than what you'd expect from any book. Notepaper sized. It's strange how wood frames pronounce the empty space that emerges from thin lines and segments of color. When you see them all lined up on the wall there is a strange sadness in the insect lines, deserts, and he wasn't even trying to be abstract. Some of them involve an image of a musical note called a fermata, which instructs a sustained pause, the prolongation of a tone, chord, or rest beyond its nominal value. He drew it on its side so it looked like a crescent moon. To musicians it is known as a bird's eye because of this elliptical shape.

Once, I fell in love with a married woman. Once, I thought that this body she left me with was able to have her live within, absorbed like an ink bird on my thigh or some secret bullet. But this is not possible anymore because I cannot stop thinking about her. Cannot stop interfering with the nature of motion, have it grow out of me, let it envelope, encircle, then gradually expand until I am freed to be nothing but an atom already accustomed to the gravity in the next phase of its world. I stutter. I don't stare long enough. I eat too much, then I don't eat at all. I buy books and don't read them. I borrow books and read them. I walk around the block and can't decide the best time to cross the street. I practice falling in love with strangers. I practice falling in love with my friends. I practice falling in love because I know that it is the only way out. That perhaps one day, I will find myself hopefully lost with the gravity of a situation like her again. And then I will know why this feeling of falling is brick red. That it is not my imagination. Because I have been practicing. Because maybe soon I will be able to say why there is a difference between secretly falling within a building of thought and actually free falling quickly, like a bright glance, the figure of a hand stretching outwards, the length of a deeply done kiss.

What's important. What's relevant? It always seems to depend on the minute of the day or nonfiction to the point of some kind of rage. A storm in the eye.

"She was talking about her soul. She was talking about the angle of her soul. The one behind hindsight, the dashboard. That walking sleepless giant chasing shadows across tables of the universe, knocking over chairs, twisting forks, teetering glasses. An animate angle that sweeps islands and airplanes into its lips at the speed of sound, and swiftly closes as if an eyelid. The speed of light. You smiled. She was talking about fascination. She is thinking about desire, how it can only grow vivid once it is left alone long enough to feel itself as one thing. Original."

The storm in the eye of my life.

I know. It's odd. But I should say that it never felt anything close to abrupt at the time. Maybe I had been in love with her for three years. And maybe those years threw themselves into a wall and broke for two weeks, the strongest and loudest that ever happened to me. It scattered molecules, feathers in an atomic living room of a slowly disintegrating, slowly regenerating physically political world.

Strange, but it happens.

Maybe if I start from the very beginning, nothing will be lost, and it would be okay. I think that if my body were a boat, to describe the ocean around me will mean that nothing will ever sink. Don't you agree?

Once there was an island that felt so alone it stopped. Got too involved with folding waves and how nothing happened to end this. It grew deaf and then violent. Then it could not tell the difference between land, flesh, blood, and water. Coldness of a flame so far below the peacefulness of the arctic circle, it burned itself down to the wick just to spite the watchful eyes of time.

Wait a minute. That was drama. But this wants to be a story about semblance and difference between the object and the subject of desire, the difference between a statue and a play, text and skin, music and motion, or an incredibly long sentence that says nothing about how one brief moment can go on to mean the world for a very long time.

So.

In six years the millennium will turn itself over and until then, anything can happen. The placement of the story, in the geometry of inclining angles of this world, becomes strangely fixated into acute and recurrent sections. Where once was science, you distill chance. Whatever the call, you leave messages and send letters from the storm. Hope that if anything, they will find a course of reference beneath the cooling screened images, between the colorfully televised warnings of hurricanes and psychology. Maps were never useful in defending against tempests.

So you write if you can, you say:

wait. Or dear miranda,

Nobody told me this world was an island. I knew that I lived on an island, but nobody said that this whole place was an island and there was an ocean and other islands. That you lived on an island around me and never knew it too. That you would leave. Sign it.

Once I was walking down Sixteenth Street, heard a nocturne being played from a car at a stoplight and actually looked to see if it was her. It was the same nocturne that I asked her to teach me. Her father was a pianist, grew her around the mathematics of music and so notes would nestle into the corners of her ears. Like painters' eyes could absorb degrees of paint. She had this ebony baby grand piano and would play it at night after she thought I had gone to sleep. Three thousand miles and still I see her face in sheets of glass, ceilings, walls of wood and plaster, cups of water, curved up like a glance. And I don't want to think it, but sometimes I feel there is no such thing as land anymore. That maybe there are just boats who believe in rivers. Drifting on the same ocean all of the time.

It's so late. To some people it is just early enough. The sun is going to reappear within a matter of hours. It has to. Motion is a habit that surrounds things that happen.

When I brush my teeth, I realize that I am twenty-seven years old. It is a very human feeling.

Run the faucet, then you don't. In an adult body, walk through the short hallway and into the angles assembled for an immediate future. Turn out the light and lie down.

It is a long fall into the fact that it is so late and uncomfortable, but you are accustomed to levels of tepidness. When it was too warm, you grew fascinations. In these deepening days, all you have are those feathers again. And you wander in them, months of curved knives.

I can't go to sleep. I don't have to. So then I will have to watch. You know, the earth is nothing but fire contained within itself by tons of ocean and degrees of thickness or acres of soil. Every plot of land, horizontal then vertical, began as an island. They say that biology began on this planet as reaction to the accidental. Pressure. A leaning in and leaning out. Chaos, chemistry, and the colorful length of desire from inertia. Survival. A self taught, half-expected emotion whose logic was not understood until millions of afternoons proved able enough to hold into evenings.

I called her three days ago. Saw her a month ago in the post office. Then I saw her at a bus stop. She was standing in a Chinese take-out shop. Then sitting on a dryer in a laundromat. Then I remembered. And it was so strange, but after I turned off the shower, parted the curtains and reached for my towel, I thought I saw her walk out of the bathroom. She left the door open.

Aloes

from *The Country of Dreams and Dust*

Russell Leong

The diving board
on which I sit
overhangs the edge
of the swimming pool,
drained of its water.
A concrete, kidney-shaped grave
swollen with the legs of odd chairs,
cracked tables,
and a hundred aloe plants
in black plastic tubs.

This derelict yard
backdrops a yellow tract house
in Little Saigon, Minh-Quang,
Temple of Shining Light,
a freeway's turn away from L.A.,
where helicopters buzz low,

overtake highways,
shopping malls, suburban tracts,
Mexican territories, and
swoop down Hollywood.
Lowriders cruise the boulevards;
pickups flood the streets.
Driven by gunshots, I hit the floor.
Am I wounded too?

On the diving board, I unwrap
my legs, locate elements of myself
in air, earth and afternoon.

Inside the temple
a monk is chanting.
His sutras unlock doors,
release windows and walls,
sweep past wooden eaves
of the western house and alight
upon aloes in the yard.

I discard another layer of my life.
A friend tells me
that seven of his buddies
have died of AIDS.
No one wants to know.

In Asian families, you just disappear.
Your family rents a small room for you.
They feed you lunch.
They feed you dinner.
Rice, fish, vegetables.

At my feet, aloes thrust green
spikes upwards from black dirt,
promise to heal wounds and burns,
to restore the skin's luster.
Pure light will arise
over suburban roofs and power lines,
illuminating the path of green aloes
by which I return.

I drink snow water
that falls from high Sierra beaches,
bleached by white shellcaps
and whale bones. Petrified waves
fathom the past
and plumb the future.

Deer
    tigers
sables
    pandas
gibbons
    lynx
monkeys
bite their tongues,
rub their eyes in the red dust.

The monk in the kitchen
is cutting cabbages
on the nicked formica table
for supper.

We must eat
and drink
in order to live.

Contributors

Writers

Lisa Asagi was born and raised in Honolulu, Hawaii. Currently, she is working on a novel in San Francisco, California.

Cristy Chung is a San Francisco Bay Area writer and editor who served recently on the editorial board for *Sinister Wisdom's* 1992 Lesbian of Color issue (#47) *Tellin' It Like It 'Tis.*

Michiyo Cornell (1953–1987) was born in Japan to a Japanese mother and a Euro-American father. A poet, writer, activist, mother, and lesbian feminist she co-founded a multicultural educational group, Kwanzaa, Inc. in 1981. She self-published a book of poetry, *Lesbian Lyrics* (1980) and published in *Azalea: A Magazine by Third World Lesbians* (1979–1980).

Elsa E'der is a descendant of Filipino plantation workers in Hawaii. She has and always will love women most.

David L. Eng received his Ph.D. in comparative literature at the University of California, Berkeley, specializing in Asian and Asian American literatures and film.

Richard Fung is a writer and independent video producer who has lived in Toronto since 1973. Born in Port-of-Spain, Trinidad, Fung has produced tapes including *Fighting Chance: Gay Asian Men and HIV* (1980) and *My Mother's Place* (1990) while contributing articles to *FUSE* magazine and *Moving the Image: Independent Asian Pacific American Media Arts* (1991). He is a graduate of the Photo-electric Arts Deptartment at the Ontario College of Art and the University of Toronto Cinema Studies Program.

Gayatri Gopinath is a graduate student in the Department of English and Comparative Literature at Columbia University and has been involved with South Asian community activism in New York City. Her essay on transnationalism and South Asian popular music is forthcoming in *Diaspora.*

Brian Green is a thirty-five-year-old African American gay man born in Chicago, Illinois. He has lived in Los Angeles for fourteen years and works in hotel management.

Lisa Kahaleole Chang Hall is a writer, activist, and doctoral candidate in ethnic studies at the University of California, Berkeley.

Alice Y. Hom, a graduate student in History/American Studies at Claremont Graduate School, has a B.A. from Yale and an M.A. in Asian American Studies from UCLA. During 1992–93 she was a fellow of the Rockefeller Humanities Asian Pacific American Generations program at the UCLA Asian American Studies Center where she did research on parents of lesbian daughters and gay sons.

J. Kehaulani Kauanui is currently a graduate student in History of Consciousness at the University of California, Santa Cruz. She recently attended the University of

Auckland, New Zealand on a Fulbright fellowship for research in Maori Studies. She received her B.A. from the University of California, Berkeley.

Aly Kim is a San Francisco Bay Area writer and editor who served recently on the editorial board for *Sinister Wisdom's* 1992 Lesbian of Color issue (#47) *Tellin' It Like It 'Tis.*

Andrew Lam is a Vietnamese American journalist and associate editor of Pacific News Service in San Francisco.

Erica L. H. Lee is a 1.5 generation Chinese American, born in Sydney, Australia and moved to the United States at age eleven. She recently graduated from Scripps College, Claremont, California with a B.A. in studio art and psychology.

R. Zamora Linmark's first book, *Rolling the R's*, was published by Kaya Production (New York: 1995).

Russell Leong is a Cantonese American poet and author of *The Country of Dreams and Dust* (1993). He edits UCLA's *Amerasia Journal* and edited *Moving the Image: Independent Asian Pacific American Media Arts* (1991). His writing is published in *Charlie Chan is Dead, Tricycle: The Buddhist Review*, the *New England Review*, and *Remapping the Occident.*

Martin F. Manalansan IV received his doctorate in anthropology at the University of Rochester.

Gil Mangaoang has a B.A. in urban studies, Loyola Marymount University. He is a writer and longtime organizer in minority, Filipino, and gay non-profit organization and groups.

Zoon Nguyen is the executive assistant to Roberta Achtenberg, Assistant Secretary, Office of Fair Housing and Equal Employment.

Trinity Ordona is a political activist and graduate student in the History of Consciousness Program, University of California at Santa Cruz.

Ric Parish is an African/Pilipino American AIDS Activist. He works as a Treatment Advocate at the Asian Pacific AIDS Intervention Team and is vice president of Being Alive People With AIDS Coalition.

Eric Estuar Reyes completed his masters thesis, ""Queer Spaces, The Spaces of Lesbians and Gay Men of Color in Los Angeles" at UCLA in 1993. His essay, "Asian Pacific Queer Space" appears in *Privileging Positions: The Sites of Asian American Studies*, ed. Gary Y. Okihiro, et al. (1995).

James Sakakura is a Yonsei (fourth generation Japanese American) living with AIDS. He has worked for the Asian Pacific AIDS Intervention Team.

Thelma Seto is a mixed-race sansei poet who lives in San Francisco.

Arlene Stein is a lesbian cultural critic and editor of *Sisters, Sexperts and Queers.* She teaches in the Department of Sociology, University of Oregon.

Dana Y. Takagi teaches sociology at University of California, Santa Cruz and is the author of *Retreat from Race: Asian American Admissions and Racial Politics* (1992). She coedited, with Michael Omi, "Thinking Theory in Asian American Studies," *Amerasia Journal* (1995).

Joël B. Tan is a pilipino paggot poët, kultural aktibist, and perpormans artist. He is an immigrant, and English is his second language. He has just completed his first collection of poëtry, retorik and perpormans entitled *(Runway) model minority.*

Took Took Thongthiraj is pursuing doctoral studies in English with an emphasis on literature by Southeast Asian women.

Daniel C. Tsang teaches "the Politics of Sexualities" and "Asian/Pacific American Alternative Media" at UC Irvine where he is a social sciences bibliographer and lecturer to the Asian Pacific American alternative quarterly, *Rice Paper.* His email address is: dtsang@uci.edu.

Kitty Tsui is the author of *The Words of a Woman Who Breathes Fire* (1983) and has just completed her first novel, *Bak Sze, White Snake.* Her writings have appeared in *Lesbian Erotics, Pearls of Passion,* (1995), *Chloe Plus Olivia,* (1994), *The Very Inside, an Anthology of Writings by Asian Pacific Lesbian and Bisexual Women,* (1994), *Lesbian Cultures and Philosophies,* (1990) and *Gay and Lesbian Poetry In Our Time* (1988).

Robert Vázquez Pacheco is a Puerto Rican gay man living with AIDS. He is a poet, essayist, community organizer, AIDS activist, visionary, revolutionary, and all-round nice guy. His work has been published in *Sojourner: Black Gay Voices in the Age of AIDS* (1993), the *James White Review* (1992) and the journal, *We the People.*

Eric C. Wat is the assistant coordinator of the student/community projects at the UCLA Asian American Studies Center and a free lance writer. His work has been published in *DisOrient, Amerasia Journal* and *On a Bed of Rice: An Asian American Erotica Feast* (1995).

Kimberly Yutani graduated from UCLA in 1992 with a degree in English and writes on independent film.

Artists

Gaye Chan is assistant professor of art at the University of Hawaii at Manoa. Her work has been featured in *AKS Photographs/Monthly Magazine* (Iran, 1992), *Art Direction/The Magazine of Visual Communication* (New York, June 1992), *The Advocate* (June 1991), *Arts Magazine* (New York, 1991), and *Amerasia Journal* (1994).

Allan deSouza is a multi-media artist and writer who has exhibited in the United States at the Houston Center for Photography, the Bronx Museum of the Arts, Whitney Museum, the Center for Photography, and in Britain at the Walsall Art Gallery, Citizens Gallery, Horizon Gallery, Embassy Cultural Center, Darlington Arts Center, and Leeds City Gallery.

Ming Yuen S. Ma is a Los Angles-based media artist, independent curator, and educator/activist. His video installations include *Between the Lines; Who Speaks?* in North American venues. His videotapes, *Aura* and *Toc Storee,* which explore aspects of queer Asian experience, have screened at Asian, Australian, U.S., Canadian, and European festivals.

Yong Soon Min is an assistant professor, School of Fine Arts at the University of California, Irvine. She has had solo exhibitions and commissions at Smith College, the Bronx Museum of the Arts, and Jamaica Art Center, and was part of group exhibitions at The Asia Society Galleries, the Queens Museum, The Whitney Museum, and the Rockland Center for the Arts.

Hanh Thi Pham received her MFA in photography. Her work is in the public collections of the California Museum of Photography, California State University, Riverside, Frederick S. Wight Gallery, UCLA, Laguna Art Museum, Long Beach State University, and South Florida University, Tampa. During 1993 she was a Rockefeller fellow with the UCLA Asian American Studies Center.

Stanley Blair Roy is an African American actor, artist, and photographer who won an Obie award for most promising new actor in a off-Broadway play, 1971. He worked as an apprentice to Alex Brodavich and has modeled for Imogene Cunningham, *Ebony, Sepia,* and *Jet* magazines.